THE MEANING OF FICTION

THE MEANING OF FICTION

Albert Cook

WESTERN RESERVE UNIVERSITY

DETROIT   WAYNE STATE UNIVERSITY PRESS   1960

other books by Albert Cook

The Dark Voyage and the Golden Mean

Oedipus Rex translated into English verse

Grateful acknowledgement is made to

the Ford Foundation for financial assistance in making

possible the publication of this volume.

for my Mother

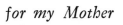

❧ PREFACE ❧

The Meaning of Fiction was first conceived, not too long after my book on comedy had appeared, as an answer to the question, "What is fiction?" This seemed the most pressing of the theoretical questions about literature, because fiction is the bulkiest and in some ways the most elusive of genres. While other critics had emphasized form, I wanted to center critically on content in such a way that form, too, might be seen more clearly in its operations. I came to feel that this new emphasis might be discussed about a genre which on the face of it was various in form and inclusive in content.

When I started, the critics who had written about the novel assumed that content pointed to form, and I could not for myself make their criterion of form stretch to include the meaning the novel carries. Lubbock's excellent book *The Craft of Fiction* applied the standards of James and Flaubert to the entire genre and in doing so begged the whole question of content. What do you do with a novel skilful in point of view, impeccable in style, coherent in presentation, but devoid of human insight? And critics, facing the novel with an aesthetic developed to handle poetry, seemed to me to lack the tools to handle any novelist with insight—Dreiser, for example—whose style or construction was bad. On a formalist set of principles you must either avoid this question or claim that in some way the style or construction is good.

Content was to be my focus; a novel, like any literary work in my view, presents the results of a cognitive act: it has a meaning. If I had chosen to write about the novel because it allowed so much by way of content, I decided to begin with the novelist who on principle allowed more detail into his novels than did anyone else: Balzac. I worked from my question to *La Comédie Humaine*, and then I had more questions, the most immediate of which seemed to focus on that very different student of Balzac, Henry James. The process was repeated, writer by writer, and the shape of *The Meaning of Fiction* gradually evolved into its present form.

My inductive approach, to see the meaning of fiction through the whatness of individual novels, may seem far at times from the theoretical interest which led me from the beginning to discuss any single writer. If so, I believe such an apparent scattering of interest is unavoidable, and I can only hope for a reader who will indulge my kind of link between theory and practice.

From the outset I have had much help, and I should like to acknowledge my gratitude to the following:

The Society of Fellows at Harvard, where the idea of this book was conceived and the earliest work begun; the Fulbright Commission for France, who gave me a grant enabling me to block out the French material; and the Fulbright Commission for Germany, on whose generous research grant I was able to work over the completed book. Wayne Shumaker and Jonas Barish, whose readings were so close as to amount to an editorial job; Josephine Miles and Warren Ramsey, who made helpful comments on the general scheme of the book as well as giving particular suggestions; George Elliott, John Jordan, John Henry Raleigh, Mark Schorer, who read parts of the book; an anonymous reader for a university press whose painstaking nine-page report aided me considerably in refining a much earlier draft.

The following periodicals, which printed parts (given in their periodical titles): *Essays in Criticism* ("Stendhal's Irony," October 1958), *French Review* ("Flaubert: The Riches of Detachment," December 1958), *Journal of Aesthetics and Art Criticism* ("The Beginning of Fiction: Cervantes," June 1959), *Criticism* ("Reflexive Attitudes: Sterne, Gogol, Gide," Spring 1960), *Modern Fiction Studies* ("Proust: The Invisible Stilts of Time," June 1958), *Nineteenth Century Fiction* ("Conrad's Void," March 1958) and *Western Review* ("The Unity of *War and Peace*," Summer 1958).

My wife, Carol, who in addition to giving me practical literary help with the manuscript has cheerfully undergone all that a serious book can impose on the pattern of a life.

Dr. Harold Basilius, Director of Wayne State University Press, for a pleasurable editorial association; and Professors Alexander Brede and A. Dayle Wallace, of Wayne State University, for perceptive editorial suggestions.

A. C.

AUSTEN	Oxford, ed. R. W. Chapman
BALZAC	Pléiade edition
BLANCHOT	*La Part du Feu*, Gallimard, Paris, 1949
CERVANTES	Viking unabridged, tr. Samuel Putnam
CONRAD	Modern Library edition (when existent); Malay edition of *Nostromo*
DOSTOEVSKY	Modern Library editions
FAULKNER	Modern Library editions
FLAUBERT	*Madame Bovary*, Malesherbes, Paris, 1947 *L'Education Sentimentale*, Gallimard, Paris, 1936
GIDE	*Les Faux Monnayeurs*, Gallimard, Paris, 1925
GOGOL	*Chichikov's Journeys* (*Dead Souls*), Reader's Club edition, tr. B. G. Guerney, New York, 1942
JAMES	(various editions, usually based on the New York edition)
JOYCE	Modern Library editions
KAFKA	*The Castle*, Knopf edition (*das Schloss*, Schocken edition)
LAWRENCE	Modern Library, New Directions edition
T. E. LAWRENCE	*The Seven Pillars of Wisdom*, Doubleday Doran, 1939
MALORY	Oxford, 3 vols., ed. Eugène Vinaver, 1947
MALRAUX	*La Condition Humaine*, Gallimard, Paris, 1946 *Les Conquérants*, version définitive, Grasset, Paris, 1949
MELVILLE	*Moby Dick*, Hendricks House, 1952
PROUST	Pléiade edition; Moncrieff translation (modified)
RABELAIS	Urquhart and Motteux translation, A. H. Bullen, London, 1904
STENDHAL	*La Chartreuse de Parme* and *Le Rouge et le Noir*, éditions du Dauphin, Paris, n.d. *Lucien Leuwen*, Bibliothéque France-Soir, Paris, 1949
STERNE	Modern Library edition
TOLSTOI	*Anna Karenina*, Modern Library edition *War and Peace*, Modern Library Giant
TURGENEV	*Turgenev Omnibus*, Knopf
WELTY	*The Golden Apples*, Harcourt, Brace, 1949

✣ CONTENTS ✣

✣ INTRODUCTION ✣

Reality is what any work of literature tries to represent. The novel, as a narrative of events purportedly past, as a large descriptive and particularizing form, confronts reality more inclusively, more extensively, than lyric poetry and the drama. In reading a novel we come away with a tingling sense of reality come alive; we feel, whether at a deathly still two AM or amid the overtones of a sleepy afternoon, that the smallest facts of our lives are clear, and real, and connected. It is this emotion, this shudder of reality, which corresponds to the katharsis Aristotle states as the characteristic emotion of tragedy. In a tragedy we feel a purification of pity and terror created out of both pity and terror fused. At the end of a novel, closing the volume in the privacy of our selfhood, we feel a withness of the self to the world, a sense not only that the given detail is faithful to our experience, but that all the details compose into an elusive, rather secret, pattern of social reality.

The novelist of our tradition presents this reality in such a way that it is felt to underlie the appearances of social life. Manners, the appearances of social custom; behavior, the appearances of habitual action; attitudes, the expressed appearances of formed opinion—these bulk very large in fiction. And the novelist follows them minutely, traces their contours, avoiding a mere naming of these appearances with moral terms alone, or representing them by a dramatic plot alone; so that in the novel, and while reading the novel, we are made aware of the very temporality and its quotidian pulse through which manners, behavior, attitudes show themselves as metamorphosing or growing or reverting or petrifying.

In holding itself close to the process and pace of everyday, a novel need not have language that shows what Charles Williams calls the ostentation, the almost tactile presence, of language in poetry; nor need a fictional plot build itself into the projective, some say ritual, force of reenactment found in drama. Fiction can, of course, use the feel of words (the poetic language of Flaubert and Joyce) or a tightly structured action (the well-made plots of James and others) for its own ends. But Western novels never fail to keep an everyday process in view, and they never fail to provide for their characters, round or flat, a kind of elusive selfhood— a secret life, as Forster (*Aspects of the Novel*) says of characters in fiction.

Narratives of earlier and other traditions do not assume for their characters the kind of self we recognize in *Don Quixote, War and Peace, Ulysses, L'Education Sentimentale, La Chartreuse de Parme, La Comédie Humaine.* In these novels the self has an inner world of longings and illusions, habits and frustrations, which it tries to work into the outer world: the attempt is a long, substantiated process, of which the character is likely to be conscious in some senses and unconscious in others. He does have some effect on the outer world—Don Quixote, Pierre, Frédéric—and the outer world on him: the novel keeps its narrative close to the minutiae of this interaction.

The *Satyricon*, closest perhaps of all classical "novels" to fiction, does not give us such selves; it remains satire only, for all its striking modernity. To be sure, Northrop Frye's taxonomic classification of elements in fiction (*The Anatomy of Criticism*) allows for Menippean satire as one mode; but this would not make all such satires fiction, any more than it would all autobiographies (one of Frye's other modes).

With an almost fictive sharpness of detail, Petronius imparts monstrous disillusionment to Trimalchio's existence: early in the *Satyricon*, Encolpius comes on him playing with a leek-green ball, in russet tunic, bald against bushy young slaves, letting dropped balls fall to be gathered in a silver bucket by two eunuchs. The sad, topsy-turvy, lavish, tasteless banquet which follows in the narrative cuts athwart a Roman world as singular and lost as that of *Guignol's Band* or Joyce's Circe episode. Yet the very rhythms of Petronius' prose do not seem to be based on those of speech, as in the novels of our tradition: his rhythms are staccato progressions always echoing the choliambics he will sometimes break into. And the characters have no inner world: their selves present a solidity that suggests the types in the later visions of Juvenal, the contemporary of Persius. Petronius is closer to them in spirit than to our prose satirists; and Swift, Peacock, and Samuel Butler are themselves much closer to each other, and to Flaubert, for all their differences, than any is to Petronius.

The *Metamorphoses* of Apuleius strings a series of quasi-Milesian tales on the thread of an Isis fable. The man turned ass is purified back to humanity by eating a rose, his spiritual dream of Isis being paralleled by the inserted Psyche legend. Apuleius in all his other writings is a Platonist philosopher, and the *Metamorphoses*, like the myths of Plato, illustrates an idea in parable form; whereas the aim of novels in our tradition is always only secondarily illustrative.

Prose even in the best of the ancient erotic tales, *Daphnis and Chloe*, does not become an instrument for revealing the process of social reality; it diffuses an essentially poetic feeling, and a metaphorical structure, in limper measure but in diction little less selective than that of the Theocritan pastorals it imitates. Animals here belong to the pastoral system; they have not yet woken from the Theocritan sleep; whereas Cervantes in his early *Colloquy of the Dogs* already characterizes even animals with the fictional verve of Tolstoi's horses, the mysterious reality of Chekov's animals.

The whole novel refers to an ideal system, as in Sidney's *Arcadia,* where the structure of reality in the prose narrative, and in the inserted poems, simply imposes a pastoral ideal on social nature. The speeches in the *Arcadia* are nothing but systems of moral abstractions; in the novels of Jane Austen the speeches are this, and something else besides. So the *Tale of Genji* seems, in English translation at least, a mere veil of incident surrounding prose equivalents for a lyric feeling more intensely given in the love poems it occasionally quotes. Nor does the *Arabian Nights* seem to present a vision different in quality from the love poems it includes. Richer in its aura of legend, its poetic feeling comes through in translation as less delicate than *Genji's.*

I wish, of course, not to comment on the literary merit of these earlier novels, but only to indicate that the imaginative vision of novels in our tradition since Cervantes gives us something they lack, a process building between social appearance and reality a secret life for the realizing (or unrealizing) selves. We might read this fictive meaning into *Genji* or the *Satyricon* or some other Elizabethan novels more "realistic" than the *Arcadia,* but we might also read this same sinewiness into a document like, say, *The Paston Letters:* such meaning is not contained or expressed in the writing itself.

"Appearance," "reality," "process,"—the generality, the very commonplace, of such terms argues for their indefinability. And it will take this whole book, as it should, to

substantiate them in such a way as to make them apply particularly to fiction.[1]

In the overall structure of this book I proceed first by
working out a term or an approach and then either refining
it or taking up its opposite. In most cases I find that one
novelist, or a pair or triad of novelists, serves as a convenient
focus for each developing point. The first chapter, for example, attempts to show how "appearance," "reality" and
"process" are found in *Don Quixote* so as to make it logically and historically the first novel. In the second chapter
I discuss how other novelists have put to their own special
uses Cervantes' practice of referring to the "appearance" of
his own novel as an appearance, an attitude which I call
"reflexive." This is on the formal side. The third chapter
concerns itself with another formal device, irony as found
in Jane Austen and (differently) in Stendhal. Moving from
form to content, the fourth chapter examines Balzac as the
most commanding example of the characteristic way in
which fiction, like history, confronts the minutiae of reality.
The fifth chapter, both form and content having been discussed, takes up the language of fiction, and introduces a
key idea about the way fictional statements relate appearance to reality to present a social process.

In the sixth chapter I return to form, this time the
thoroughgoing formalism with which Flaubert endowed
the novel. His followers either tighten the dramatic structure of the novel or attend to a figurative texture. The chapter (VII) on "the specializing sensibility" discusses the second procedure, that on James (VIII) takes up the first.

[1] Trilling (*The Liberal Imagination*) suggests "appearance and
reality" as the basic theme of fiction in its concern for "manners";
yet he discusses only the most superficial manifestations of their
interaction in the novel, class and money. Georg Lukács (*Die
Theorie des Romans*) uses the term "process" in a way somewhat
too general for a convincing application to the novels he would
discuss, just as his other terms—"irony," "balance" (*Gleichgewicht*)
—marvelously suggest, yet somehow beg, rather than solve or even
fully raise, all his pointed Hegelian questions.

In the second half of the book I proceed more directly to the implications of critical notions usually applied to the novel. First (Chapter IX) I discuss idea by treating three novelists in whose work idea plays a special role. The next (X) is a chapter on character, centering largely on Tolstoi, though plot is touched on (as it must be in a discussion of character). Chapter XI, the longest, discusses plot by taking up three major novelists whose plots as such present particular problems; the chapter (XII) on romance treats of a special kind of plot in the novel. The next chapter takes up sentimentality, a tone that will come off in no other genre than fiction and that critics have sometimes erred by categorically censuring in fiction. Then (Chapter XIV) I discuss the relation between the life of the novelist and his work, and then (Chapter XV) the novelist, Proust, who most completely—and at the same time artificially—identified his life with his work. The last chapter summarizes and generalizes.

❦ I ❦

THE BEGINNING OF FICTION

CERVANTES

Don Quixote shows a particular concern with appearance and reality, a concern so pervading later novels that a striking number of great novelists themselves have felt under the shadow of Cervantes. We need not decide between Cervantes and the point at which our fiction can begin: they are indistinguishable. What Cervantes discovers and embodies in *Don Quixote* is precisely the beginning of fiction.

The romancers who preceded Cervantes, some of whom he parodies, posit a reality not only perfect but fixed. In Boccaccio's writing the defections from fixity may occasion a prose equivalent for comedy of manners; for Lyly, fixed maxims may be illustrated by an almost allegorizing dialog. But Cervantes takes the plot of a romance and makes it something more than fixity: reality grows as Don Quixote expands his illusion for so long that the surrounding society accords it a quasi-reality; and his secret self comes into its own in the very act of renunciation, just as a third reality is powerfully intimated in the process built up between inner illusion and outer fact.

In the Renaissance the question of appearance and reality arises from the birth of a particular kind of consciousness of the self. This "new" self appears in the scepticism of

7

Montaigne, in the perspective of painting, in drama, before it gets into fiction.

In painting, introspection is, as it were, projected on the world to produce the distances of perspective, and we move from the solidities of Giotto to one culmination in Leonardo, another in the *Tempest*-like cloud color symphonies of Titian and Tintoretto (Malraux calls this chief element in Renaissance painting precisely "fiction").

In philosophy, sceptical introspection evolves into the *cogito* of Descartes, and epistemology, the question of what the self can know, develops as the central problem of philosophy, a development which goes hand in hand with that of the art form we are discussing. Indeed, many novelists have utilized or paralleled epistemologists; Sterne echoing Locke and Proust at least partly paralleling Bergson.

In soliloquy the Elizabethan drama brings introspection for the first time onto the stage. A fair share of Shakespeare's speeches have some of the character of soliloquy, and his "cloud capped towers," house men "such stuff as dreams are made on," a world as shadowy against the solidity of Dante's very shades as a Titian cloud against the gold sky of Giotto.

Shakespeare is, among other things, a moralist who reads Montaigne. The fixed categories of medieval "faculty psychology," which the Barber and the Curate show as defective when they apply them to Don Quixote's illusion, likewise dissatisfy Montaigne, who sees the human spirit as *ondoyant et divers*. This phrase is echoed centuries later by the Goncourts, who say they want their Journals to represent what evidently they at least found their novels could not, *l'ondoyante humanité dans sa vérité momentanée*.

In *Don Quixote* the prose romance, not for centuries to get at the texture of the *vérité momentanée*, the quotidian, can yet render the quality of its process. Introspection into the self's secret life turns to the world and envisions how between the two is set up an interaction of appearance and reality. Of course Don Quixote is the very opposite of introspective: he is psychotic, unconscious of his true self by definition. All the more, and for this very reason, does the secret life of his self mount silently behind his illusory philosophizing speeches and find its outlet in the process of an action it tacitly motivates. That his action is bound up with his lack of self-consciousness makes for what Americo Castro[1] calls the novel's "incarnation." The absoluteness of his illusion generates the incisive sadness of his unrequited devotion and also his final success. To borrow Auden's terms (*The Enchafèd Flood*):

> Man's being is a copulative relation between a subject ego and a predicate self. The ego is aware of the self as given, already there in the world, finite, derived, along with, related and comparable to other beings. It is further aware of the self not only as existing but also as potential, as not fully actual but as a self which becomes itself.

We may apply these terms specifically to Don Quixote, as Auden does not (though here writing on Don Quixote). By shutting out completely his ego (Alonso Quisano) for an illusory self (a romantic knight), he creates a totally new private ego (Don Quixote). The new private ego then becomes the public self, and through madness is achieved the totality of one's vocation, the identification of the private ego with the public self. The paradox of inner illusion and outer reality is mirrored in the sad paradox of madness and success. Retiring to La Mancha at the end, recognizing one's illusion, acknowledges rather than destroys this roundabout success.

Don Quixote is an archetype of its genre because fiction always exhibits the emanations of the ego in its relation with other egos, all trying, in distinct ways, with varying success, to turn the appearance of the ego into the reality of

[1] This and other critical references in this chapter are to writers included in *Cervantes Across the Centuries*, ed. Angel Flores and M. J. Benardete (New York, 1947).

the self. Drama, contrastingly, deals with selves, not egos, public personae completely present on the stage: they have, strictly speaking, no secret lives; all we know of them is what they say in their speeches. Hamlet, a limit for drama, is caught between the ego and the self. In the drama his madness cannot, like Don Quixote's, become incarnated into the structure of outer reality. It remains internal, the ego is isolated from the self as it comments on the self.

Cervantes mirrors his unconscious self, Don Quixote, in a style as unstylized as (idealized) conversation, a common style. Prose to begin with is the language of everyday, so baldly real, so unintrospective, that we laugh when Molière's philosopher brings M. Jourdain to realize introspectively that he has been speaking prose all his life. Cervantes abandons literary prose for a common style, the language of everyday in its real *vérité momentanée.* The style no more states that Don Quixote feels the introspection that it builds up silently through the action of the plot it simply presents. "All affectation is bad," says a disguised puppet master in *Don Quixote.* Cervantes' style is an antistyle, he tells us in his prefaces, a reality which sets itself against the artificial styles it exploits to create a contrast for Don Quixote's idealizing speeches and for the more elaborately wrought style of *El Curioso Impertinente:* if his composition of narrative is, as Casalduero tells us, baroque, his prose is deliberately anti-baroque. It is stylized; of course, as any successful literary prose must be, even that which cries in direct tones "literature!" as Cervantes does at the more fulsome artifices of his day. In the process of parodying knightly narrative, he creates a new, and appropriate, mode for narrative prose; the living fiction meaning resides in the very neutrality and simplicity of a style which transforms romance through a process analogous to that by which Don Quixote transforms in the madness of his life the knightly illusion into a higher reality.

Only in Cervantes is the common style put to the task

of narrating life's process. Vinaver calls Malory's common
style "more realistic" than that of his sources. Yet Malory's
romance has not yet added the third dimension of introspection between its concrete world of narrative and its
fixed categories of moral abstraction. Malory finds no
meaning and states no motive for the madness of Tristram
beyond the physical details of his madness. A modern critic
interested in myth could read the meaning into the myth
and relate this madness to Tristram's love, but for Malory
the meaning of the romance's myth was statable, if at all,
in the categories of his style. Consider this passage from the
beginning of *The Poisoned Apple:*

> Than, as the booke seyth, sir Launcelot began to resorte
> unto quene Gwenivere agayne and forgate the promyse and
> the perfeccion that he made in the queste; for, as the booke
> seyth, had nat sir Launcelot bene in his prevy thoughtes and
> in hys myndis so sette inwardly to the quene as he was in
> semynge outewarde to God, there had no knyght passed
> hym in the queste of the Sankgreall. But ever his thoughtis
> prevyly were on the quene, and so they loved togydirs more
> hotter than they ded toforehonde, and had many such prevy
> draughtis togydir that many in the courte spake of hit, and
> in especiall sir Aggravayne, sir Gawaynes brothir, for he was
> ever opynne-mowthed.

The psychology here is lucid and sensitive, but not
fictive. It weaves a tale of fixed moral types or situations,
"promyse," "perfeccion," "queste," etc., like the *Roman de
la Rose* as described by C. S. Lewis in *The Allegory of
Love.* Launcelot's "myndis" are "sette," fixed, and the
"semynge outewarde" does not differ qualitatively from the
"prevy thoughtes"; the narrative makes them almost solid,
palpable—as in the allegories where they are palpable—
characters. No dialectic between appearance and reality,
"inwardly" and "outewarde," here! "Inward," is "sette"
with the same look and feel, the same cast, as "outewarde."
Launcelot is not a round character or a flat one (think of
the difference in this respect between him and Mr. Pick-

wick, whom Forster calls flat!) but a bundle of fixed attributes. So too Gwenivere. Here adulterous love knows no
process of metamorphosis: the change is always simple, flat,
fixed, external, "they loved togydirs more hotter" simply,
from one moral type to another. Whereas in true fiction,
from *La Princesse de Clèves* through *Ulysses*, the psychology of love is a whole tenuous, internal, shadowy, introspective world.

Romances, to be sure, always typify characters; yet we
have only to compare Malory's Launcelot with Captain
Ahab or Judge Pyncheon or K or HCE to perceive how
much more introspective and internal characters are in true
"fictive" romances than in allegorizing romances like Malory's or Bunyan's. One could find nascent fictive elements
in the *Morte D'Arthur*, as Dorothy Van Ghent (*The English Novel*) has found them in *Pilgrim's Progress*, but these
occupy no commanding imaginative center in the narrative.

A romancer who was one of Montaigne's early contemporaries represents the *ondoyant et divers* by a vast sati-
rizing, transmogrifying catalog and gets something like a
fictive gusto into his tone by thickening grotesque specifici-
ties around his giants. Modern French critics like Léon-
Paul Fargue stress the poetry of Rabelais' language, comparing it to the plastic language of *Finnegans Wake*. The
poetry of Rabelais' cataloging narrative almost envisions
extensively, "horizontally," what Cervantes' far simpler and
far deeper structure probes "vertically," a fictive world.
Here is the birth of Pantagruel:

> Just such another case fell out this same yeare: for on
> a certain Friday, when the whole people were bent upon
> their devotions, and had made goodly Processions, with
> store of Letanies, and faire preachings, and beseechings of
> God Almighty, to look down with his eye of mercy upon
> their miserable and disconsolate condition, there was even
> then visibly seen issue out of the ground great drops of
> water, such as fall from a puff-bagg'd man in a top sweat,
> and the poore Hoydons began to rejoyce, as if it had been

a thing very profitable unto them; for some said that there
was not one drop of moisture in the aire, whence they might
have any rain, and that the earth did supply the default
of that. Other learned men said, that it was a showre of the
Antipodes, as Seneca saith in his fourth book *Quaestionum
naturalium*, speaking of the source and spring of Nilus: but
they were deceived, for the Procession being ended, when
every one went about to gather of this dew, and to drink of
it with full bowles, they found that it was nothing but pickle,
and the very brine of salt, more brackish in taste than the
saltest water of the sea: and because in that very day Pantagruel was borne, his father gave him that name; for *Panta*
in Greek is as much to say as all, and *Gruel* in the Hagarene
language doth signifie thirsty; inferring hereby, that at his
birth the whole world was a-dry and thirstie, as likewise
foreseeing that he would be some day Suprem Lord and Sovereign of the thirstie Ethrappels, which was shewn to him
at that very same hour by a more evident signe; for when
his mother Badebec was in the bringing of him forth, and
that the mid-wives did wait to receive him, there came first
out of her belly threescore and eight Tregeneers (that is,
Salt-seilers,) every one of them leading in a Halter a mule
heavy loaden with salt; after whom issued forth nine Drom-
edaries, with great loads of gammons of bacon, and dried
neats tongues on their backs: then followed seven Camels
loaded with links and chitterlings, Hogs puddings and sal-
ciges: after them came out five great waines, full of leeks,
garlick, onions and chibots, drawn with five and thirty strong
Cart horses, which was six for every one, besides the
Thriller. At the sight hereof the said midwives were much
amazed, yet some of them said, Lo, here is good provision, and
indeed we need it; for we drink but lazily, as if our tongues
walked on crutches, and not lustily like Lansman dutches:
truly this is a good signe, there is nothing here but what is
fit for us, these are the spurres of wine that set it a going.

The drought is here deceptively alleviated by the *grosses
gouttes d'eau*, which turn out to be *saulmure*, and that this
liquid is actually the broken amniotic fluid of Badebec is
only insinuated, suggesting the satirical connection between
the cataclysmic birth of Pantagruel and the expectant, dis-
astrously disappointed world he "entirely alters" (also a

pun on *altérer*, "to arouse thirst") in the parody etymology
of his name. This parody suggests connections as well with
the Greek of the classicists and the "Hagarenes" (Arabs as
supposed descendents of Hagar), extending the world laterally, geographically, by verbal references about the imagined protagonist. Parody, then, in Rabelais, serves not the
end of complicating paradoxes, as in Cervantes and most
succeeding fiction (except in Joyce, who returns to the
method of Rabelais). Rabelais' parody is a poetic method
of extending the world fantastically; a fantasy continued
in the splendid, almost surrealist, poetry of the nine drome-
daries loaded with hams and smoked ox (not "neats")
tongues, the seven eel-carrying camels, and the other de-
lectables which follow Pantagruel out of Badebec's womb
to *altérer le monde*. The midwives are at first struck dumb;
but through the natural virtue Rabelais continually celebrates, the good sense of some gradually recovers, and one
notes that the provisions will be useful; further, they bode
good for the world, the quoted speaker herself puns in almost Joycean fashion, *lâchement, nom en lancement*. Again
is insinuated, one feels, the inadequacy of this common
sense statement to the prodigy that has just been born. But
Hope, not present, is future; all the things to eat out of the
womb are *aiguillons de vin* (spurs of wine)—if salt has come,
can water be far behind? The method here is specifying in
its free catalog of concrete particulars, analogical in the
narrative devices—parody, etc.—by which it purveys them.
The hams and cabbages and camels and philosophical tracts,
all the particulars of the *ondoyant et divers*, render a sinewy
world fictive in its *vérité momentanée*. The insinuations of
the satire, the fantasy and otherworldliness of these unreal
giants moving across a real France, are already big with the
fictional vision.

More simply, perhaps more searchingly, with more absolute "fiction," did Cervantes employ his language and
deploy his incident:

Now, fate would have it that as they were engaged in this conversation one of the company should come up, dressed in a mummer's costume, with many bells and with three cow's bladders on the end of a stick. Approaching Don Quixote, the clown began brandishing his stick, beating the ground with the bladders, and leaping high in the air to the jingling accompaniment of his bells. This terrifying apparition so frightened Rocinante that, without his master's being able to restrain him, the hack took the bit in his teeth and started off on a run across the plain, more swiftly than one would ever have thought possible, viewing the bones of his anatomy. Perceiving that his master was in danger of being thrown, Sancho leaped from his gray and ran with all haste to help him; but by the time he reached the spot both horse and rider were on the ground, which was the way it usually ended whenever Rocinante showed any signs of life.

Hack (rocín) for hidalgo, lean nag for starveling, Rocinante is a metonymic metaphor for Don Quixote himself. The Don's courage does not prevent his horse from shying, just as his total dedication to an illusion cannot mitigate, except in the whole process of life, the hard reality of the world: his horse, planted firmly beneath him on the ground, stands for the concreteness of this reality. Sancho, as commentators urge, is also dedicated to illusion, but pragmatically: he hopes to get an island. Earlier, in an unexplained pure act (all acts are unexplained in *Don Quixote:* it is at once their fictive reality and the dimension of their sadness that they happen mutely in process), Sancho has tied the forelegs of Rocinante and forced his tired master to sit up all night as the smell of Rocinante's dung rises to his nostrils.

Sancho, with enough selfish prudence to leap from his own ass to earth, has enough devotion to seek out his master. But common sense arrives too late. Sancho is common sense, and yet the metaphors of the romance plot here do not stand for some allegorized meaning: they create, in the simple, direct narrative line, the very feel of a secret life's process. The internal is made external in the action which Cervantes narrates.

What frightens Rocinante is a kind of illusion: we measure the otherworldliness of the belled mummer by his effect on an animal; his mummery is the Parliament of Death. The concreteness of those "three cow's bladders on the end of a stick" helps to make the scene existential. It does not do the work of Rabelais; Cervantes carefully keeps his detail to a minimum; it would be long before detail could become imaginative in ways proper to fiction, through the discoveries of Balzac and Flaubert. Here in Part II, indeed, Cervantes is writing against Avellaneda, who, as Stephen Gilman shows, clogs his apocryphal Part II with just such details.

Don Quixote is internally consistent, and he manages to land on both feet after any tumble. In the very next chapter he will apply this experience through the all-the-world's-a-stage metaphor and find proper this kind of separation between appearance and reality. "It is only right that the accessories of a drama should be fictitious and not real, like the play itself." How literature other than courtly romances relates to life Don Quixote knows well; but the illusion of his favorite tales is a higher reality which he makes substantial in his own life; understanding becomes action, precisely because it cannot be introspective, cannot acknowledge itself illusion. The secret life here is so completely expressed in the plot of a romance that it exists as in real life, mute but for its action. How is this achieved?

A plot, it is said, is a story whose incidents proceed in causal sequence. In one very important sense there are as many plots as there are literary works that use them, but in another sense we can distinguish between plots whose causality seems contained in their beginning and plots whose causality generates itself anew through the middle and the end in such a way that by the end we are on totally unexpected ground. *Oedipus Rex* has a plot of the first kind; the drama advances by trying to reveal/conceal the implications of an action given but not understood at the very beginning. The outcome is unknown, to be sure, but not unexpected, particularly to the Greek audience, the only one conceived of by Sophocles. They knew, we must presume ourselves to know, the myth at its very beginning. Oedipus has only to look at his feet, to remember his homecoming trip of exile, to resolve the plot. However large the scale of the action in plots of the first type, the end is causally implied in the beginning; the *Agamemnon* demands the middle of the *Choephorae*, the resolution of the *Eumenides*; the poetry of *Prometheus Bound* surges with implications of a resolving optimism to come in the lost concluding plays.

In plots of the second type, those whose causality generates anew through the middle and the end, we move as we read into ground both unknown and unexpected. Qualitative change, metamorphosis, is constantly taking place. After twelve years and over a thousand pages Pierre in *War and Peace* has attained a staunch wisdom and genial penetration inconceivable for the bumbling egotist of the novel's beginning. This metamorphosis can take place in novels even with undeveloping characters, those of a romance. Don Quixote does not develop. But how unexpected is his setting forth, his return, his gradual backhanded acceptance on something like his own terms, his death!

We may call the first type plots of "design," the second type plots of "process." These are roughly characteristic of genres: we tend to find plots of design in dramas, particularly tragedies, plots of process in novels. Even exceptions are instructive: when novelists use plots of design, they do so, one might almost say, for imaginative ends which are really those of process; the design of Madame de la Fayette sets up a rigid, inexorable pattern—of time, of ethics—

through which the process of the protagonists' feelings evolve: Racine, conversely repatterns a similar process of the emotions into the paradoxical designs of dramatic plot. Hardy employs plots of catharsis-evoking tragic design as an imaginative window on a moral process which is essentially fictional; James uses design plots to get at the nature of time's process.

Design suggests the spatial arts, a spatial order in the plot, and process, a temporal order. Time is of the essence in fiction, and more than one novelist has exploited it. Through time, toward natural death, is the process plot of *Don Quixote* moving; its attention to process, as well as its theme, distinguishes it from the plotlessness of haphazard picaresque, from the design plots, suggestive of a spatial tapestry, in allegories and chivalric romances. The idle peregrinations of pastoral and chivalry it transmutes into a vehicle of meaning. The expanding circles of *Don Quixote*'s seemingly random, destined journeys possess a baroque order, as Casalduero has shown; more important, they illuminate the reality/appearance of process in life, and its finality, giving a tragic dimension to the everyday.

In *Don Quixote* Cervantes employs design with the inserted tale of *El Curioso Impertinente* for contrast to his main action; there is a correspondence between the fate of Anselmo and the illusion of the Knight of the Doleful Countenance, but it is one which has been turned inside out, so that there is no one thing that Camila matches except the illusion of the Don's destiny (though in a way she stands for Dulcinea, who to be sure is an illusion); and what shall we call Lotario? Design, the plot of the inserted tale, is made here to reflect on process, the main line of narrative; we measure the slowness, the unfolding, of the process by the relative fixity, the artifice of the design.

Don Quixote eases into a situation that will become irreversible, like the process of time itself, strong as death, requiring the imminence of death to effect its *desengaño*.

Arid La Mancha is a magnet for a widening series of sallies; its citizens with their real love for the Don and their perhaps equally illusory, surely inapplicable, moralizations about him, constitute the real world away from which, and toward which, he is all the time moving; if he takes too long they will fight illusion with disguise and trap him by pretending to assume his illusion. The very titles Samsón de Carrasco takes, "Knight of the Mirrors," "Knight of the White Moon," etc., ape the introspective self-consciousness of the Knight of the Doleful Countenance. And Don Quixote's shield device is not an allegorical lion or flaming sword but the face of his own selfhood.

The movement Dorothy Van Ghent traces from the rugged mountains and country landscape of Part I to the populous cities of Part II reflects the gradual persistence of Don Quixote from loneliness into a kind of acceptance. The world grows more real as he persists; it is simple in the first sally, more complex in the second sally, swarming with life the length and breadth of Spain in the third. If life is strong, so is he; and the paradox of illusion and reality in his idea is matched in his character by the paradox between his lean destitution and his real might; he has intrepid courage, and he usually bests the combatants he encounters in his voyages.

The world through which Don Quixote moves in the process of his wilful total illusion is peopled by characters whose individualities are etched in by their reaction to him. As in *Dead Souls* and *The Confidence Man*, the denizens of this fictive world reveal themselves by their unique responses to what is basically the same situation, the same person, for each. Their lesser illusions, their rejection of illusion (implying their rejection of life's sad mystery), crystallize around his grand illusion: this is the Pirandello aspect of Don Quixote which Jean Cassou notes. In no novel do the characters rationalize their conduct so persistently in the attempt to sway those about them, chiefly Don Quixote

himself. Yet no one is convinced. Each reacts uniquely in
the process of fulfilling his own destiny.

Sancho Panza's response is to serve Don Quixote, osten-
sibly in hope of an island, though his hard good sense must
realize this will probably not be forthcoming, and no one is
more surprised than he when in a byplay of action it suddenly materializes. His desire for an island is only a mask for
a real illusion of his own, one only dimly perceived by himself, perhaps a desire to get some fun out of life. When he
wakes up to the fact that he has got himself into deeper
waters than he bargained for, he grows fearful, and resent-
ful, of Don Quixote; he hobbles Rocinante. This act, too,
seems to comment on his master; in fixing him to a dead
stop, it underscores ironically the inadequacy of an *idée
fixe*, the ideals of knighthood, in the process of life: Rocinante will not be allowed to proceed, while Don Quixote,
as Coleridge defines his madness, acts "in eddies, the circling of a stream which should be progressive and adaptive."
Everything is mentioned but the basic fact which has motivated Sancho, that his master is riding an illusion. The illusion is too strong for Sancho here and at the beginning of
Part II, when he reluctantly re-enlists for the third sally.
He eventually enjoys himself, ultimately glorying in his
found kingdom. But he has no stomach, and no head, for
his own Cave of Montesinos, and his only salvation when
his ass falls into a dark pit is Don Quixote himself, whom
fate has riding by at the crucial moment. The stereotypes
of this novel's romance plot invite formulations of Sancho
Panza's character: he is fat for Don Quixote's leanness, common for his threadbare nobility, prudent for his illusion, realistic for his ideals; all this, like the romance plot itself, is
true, but not final, as it would be in Malory or even Rabelais;
it is merely the framework into which the individuality of
Sancho's character is ordered, an individuality that finds
expression in the uniqueness of his own action's process.

He, too, meets opposition; the scorn of other wayfarers; the loving truculence of his wife Teresa. So he, like no one else, can bask in Don Quixote's reflected glory. He loves Don Quixote; so, in their distinct ways, do the other townspeople: his fretting but docile housekeeper, the garrulous, meddling Barber and his companion the kind but overweening Curate, who lead Don Quixote back in a cage at the end of Part I. Don Quixote's chief antagonist, the educated, soft-spoken young man who tames—instead of mythically supplanting—the half-baked quinquegenarian, is his most devoted, and most detached, friend, the Bachelor of Arts Samsón de Carrasco. Samsón fights ideas with ideas; and as the Don's involvement in reality waxes with time into a stubbornness which the very process of events has fortified, Samsón invents a deeper benevolent disguise, exacting not the Don's total return to La Mancha, but a vow that he will abstain from sallies for a year. In Part I the simple Barber and Curate suffice to lead the errant knight back to La Mancha; by Part II it takes all the artfulness of a Bachelor of Salamanca; and even then, before he succeeds, he is twice unmasked as "the very countenance, form, aspect, physiognomy, effigy, and image of the Bachelor Samsón Carrasco."

While his townspeople cherish Don Quixote, those he meets on the road are out for what they can get from him, in the way of money (the innkeeper), brutal amusement (Maritornes, who makes him bellow like a bull), or gentle humoring delectation. Only Don Diego and Gines de Pasamonte, an older, more buffeted counterpart of Samsón de Carrasco, are really disinterested; like all the others, Gines has an illusion of his own which brings him, symbolically, across the knight's path again and again from the time Don Quixote frees him of a galley slave's chains till the time he encounters him disguised as the master of a talking ape in Part II. As always, Gines' meaning is incarnated so completely into his action that to call him an adventurer or an out-at-elbows literary man or a cynic of trenchant superiority to events is to oversimplify an individuality that the fiction has created.

All these characters, even Gines, reflect around Don Quixote's illusion; he gives meaning even to the duenna who shows herself gullible by coming to him for aid, the ecclesiastic who shows himself insensitive by saying at a dinner where he is being humored, "Where in the name of goodness did you ever come upon any knights-errant living or dead? Where are there giants in Spain, or bandits in La Mancha, or enchanted Dulcineas, or any of the other silly things they tell about in connection with you?"

There are none, of course, "really." The text, for all its paradox, evolves its complexities from the dead certainty of Don Quixote's madness. In Cervantes' exemplary novella, *Man of Glass*, a madman who thinks himself transparent utters statements of lucid social insight; Don Quixote is the reverse: both opaque, and, of his essential sadness, inarticulate. His endless idealizations of knighthood only make this sadness more articulate in the action; and his opacity serves, more completely than the man of glass's transparence, to reflect the fictive world which he defines as he moves through it.

Within his madness the knightly ideal is a rational, empirical universe: Don Quixote reasons deductively about cases, inductively according to the precedents of the knightly romances he can cite in great detail; and his madness is dedicated to virtue. Yet he is mad, and must be unequivocally mad, for the plot to carry its full weight of sadness. Cervantes' certitude on this point has misled many commentators, including myself in an earlier essay, to think him hostile toward the ideal which is so totally defeated in the brute reality of the novel; Don Quixote is at first buffeted, wounded, mocked, caged; then twitted and humored; he recants on his deathbed. Yet through all this comedy in the process of its plot emerges the fictive tragedy of a world. Don Quixote's sadness is bound up with his lack of self-consciousness. His madness is his strength. His success finally, his heroism against the ordinariness of every-one else, is the sincerity left, as the residuum of his illusion, in his recantation; the very sincerity which made him recant made him dedicate himself totally to an idea; what makes this sad is that in the reality of the world which fiction explores all ideals are a kind of illusion. Illusion is not a higher reality; Don Quixote is always mad. But the inter-action between his illusion and the world's reality generates a higher reality, one fictively tragic. This reality uses the means of a new genre, fiction, for the ends of the new genre, a mirroring of the illusion in reality through the temporal process of the inner life as it marks itself in its blind process of action. The certitude about Don Quixote's madness makes his ambiguities more, not less, unresolvable. His comedy is his tragedy, his reality is his illusion, the ap-pearance he sees becoming reality, which Cervantes has worked into the structure and style of his book and even related to his own life.[2] Don Quixote's illusion, at the end, seems a *Tempest*-like veil of reality over the mystery of life's process. Its comedy has a tragic note, but its final mood is not sorrow so much as a sad vision of reality; one so original that on all succeeding fiction it makes its mark, if only by serving, as its central character does within itself, as a mirror for the appearance-and-reality which again and again permutes in the root conception of novels after it.

[2] Not only does Cervantes state for his fictive purposes that he is copying the data of an Arabic historian, Cid Hamete Benengali, but in Part II he has doubled his own life with the fiction by his constant asides against the apocryphal Part II of Avellaneda.

✣ II ✣

REFLEXIVE ATTITUDES

STERNE, GOGOL, AND GIDE

All art, of course, envisages reality: any work of art is, among other things, an intuitive statement about our experience of the world. And any work of art, at the same time, interests itself in appearance; first in the sort of appearance to be found in the "sheen" of things, the way they appear; second in its own appearance, the artifice it constitutes of paint or sound or words organized.

The novel generally puts social appearance and reality, as well as the fine process through which both change or interchange, at the center of a given theme. We have seen Cervantes doing this; Don Quixote as a person is thus centrally placed. The novel, to begin with, because of its mere length, stands closer (makes an appearance of pretense to stand closer) to actuality than other genres just by going along at a slower pace even than epic and moving through minutiae. The problem the novelist faces then, of inventing a coherent artifice, an appearance, is bewildering just because of the mass of detail or experience he must contemplate. This condition of the genre sometimes gets worked into the tone of the writing. Cervantes, and many another novelist, refers ironically to the appearance of his own novel, the artifice which it must perforce be as selected and, hence, in one sense distant from reality. Fielding, to a lesser extent Thackeray, Trollope occasionally, speak of their make-believe as a make-believe. This artifice is in the initial conception of *Tristram Shandy*, *Dead Souls*, *Les Faux Monnayeurs*, as well of *Don Quixote*; and it is implicit in the formalism of most well-made novels since Flaubert.

We shall call this artifice reflexivity, partly by analogy to the reflexive voice of an inflected verb. Partly, too, this term may serve to indicate something of the introspective character in the inner lives that go on in novels; introspection is reflexive in being reflective: it *considers itself*. One captivated by this fact might find an obscure connection suggested in noting that the modern language most fertile in reflexive verbs is the language in which the most formal novels are written, including the most thoroughly reflexive novel of all, *A La Recherche du Temps Perdu*.

Reflexivity, like any literary device, does not or should not operate in a void; artifices would be vain if they could be purely artificial; they cannot because they must in some way designate the reality from which they spring. When a novel uses reflexivity it must discover a reality. Otherwise we feel it to be gratuitously artificial: *Euphues* seems more artificial than *Don Quixote* because it embodies a reality less deep, though actually the reflexivity of Lyly's proto-novel is far simpler than Cervantes'.

As a sequence of words, as a narrative of successive events, the novel is subject to time as a formal condition; in this its artifice resembles the reality of life even more than do less expansively temporal genres, and the similarity has often been exploited. Sterne's reflexivity about the time of his narrative reveals some of the tenuousness of living time. In *Tristram Shandy* the improvisatory tone of "I'm making it up as I go along," allows a meandering narrative which can constantly interrupt itself to give Rabelaisian catalogs, introduce diverse details and characters, inject a capriccio into the rhythm, and have its characters philosophize on all manner of contingent subjects. Uncle Toby and Walter Shandy discuss the relation of time and eternity to the pretended wonderment of the narrator. He, too, speculates on the difference between the time of reading the narrative and the time of the events of the narrative, ironically playing fast and loose with the fact that in his seemingly topsy-turvy book world reading takes longer than doing. In *Tom Jones* Fielding expresses the relative difference between duration and clock time by disquisitions on the subject and by book headings ("Containing Twelve Hours," "Containing Three Days," etc.). Centralizing Fielding's point, that moments of stress slow the clock, Sterne pits the dullness of the clock against the infinite fits and starts of an odd fictive world.

Through his reflexivity toward time Sterne is able to express the essence of his unique humor; this, in Coleridge's definition (cited by Dorothy Van Ghent in *The English Novel*), is "a certain reference to the general and the universal, by which the finite great is brought into identity with the little, or the little with the finite great, so as to make both nothing in comparison with the infinite." Reflexivity is an irony toward one's self as narrator. In Sterne, to apply Coleridge's summation, the presence of infinity implied by the narrator's constantly asserted freedom to go into ever greater details, or to digress, ironically qualifies the nature of the finite, revealing it as capricious, irregular, half melancholy, shoring up pitiable but lovable ideas and quirks to weather out its fond and foolish existence.

The associative laws of the Shandean universe are quite different from those of Locke, which they satirize as part of the irony. By a principle of distortion comparable to that in *Gulliver's Travels*, Sterne envisions the nature of sentiments: instead of altering the size of the people he distorts their psyches from inside out by deflecting the conjunctions of fancy from one incongruity to another; if incongruous in the appearances of time, congruous in the reality of an imagined eternity. The reflexivity toward time helps underscore the temporal arbitrariness, and thereby the spirituality, of the conjunctions. "Digressions," Sterne says, "incontestably are the sunshine;—they are the life, the soul of reading!—Take them out of this book, for instance,—you might as well take the book along with them."

As *Tristram Shandy*'s time-play is essential to its fancy, its fancy is at once a chief meaning and a chief mode of characterization. Eschewing the other descriptive methods he enumerates, Sterne declares, "I will draw my Uncle Toby's character from his Hobby-Horse." Uncle Toby, Walter Shandy, his wife, Obadiah, Slop, Yorick are helpless before the infinite because they are fanciful; Uncle Toby's impotence and his hobbyhorse of reconstructing the siege of Namur equally reveal his dependence on the warping past (he was actually wounded in the groin). What the structural irony does, as Dorothy Van Ghent indicates, is keep "the sentimental and the emotional and the pathetic in the same human world with the obscene and the trivial and the absurd." Impotence leads to love: Uncle Toby feels pity for the fly he releases from his hand, the most impressive event of the narrator's boyhood, because of his wound, perhaps; and the Widow Wadman's amorous interest arises from a pleasurable commingling of curiosity and pity in her impressionable breast.

For the clergyman Sterne, as for Montaigne and Cervantes, the soul is infinite, too evanescent in the reality of its appearances, too fictive, for such coarse meshes as the theological categories of Latin theologians, the chief butt of satire in the novel. And because man in this life has intimations of immortality, the body is the mansion of the soul, and noses and whiskers are windows on a secret life:

—There is, continued my father, a certain mien and motion of the body and all its parts, both in acting and speaking, which argues a man well within; and I am not at all surprised that Gregory of Nazianzum, upon observing the hasty and untoward gestures of Julian, should foretell he would one day become an apostate;—or that St. Ambrose should turn his amanuensis out of doors, because of an indecent motion of his head, which went backwards and forwards like a flail;—or that Democritus should conceive Protagoras to be a scholar, from seeing him bind up a faggot, and thrusting, as he did it, the small twigs inwards.—There are a thousand unnoticed openings, continued my father, which let a penetrating eye at once into a man's soul; and I maintain it, added he, that a man of sense does not lay down his hat in coming into a room,—or take it up in going out of it, but something escapes, which discovers him.

(The whole of modern fiction uses narrative detail in accordance with this principle.)

Uncle Toby's concupiscence is as odd and archaic as the siege of Namur; which, according to the principle held in this passage, may be why he lost his manhood there. The force of love dominates him, in all its nervous imperiousness, as it does his brother and his sister-in-law. Love is an oblique angle that best illuminates him, as birth and a "sentimental" trip to France, where he reacts to the pathos of love, best highlight Tristram. The novel's theme turns on that principle which incarnates the sentiments' appearances into bodily reality, bringing new people into this soulful world. Love, as Freud was later to discover, picks up like a ball of tar all the oddments of this life. Sterne expresses the immortal strangeness of this ball of tar by amusedly describing the mortal oddments it has picked up.

No love, no incarnation. Names are significant, Walter Shandy urges, and his son, who was to be called Trismegistus, got the name Tristram through the all too human bungling of a chambermaid "with a memory like unto a sieve." Human contingencies turned him who was to be

Trismegistus—an arch permuter of hermetic correspondences which suggest those of *Tristram Shandy* without the
love—into Tristramgistus, a knight of love who learns the
gist of life in the process of living. The dependencies of love
are a thralldom no one can escape, down to their very errors. "The original of society," Walter Shandy says, "I'm
satisfied is, what Politian tells us, *i.e.*, merely conjugal; and
nothing more than the getting together of one man and
one woman."

Love occasions the delicate feelings observed by a
mature Tristram in France; love makes this lopsided
Shandean world go round, and love properly occupies the
center of the novel, which begins with the conception of
Tristram and ends with the courtship of Uncle Toby. All
the relationships in the novel are occasioned by blood ties,
amorous attraction, or attendancy on the birth of Tristram;
and the parturient consequences of love bring Dr. Slop and
the midwife, Yorick and Susannah and Obadiah, into the
narrative.

The very time of the narrative in its congruous incongruities rises out of love. So Sterne declares that he will
tell his story, "as Horace said," (actually contrary to Horace's dictum) *ab ovo*, from the egg; and this particular egg,
the homunculus, is fancied weak and melancholy, Shandean
that is, because one of the haphazard congruities in time,
the connection of winding a clock with the act of love, has
been interrupted. The sense of life must evolve in a process
as circuitous as the wobbly lines drawn by Sterne to illustrate the course of his narrative. "I am not obliged to set out
with a definition of what love is," he says. "And so long as
I can go on with my story intelligibly, with the help of the
word itself, without any other idea to it, than what I have
in common with the rest of the world, why should I differ
from it a moment before the time?—When I can get on no
further,—and find myself entangled on all sides of this

mystic labyrinth,—my Opinion will then come in, in course,
—and lead me out." The last statement is ironic, for according to the novel's epigraph—

Ταράσσει τοὺς ᾿Ανθρώπους οὐ τὰ Πράγματα,
᾿Αλλὰ τὰ περὶ τῶν Πραγμάτων Δόγματα

it is not facts (realities) which disrupt mankind but opin-
ions about facts (surmises on appearances); and, in this
novel which deals with opinion only to satirize it, the
"mystic labyrinth" of life is embodied in the facts themselves of love's incongruous progressions.

Modesty is a necessary and revelatory incongruity,
an indestructible absurdity which somehow keeps the physical fact of love in its proper place; this place may seem
improper to prudery, as life's mystery seems incongruous
to mortal, unimaginative eyes. The Widow Wadman
blushes, but she must have Uncle Toby's manhood confirmed, and fame spreads the report through all the parish
as to "what were the secret articles which had delayed the
surrender."

The narrative in its reflexive caprice is divergent to
the last. We end not with the implied, expected wedding
of Uncle Toby but with the impotence of Walter Shandy's
stud bull. Walter Shandy is just getting under way, and
bogging down, in an endless anecdote about the bull when
Mrs. Shandy says, "L—d! . . . what is all this story about?
—A Cock and a Bull, said Yorick—And one of the best
of its kind, I ever heard." The fiction ends by calling itself
a make-believe cock and bull in a digressive anticlimax: this
points up, like all else, the evanescent reality of love under
its temporal appearances. Such a meaning is fictive in its very
tentativeness and indirection; in its own peculiar way it
demonstrates the queer reality of appearance by reflexively
calling itself an artifice at every step.

Gogol uses a different kind of reflexivity for an appropriately different end. His most characteristically reflexive device, which Dorothy Van Ghent notes too in Sterne, is his use of the expanding metaphor. He plays with the vehicle of the metaphor so reflexively that it becomes a little world in itself, changing to the tenor before our very eyes till it collapses back again into its real character as a trope of language. "The peripheral characters of his novel," Nabokov says (*Nikolai Gogol*), "are engendered by the subordinate clauses of its various metaphors, comparisons and lyrical outbursts. We are faced by the remarkable phenomenon of mere forms of speech directly giving rise to live creatures." A world pullulates into being before Chichikov's, and our, eyes as he arrives at the governor's party:

> Upon entering the main hall Chichikov was compelled to narrow his eyes for a minute or so, since the brilliance of the candles and lamps and the ladies' gowns was terrific. Everything was flooded with light. Everywhere one looked black frock coats flitted and darted by, singly and in clusters, as flies dart over a white, gleaming loaf of refined sugar in the summer season, on a sultry July day, as an aged housekeeper standing at an open window cleaves and divides the loaf into glittering, irregular lumps: all the children, having flocked together, are looking on, curiously watching the movements of her roughened hands as they lift up the maul, while the aerial squadrons of flies, held up by the buoyant air, fly in boldly, as if they owned the whole place and, taking advantage of the crone's purblindness and of the sun that bothers her eyes, bestrew the dainty morsels, in some places singly, in others in thick clusters.

Here the flies, a mere comparison, come into a life of their own, like the dead souls whose exchange gives the plot its main line. Appended to them, as the owners to the dead souls, are a housekeeper out of nowhere and even some gawking children ("second generation now!" Nabokov comments).

In the playfully significant names he gives his characters, too, Gogol is reflexive, and in his occasional author's
asides throughout. Reflexive, as well, perhaps, is his cavalier-
ness with the plot. Where Sterne flouts Horace by com-
mencing *ab ovo*, Gogol plunges so protractedly, so playfully, *in medias res* that we are within a third of the end
before we know Chichikov's origins and purpose. What
remains a mystery for so long is why he wants to buy the
dead souls, the deceased serfs, who will retain a fictive life
till the next census in the government audits. The reason
for buying them is deliberately left in obscurity, because,
in the mere legal fiction of their existence, they constitute
the central reflexivity of the plot: it is so fictive as to be
about nothing, as the gallows humor Gogol continually
extracts from the situation keeps reminding us. " 'After all,
what sort of a parable is this, really,' ask the townspeople,
in a nameless fictive town of N——— which is on the
road to the real cities of Moscow and Kazan. 'What sort
of a parable are these dead souls? There's no logic to dead
souls; how, then, can one buy up dead souls? Where would
you ever dig up a fool big enough to buy them? And what
sort of fairy gold would he use to buy them? And to what
end, for what business, could one utilize these dead
souls? . . . All this is simply the Devil riding on a fiddle-
stick, so much moonshine, stuff and nonsense, pigeon milk
and horse feathers!' "

" 'And how on earth has the governor's daughter got-
ten mixed up in here,' they wonder." What has attracted
the governor's daughter is the same confidence fraud to
which the prospective sellers give such varying, such fictive,
value. The fraud, the pivotal situation of the plot, turns
this world inside out, as do the expanding metaphors, to
show the estates of the town in all their elusive, swarming
concreteness. Their owners in all their individuated roundness change before our very eyes, like the metaphors, as
Chichikov makes them his fictive proposition. The nothing-

ness of the dead souls measures and qualifies them, and they fall into sharp relief by the varying manners Chichikov uses to make the identical proposal to each, by the worlds of differences among their households—above all, by their responses. Since souls have no value, each betrays the secret constellations of his psyche by his reaction to this fiction. The generous, modest, anxious Manilov, at first so shocked and deferential toward the dead that he cannot understand the request, gives them gladly, even paying for the title deeds, while the fussy widow Korobochka, with her clumsy slyness, bargains Chichikov up to fifteen roubles for the lot and tries to sell him honey, grain, and feathers into the bargain. Nozdrev, at first almost ruthlessly, insists on gambling for the souls, cheats at checkers, and is about to order his bullies to thrash Chichikov when a police officer arrives to arrest him for a brutality. Where the tough, suave Sobakevitch anticipates the proposal and exacts the highest price, two and a half roubles a head, Plushkin, whom he has maligned as a miser, rubs his hands with glee at the opportunity to dump the "dead weight" from his tax rolls. They are individuated as well, later, in their reactions to the police inspector's investigation of Chichikov's activities; Korobochka imperceptively tells all, Sobakevitch takes Machiavellian umbrage and goes on vacation, etc. Their lists are as different as the compilers: "Every one of these memoranda seemed to have some sort of character of its own, and because of this, it seemed as if the muzhiks themselves took on their own characters. The muzhiks belonging to Korobochka had, almost to a man, supplemental qualifications and nicknames. Plushkin's memorandum was distinguished by its conciseness of phrase: frequently only the first syllables of his dead serfs' first names and patronymics would be written down, followed by two dots. Sobakevitch's list struck one by its unusual fullness and particularization: not one of the muzhiks' qualities had been passed over; of one it was said: *a good Joiner;* another had a notation opposite his name: *Knows his Work and doesn't touch spirits.* . . . 'And what muzhik is this? Elizavet' the Sparrow! Hell and damnation and the bottomless pit—a wench! How did she ever get shuffled in here? That Sobakevitch is a scoundrel; even in such a thing he had to take me in!' "

Why Chichikov wants only male serfs is deliberately left obscure, like much else. Perhaps because men are stronger and handier than women; but these are all dead! In these deliberate obscurities, as in its central situation, *Dead Souls* resembles Melville's *The Confidence Man.* What makes Gogol's book weirder is the playful reflexivity of his metaphors and style and the related partial reflexivity of his central situation.

Gogol burned the rest of what he had finished of his novel in a fit of touchingly fanatic zeal. In a sense, though, it could go on indefinitely, the central conception could make it theoretically interminable. In Part II Chichikov slows down in a way reminiscent of the perpetual slowing down in *Tristram Shandy*. He buys an estate and settles for a long moment. Chichikov's plot, by the very fact of its being an endless repetition with variation, has no design; it is all process. The lightness of the reflexivity, in its improvisatory tone, allows Gogol to shift it at will from the dead souls' confidence tour to life on a purchased estate, then to prison where Chichikov has been sent for forging a will. History has made it conclude, if fittingly, only tentatively, on the prince's unfinished panegyric of Russia, ironic in Gogol's context, though not in the mouth of the prince. A perhaps endless fictive world has been stopped in process; but its character has been generated by a reflexivity of metaphor and plot, a world as different in its weirdness from the preternaturally cluttered one of *Tristram Shandy* as Gogol's use of reflexivity differed from that of the author he admired.

In *Les Faux Monnayeurs* Gide injects a functionless reflexivity that mars what is otherwise his best novel. For his chief observer, Edouard, to be writing the same novel has no relation other than a wilfully stated one to the imaginative center of Gide's novel. For the rest, *Les Faux Monnayeurs* is an excellently plotted fiction which explores the psychological genesis of moral falsity in the illegitimacy of Bernard and Boris; the adulterate pregnancy of Laura; the self-destructiveness of Vincent and Lady Griffiths; the literary adventurism of Olivier, Edouard, and the Comte de Passavant. The moral lives of all these people and others are acutely presented through incisive incident and portraiture, and the counterfeit money serves neatly, if somewhat factitiously, dramatically as a *ficelle* binding them together and pictorially as a metaphor for moral falseness.

But counterfeiting, literal and figurative, calls for reflexivity in a novel only by a logical trick. Even the appearance of an angel at a moment of Bernard's contrition, miraculously achieving his conversion from the falseness of his past, seems validly expressive of the moral life of the novel, and therefore legitimately borrowed from Dostoevsky (its counterpart being Ivan Karamazov's discourse with the devil). What, after the very extremism of Bernard's lying past, could the miracle of contrition conjure up in sufficiently strong opposition to it but an angel? Bernard's decision almost demands one. Yet to have the monstrously jejune speculations of Edouard's journal follow on the horror of Boris' suicide is to cap a realized fictive finality with a bungling anticlimax.

Forster's critical discernment (*Aspects of the Novel*) has guided us in separating the good from the bad in Gide's novel. But his reason is the wrong one: "It is like trying to lay an egg and being told you have produced a paraboloid—more curious than gratifying. And what results when you try to lay a paraboloid, I cannot conceive— perhaps the death of the hen. That seems the danger in

Gide's position—he sets out to lay a paraboloid." What ails Gide's novel is not that it uses reflexivity, a legitimate and indeed, as we have been saying, a radically fictive device, but that it fails to use it imaginatively. The feeling of fate Gide achieves now and then by brusque transitions to the third person of an overseeing author, lending a piquancy to the style, needs not such *postiche* Pirandello mechanisms. For Gide's theme was not Pirandello's infinitely self-reflecting mirrors, though he declared it to be that, but the analysis of a kind of moral evil. It deals with Mme. Sophroniska's "questions de psychologie et à ce qui peut éclairer d'un jour nouveau l'âme humaine," and not with Edouard's grandiose "lutte entre les faits proposés par la réalité et la réalité idéale," or his "rivalité du monde réel et de la représentation que nous nous en faisons."

Reflexivity is a precarious device just because it relates so radically to the nature of fiction. Gide struggled over-ambitiously to turn his sharp minor moralist's gift into the equipment of a major novelist, but it takes a Sterne or a Gogol to present a world of fiction with breadth and temper sweeping enough to include a reflexivity beyond the scope of *Paludes*, the acute *jeu d'esprit* in which Gide fictionalizes on a smaller scale the problems of the novelist.

Gide, who calls *Les Faux Monnayeurs* his first novel, had at least the good sense to confine himself to the *récit* till he could take on a more ambitious, and as it turned out slightly too ambitious, form. Yet never in his career as a writer does he stop floundering to add the impossible cubit to his stature; he goes from the calculated limitations of a journal like the Goncourts' to the magic of myth in *Thésée*. The last, to be sure, matches the modest success of *L'Ecole des Femmes*, *Les Nourritures Terrestres*, and others, and it is to Gide's credit that in the over-blown partial failure, *Les Faux Monnayeurs*, he can surpass his smaller works.

If Gide is imperfect, he is to the extent of his imperfection amateur rather than professional, and there is an irony of history in the fact that as an editor he rejected impulsively, almost compulsively, on the grounds of amateurism, the manuscript of the most thoroughly professional novelist of his, perhaps of any, literary generation.

There is a further irony that Proust could, as Gide could not, put reflexivity to consummate imaginative use. In Proust's novel, the identity of Marcel (I of the narrator) converges at the end with the identity of Proust (I of the author). The book is about the man who is writing the book about the man who is writing the book. . . .

For Proust, reflexivity becomes thematic first through perspective; for Sterne through narrative time; for Gogol through plot and metaphor. These uses of reflexivity, as well as the equally distinct ones of Cervantes, Fielding, and others, while they are as unique as the novels where they occur, have in common a revelation of a sense about events which is germane to fiction in general. A make-believe sequence of happenings that ring true calls itself make-believe so as to call into play felt qualities of both appearance and reality.

℥ III ℥

MODES OF IRONY

JANE AUSTEN AND STENDHAL

Like reflexivity, irony is a formal device by which a literary work can contrast appearance with reality, and consequently novels often use it. Irony in poetry, indeed, when it has people in view, just by setting up an interaction of appearance and reality, makes its characters look much like those in novels. Juvenal's unscrupulous metropolitans, Pope's narcissistic socialites, Laforgue's starry-eyed sophistic languishers, could appear in fiction with minimum adjustment.

The forms of irony in the novel are various. One form is the irony of statement. Jane Austen's remark in *Mansfield Park*, "They had their faults, and Mrs. Norris soon found them out," implies many contrasts between appearances and realities. True, the Grants ("they") did have faults, but not of the sort Mrs. Norris, the most insensitive person in the novel, could appreciate. What Mrs. Norris considers a fault, extravagance about the table, has a relation, though unperceived by her, to the fault, the gluttony, of the Grants. They seek affection through some other means than the sole Austenian one of enlightened altruism, as does the greedy Mrs. Norris herself. The ironies of Jane Austen's statement touch on contrasts between Mrs. Norris' ignorance and her self-imputed wisdom, between Mrs. Norris and Fanny, who perceives the Grants' true character, between Mrs. Norris and the Grants, between Mrs. Norris' initial hostility and subsequent respectfulness towards the Grants, between Dr. Grant's incapacities as a clergyman and Edmund's later capacity when appointed to the same living. The complexities, the ironies of the statement, rival the complexities and ironies of the whole novel.

A second form, dramatic irony, exhibits contrasts between a real state of affairs and the knowledge of some character who cannot see beyond appearances. Mrs. Norris is ignorant of reality throughout *Mansfield Park*, and her ignorance ironically both characterizes her and furthers the plot by incapacitating her; she has not the discernment to be as meddlesome as she would like (though enough to check Fanny at many points). Both Fanny and Edmund are ignorant of the real state of their hearts till the end of the novel, and this ignorance is a dramatic irony, a contrast between what is thought real and what is actually true. The irony, perpetuated throughout the drama of the plot, reveals the delicacy and the crucial importance of the knowledge they share, and its identity with their love for each other. Also in *Sense and Sensibility*, *Pride and Prejudice*, *Emma*, and *Persuasion*, the protagonist's crucial ignorance about the real nature of others, and preeminently of the suitor, is pivotal to the plot's contrivance of appearances.

A third kind of irony, distinguishable from both irony of statement and dramatic irony, is what we may call irony of event. At the beginning of *La Chartreuse de Parme* the political prisoners from an infamous prison are released to join a procession celebrating Marengo: "Leurs figures pâles, leurs grands yeux étonnés, leurs membres amaigris, faisaient un étrange contraste avec la joie qui éclatait de toutes parts." (Their pale faces, their great bewildered eyes, their wasted limbs, contrasted strangely with the joy which was bursting out on every side.) This is an irony neither of

statement—Stendhal says what he means—nor of drama—
nobody is presented as unaware of anything (in fact the
"grands yeux" of the prisoners are doubtless "étonnés"
out of awareness of the contrast). The irony is one of contrast between two events designated in the plot, here between the past condemnation and present praise of the
prisoners by the citizens of Milan; an irony of event with
overtones of worldly wisdom, and of otherworldly wisdom
(in the hidden parallel to the Crucifixion and the Resurrection, a parallel the clerical subject and title of the novel
invite us to draw—as only one term of its irony, however).
The irony of this event generates another irony of event:
"Leur arrivée fut le signal du départ pour les familles les
plus compromises." Up go the prisoners, down go the slug-
gish among the best families. This ironic contrast, in turn,
through its surprise and rapidity suggests what in fact will
happen, that the caprice of fortune will cause still another
ironic reversal. Stendhal's narrative is a vast tissue of such
interrelated ironies of event.

Always irony contrasts appearance with reality: a
statement says one thing and means another; a character
believes an appearance which is contradictory to reality;
one event shows up the reality of another as merely an appearance, making a new reality of both together.

Jane Austen's novels posit a central irony between social
status, a kind of appearance, and love, a kind of reality,
between egoism and altruism. Each of her plots reconciles
the contrast, and it gets into her diction as an interplay
between terms of precision and terms of what we shall
call "resonance."

The terms of precision have been carefully quarried
from *Persuasion* by Mark Schorer, who perceptively discusses her use of "metaphors of the counting house":

Time is *divided*, troubles *multiply*, weeks are *calculated*, and even a woman's prettiness is *reckoned*. Thus, one's independence is *purchased;* one is *rendered* happy or unhappy; one is on *terms*, friendly or unfriendly, with others. Young Mr. Elliot has "nothing to *gain* by being on *terms* with Sir Walter," but Lady Russell is convinced that he hopes "to *gain* Anne" even though Anne cannot "know herself to be so *highly rated*." We are asked to "take all the charms and perfections of Edward's wife upon *credit*," and "to judge of the general *credit due*." Captain Wentworth thought that he had *earned* "every blessing." "I have *valued* myself on honorable toils and just *rewards*." [1]

In all of Jane Austen's novels some income is the *sine qua non* for affection, and in a sense nubile girls are marketed. Yet for her perceptive heroines, an estate of some substance is only the substratum on which inclination is built. Her villains are, like Frank Willoughby, Lucy Steele, and Mary Crawford, those who are exclusively interested in the fortunes to be had through courtship, or in egoistical physical pleasure, like Mr. Collins and Maria Bertram. In her more charitable characters perception rises from a tension between acknowledging the reality of money and discovering the reality of love. Elinor in *Sense and Sensibility* equals or exceeds her sister Marianne in sensibility, as well as in sense, though she has the sense not to be so impulsive and vocal about it; her sensibility is the greater for her sense, not the less. Money without love is hard, insensitive, while love without money is not sensible. In Jane Austen's diction, consequently, we find, not only terms for sense, the "metaphors of the counting house," but also terms for sensibility. Often these terms of resonance describe praiseworthy mental attitudes, like "sensibility" itself, a term of praise when counterbalanced by "sense." The end of *Persuasion* well illustrates how the two kinds of terms interact and compose:

[1] Mark Schorer, "Fiction and the 'Matrix of Analogy,'" *Kenyon Review*, XI, Autumn, 1949. The italics are Schorer's.

> Her spring of felicity was in the glow of her spirits, as her friend Anne's was in the warmth of her heart. Anne was tenderness itself, and she had the full worth of it in Captain Wentworth's affection. His profession was all that could ever make her friends wish that tenderness less; the dread of a future war all that could dim her sunshine. She gloried in being a sailor's wife, but she must pay the tax of quick alarm for belonging to that profession which is, if possible, more distinguished in its domestic virtues than in its national importance.

Here, to be sure, we have "worth," and "pay the tax." But we have also "spring of felicity," "glow of her spirits," "warmth of her heart," "tenderness," "dim her sunshine," and "gloried." Light imagery is so frequent in these terms that we might almost call them metaphors of illumination. Not only in this passage but throughout Jane Austen's novels, these terms of resonance, or of illumination, counterbalance the "metaphors of the counting house" to express in the style the tensions which allow the novels to present their meaning of sociable loving-kindness.

Precision is ironic with reference to illumination: each kind of term, as a statement, qualifies the other. The ironic contrast in Jane Austen's diction provides a set of verbal coordinates to locate the characters, who, in their multifarious ways, reveal their moral life by their expressed attitudes and actions toward the contrasted ideas. While precision of intellect demands awareness of the group of ideas centered in money and self-interest (property, social class, self-protection from denigrators or seducers), the illumination of the heart can only be satisfied by the group of ideas centered around love and altruism (mutual inclination, filial piety, thoughtfulness). "Her head and heart were soon the better for such well-timed kindness." "Kindness" must needs have the head's precision of "well-timed," "well-timed" the heart's glow of kindness.

Each group of terms has its appearance and its reality. Money seems appearance, but it has a hard reality which can be underemphasized by an Emma Woodhouse in her egotistical patronage of Harriet Smith, overemphasized by Anne Elliot through listening too closely to her hardheaded relations.[2] Love's appearance is the form through which it must operate for its own protection. Devaluation may result if girls reveal too openly the hard reality of their necessity, physical and economic, to marry. Doubtless girls are impressionable, but if they give their feelings away like Marianne Dashwood they lay themselves open to abandonment, besides failing to recognize the reality of deep love through the decorous appearance of a Colonel Brandon or a Mr. Knightley. These errors of love, however, are adjustable in the society; Jane Austen's novels center on their adjustment in the process of courtship. Errors on the side of money, too great a hardheaded respect for its appearance, are less likely to be adjusted because they betray an egoism which in the course of a plot's events grows into the monstrous coldness of a Mrs. Norris or a Mrs. John Dashwood. Likewise sexual egoism will erupt and betray itself in a Mr. Collins, a Mr. Elton, a Frank Willoughby. The potential sensitivity of the latter, like Henry Crawford's, can be deliberately sacrificed by egoism; only in the deed of altruism does balance become refined. And no virtue can exist without love. The candidness of a Mary Crawford, engagingly frank to the modern reader who like a Marianne Dashwood romantically takes frankness at its face value, conceals an egoism not only far colder, but less perceptive, than Fanny Price's true humility. A Darcy, meeting the test of an Elizabeth, thereby refines both himself and her; Mary Crawford chills herself through refusing the kindness of Edmund in opposing his commitment to orders (the profession of Jane Austen's own family).

---

[2] The financial sufficiency of the truly sensible may come, as Elinor twits Marianne in their interchange about a sufficient income, to fewer pounds per year than the exhibitionist of sensibility may feel he needs.

Money and love, the two halves of the ironic contrast between appearance and reality, are reconcilable. Each of the
serious novels ends with such a reconciliation crowned by
the wedding it sought.

What makes the reconciliation difficult and keeps the
contrast strong is the imperfection of characters toward at
least one of the terms. Not only the Misses Bertram, but
nearly all, lack "the less common acquirements of self-
knowledge, generosity, and humility." The simple social
occasions a handful of interrelated families produce, and
the ordinary vicissitudes of courtship they react to, evoke
attitudes imperfect and imperfectly perceived as so by
others. Jane Austen makes her plot evolve, usually, by having a social event take place, with nearly everyone present.
Out of the lightness of appearance is evolved an urgency
of reality. The newness of each event brings to the surface
the most sensitive and most pressing feelings, Emma's
toward Jane Fairfax, say, or Mr. Elton's to Emma; then
everyone reacts to what has newly happened, or is strategi-
cally ignorant, or keeps prudent silence, about it. As the
people become intricated the sensed time slows down as in
real life. The plot, as a mirror of the socializing process,
reveals Emma changing at the same time as, and through,
her perceptions of Mr. Knightley. Often an innate disposition, Sir Thomas's slowness of mind, Mr. Woodhouse's
irritable hypochondria, acts as a further check to keep
the plot from evolving as quickly as it might if the earnest-
ness of the young were allowed free rein.

Besides the light irony of her terms and her tone, Jane
Austen keeps a fine dramatic irony going through her story,
an irony that gains tension by defining a character's partial
ignorances and imprudent aspirations. This it does by referring them back through all the other characters. In most
novels the characters do not interrelate dynamically: Wal-

ter Shandy's acquaintance with Yorick does not much affect his reaction to the Widow Wadman; Stephen knows Bloom and Mulligan, but neither of these friends through or because of the other. In *Emma*, though, as in Jane Austen's work generally, the tension remains fine and avoids an impression of stiff structure because the characters have been made to react supply and complexly through each other as well as to each other. From her very first discussion with Mr. Knightley, interpreting the circumstances of Miss Taylor's marriage in the presence of her father, Emma reaches unawares through her friend to the decorous silent love of Mr. Knightley. And all the others are gradually revealed through a like multiple relation. Because Miss Taylor has become Mrs. Weston, this new state of affairs causes Emma to befriend Harriet, causing Mr. Knightley to take new bearings on her, to advise her against matchmaking, to keep silent while she lets the Mr. Elton she had planned for Harriet propose to her. Each point affects and changes, sequentially and ironically, all the dynamically changing relationships. Emma hurts Harriet, which hurts Mr. Martin, which silences Knightley, which betrays Mr. Elton into innocent imprudence, which gives an opening to the thought of Frank Churchill . . . which finally brings Emma round to Mr. Knightley, after everyone has taken everyone's measure using everyone else as a changing yardstick while the measure itself has been changing.

Thus Jane Austen's dramatic irony crystallizes the bearing of intelligence on feeling, of sense on sensibility, of money on love. So prismatically does she do this, with each character a facet of the growing crystal, that the reality of the feelings evolves, and is revealed, through the slow process of appearances. One moves finely from moment to moment not through dramatic structures, which more crudely handled dramatic ironies would produce, but in a free and fluid gradual disposition of interactions. The outcome's fullness of ironic knowledge cannot have been realized either quickly or abstractly by adding up the characters in the double entries of money and love; it must have come about through the quirky meanderings of small social actions. The controlling dramatic irony seems improvised only because it manages a lightness of hold on the rein in so masterfully fictional a way.

The appearances and realities of people and events are many-dimensional. In their freedom an individual can change, but the freedom of his love has a context of social status: "We cannot choose whom we are free to love." The successful protagonist is more, not less, loving for the tempering irony of the social context (money) in which Jane Austen places him. He merges up toward the *numen* (to borrow Blackmur's terms), moral illumination, in the sociable loving-kindness of Edmund and Fanny, of Anne and Captain Wentworth, or down toward the *moha*, the horrible social degradation of Mrs. Norris, of Maria Bertram.

The structure of Jane Austen's irony is as simple as her plots are restricted. Yet her observations are so searching, the relations of her people so powerfully evolved, that on her "two inches of ivory," as she called her writing, Jane Austen has created a series of similar worlds in which the appearances of surface and the reality of depth are one, as are justice and mercy, prudence and passion, irony and honesty. In these worlds, as in the landscape of the country where she so tellingly, so unostentatiously places her characters, gentleness refines intensity, intensity fortifies gentleness.

Irony defines in Jane Austen, refines in Stendhal. Jane Austen's ironies of statement reinforce her central dramatic irony to define what the successful need to reconcile. Once achieved, reconciliation holds: we can imagine Mrs. Emma Knightley, Mrs. Anne Wentworth, Mrs. Elizabeth Darcy describing or chiding the unenlightened with mild ironies of statement; for themselves there will be no further dramatic irony; once refined through the acts the irony has allowed them to define in process, they are defined, they step out of irony into the light of sociable loving-kindness.

No relief, though, for a condemned Julien Sorel, a bored Lucien Leuwen, a Fabrice del Dongo withdrawn to the vow of silence, a betrayed Abbesse de Castro or Mina de Wangel, an impotent Octave, an exiled Jules de Branciforte. Irony in Stendhal not only defines but continually refines. He who does not submit to the refining process, or does not perceive the necessity of submission, is lost, wittingly or unwittingly excluded from "the happy few." In Jane Austen ironies of statement can be cleared up by understanding; dramatic ironies, resolved by discovery; Emma ceases to be ignorant, the scales fall from her eyes, and the dramatic irony is gone forever. But what, consistently, can Stendhal's ironies of event generate but further ironies of event? When the scales fall through the maturing process, the irony is all the stronger.

Irony is just getting under way for Lucien Leuwen in his first days at Nancy:

> Notre héros fut obligé de répondre. Pendant qu'il est engagé dans la maussade besogne de rendre poliment dédain pour dédain au capitaine Henriet, nous demandons la permission de suivre un instant le lieutenant général comte N . . . , pair de France, chargé, cette année, de l'inspection de la 26e division militaire.
>
> Au moment où sa voiture passait sur le pont-levis de Nancy, chef-lieu de cette division, sept coups de canon annoncèrent au public ce grand événement.
>
> Ces coups de canon remontèrent dans les cieux l'âme de Lucien.
>
> (Our hero was obliged to answer. While he is engaged in the gloomy task of politely giving back snub for snub to Captain Henriet, we request leave to follow for a minute Lt. General Count N . . . , peer of France, charged, this

year, with inspecting the 26th Division.

At the moment his carriage was passing over the draw-bridge to Nancy, capital of the district, seven guns pro-claimed this great event to the public.

These guns elevated Lucien's soul to the skies.)

The "maussade besogne de rendre poliment dédain pour dédain" is a necessary task in the exacting comedy of Stendhalian life. *Dédain* mocks a previous *dédain* into irony, and both together are a cold ironic appearance, hence *maussade*, in contrast to the frankness and reality of a con-stantly implied sensitive love. While *maussade*, it is none-theless, ironically, a *besogne*, an obligation to be slighted at peril. Lucien attains maturity by recognizing and meeting such obligations. The otiose commas in such passages as "chargé, cette année, de l'inspection," serve to underline the irony by suggesting contrast with further events: one would think from the magnificent welcome of the cannon shots that Count N were entering into a situation of fixed and eternal emoluments; the commas around "cette année" hint that perhaps another year will bring, in time's irony of event, another self-important nobleman to the important post.

Ideal conduct will be a complete, Stendhalian irony, continuing under all circumstances. Lucien is only a novice, or the cannon shots, announcing a "grand événement" only to the naive, would not have raised his soul to the skies. He is in need of further lessons. Life is a series of such ironic lessons to Stendhal, a sort of Salzburg salt mine. When Lucien is bored enough by Nancy, his sensitivity will need something, the love of Madame de Chasteller; but he will not recognize this till he has advanced a little in the school of irony. The salt mine, Nancy, is necessary as a bitter en-viron to the love, as Stendhal's marginal notes on the manu-script show. It is in the salt mine that love will crystallize on the branches of the spirit, though the crystals are still necessarily salt crystals and the love partakes of the same ironic insights, become a source of delight through mastery, as in the art of Stendhal which portrays them.

If events succeed one another thus ironically, if a Mosca or a M. Leuwen feel ironic in cavalierly calling events into being, there is an infinity of contrast among events, as between the appearance of the conventions through which they operate and the reality of their existence as facts. Perhaps Stendhal meant this when he spoke of "réalité voilée et dévoilée par les faits." [3] The reality is inseparable from the appearance; the conventions of love create love; mere physical love, Lamiel discovers, is perfectly inconsequential without the crystallization she will later learn to know; crystals are artifice on the reality of the branch, but branch and crystals are one.

There is so much make-believe in life's ironic events that life exists beyond belief. Stendhal, the "incrédule" as Alain calls him, is at one and the same time, and ironically, credulous of the meaning that flashes beautifully through the meaningless ironies of life. Belief and disbelief become one. Does Stendhal, for example, believe, or disbelieve, in fate, in astrology? Let us consider the ironies implied in his quotation from Ronsard, at the beginning of Chapter II of *La Chartreuse de Parme*. This comes just as the stage has been set and the action can really get under way. The quotation has an added importance as the only epigraph in this novel; its relation to artifice is suggested by the use to which epigraphs are put in the earlier *Le Rouge et le Noir*, where almost always they are oblique, ironic expressions of Stendhal's theory of fiction:

. . . Alors que Vesper vient embrunir nos yeux,
Tout épris d'avenir, je contemple les cieux,
En qui Dieu nous écrit, par notes non obscures,
Les sorts et les destins de toutes créatures,
Car lui, du fond des cieux regardant un humain,

[3] I owe this citation to a series of lectures by Maurice Merleau-Ponty.

Parfois, mû de pitié, lui montre le chemin;
Par les astres du ciel qui sont ses caractères,
Les choses nous prédit et bonnes et contraires;
Mais les hommes, chargés de terre et de trépas,
Méprisent tel écrit et ne le lisent pas.

Le marquis professait une haine vigoureuse pour les lumières.

(When Vesper comes embrowning our eyes, all captivated by the future, I contemplate the skies, in which God writes for us, in characters that are not obscure, the lots and destinies of all creatures. For he, looking at a man from the depth of the skies, shows him the way sometimes, moved by pity; by the stars of the sky, which are his letters, he foretells things to us, good ones and the opposite. But men, laden with clay and with sins, scorn such writing and do not read it.

The marquis professed a vigorous hatred for enlightenment.)

There is, in the first place, a reflexivity in Ronsard's poem: the artifice asserts it is artifice by speaking of a classical god, Vesper, embrowning our eyes, whereas actually Ronsard does not believe in Vesper. The reflexivity allows Ronsard to inject with the irony of wit the nostalgia of the twilight he is describing, very much as Stendhal, here quoting Ronsard, refines love by the irony of events. Love is the more nostalgic for irony in Stendhal, as nostalgia is the more regretful for wit in Ronsard.

The poem is an artifice, as opposed to the reality of the prose narrative which follows, all the more artificial because the Ronsard quotation has the most oblique connection to the statement immediately following. The Marquis del Dongo "professait" (professed: that is, how could such a dolt actually feel a hate, do more than profess one, Stendhal ironically implies) a hate for Stendhal's beloved enlightenment, "les lumières," and Ronsard's quotation, as poetry, has some of the refined sensitivity the marquis is rejecting. The statement of Ronsard, then, itself contains an irony which parallels that of Stendhal's novel; Stendhal uses this irony ironically against the marquis. But there is the further irony that Stendhal seems to be quoting the statement only to dismiss it. Surely Stendhal identifies himself partly with "les hommes, chargés de terre et de trépas," who "méprisent tel écrit et ne le lisent pas." "Do not read it, as well they might not," Stendhal ironically hints, using the quotation as an irony of statement which implies its opposite, "unless they happen to be lovable dotards like the impassioned astrologer Abbé Blanès."

Only partly, though, only ironically, only in one of the reality halves of an artifice-reality equation ("réalité voilée et dévoilée par les faits"), is Stendhal rejecting the statement. In one sense the Abbé Blanès is a dotard, but how is one to account for the fact that with his astrology he actually does predict the truth, not some inconsequential truth, but our whole plot, first Fabrice's adventures at Waterloo, next his imprisonment in the Chateau de Grianta? Where does Stendhal stand toward Fabrice here?

> S'il ne faut pas croire à l'astrologie, reprit-il en cherchant à s'étourdir; si cette science est, comme les trois quarts des sciences non mathématiques, une réunion de nigauds enthousiastes et d'hypocrites adroits et payés par qui ils servent, d'où vient que je pense si souvent et avec émotion à cette circonstance fatale? Jadis je suis sorti de la prison de B . . . , mais avec l'habit et la feuille de route d'un soldat jeté en prison pour de justes causes.
>
> Le raisonnement de Fabrice ne put jamais pénétrer plus loin; il tournait de cent façons autour de la difficulté sans parvenir à la surmonter. Il était trop jeune encore; dans ses moments de loisir, son âme s'occupait avec ravissement à goûter les sensations produites par des circonstances romanesques que son imagination était toujours prête à lui fournir. Il était bien loin d'employer son temps à regarder avec patience les particularités réelles des choses pour ensuite deviner leurs causes. Le réel lui semblait encore plat et fangeux; je conçois qu'on n'aime pas à le regarder, mais alors il ne faut pas en raisonner. Il ne faut pas surtout faire des objections avec les diverses pièces de son ignorance.

C'est ainsi que, sans manquer d'esprit, Fabrice ne put parvenir à voir que sa demi-croyance dans les présages était pour lui une religion . . . et il eût éprouvé une répugnance invincible pour l'être qui eût nié les présages, et surtout s'il eût employé l'ironie.

("If one ought not to believe in astrology," he came back, trying to distract himself, "if this science, like three fourths of nonmathematical science, is a union of enthusiastic fools and clever, self-seeking hypocrites, how is it that I think so often, and so strongly, of that fatal circumstance? Once I did get out of the prison of B, . . . but with the dress and travel papers of a soldier who had been justly imprisoned."

Fabrice's reasoning could get no farther; he circled the difficulty a hundred ways without getting over it. He was still too young; in his leisure moments his spirit revelled in the sensations produced by romantic circumstances such as his imagination was always ready to furnish him. He was far indeed from using his time to examine patiently the real details of things in order to divine their causes. The real still seemed to him flat and muddy; I conceive that it was no pleasure to examine it, but then one ought not to reason about it.

This is the way that Fabrice, without lacking intelligence, could not come to see that his half-belief in predictions was a religion for him. . . . And he would have felt an invincible repugnance for a being who denied predictions, above all if he used irony.)

Stendhal seems to be mocking Fabrice's belief in astrology, much as he seems to mock Ronsard's: "Il était trop jeune encore"; and who is meant by the last statement, one who "employé l'ironie," whom Fabrice would have hated so invincibly, but Stendhal himself, ironic here and throughout.

Yet, again, Stendhal is not actually dismissing the astrological ideas his artifice makes him seem to. Not much later the Abbé Blanès really predicts everything, and he goes on to warn Fabrice against just the dark deed which is to materialize as the murder of Giletti.

Stendhal neither believes nor disbelieves in fate; nor are his ironies a simple suspension of belief. They are an irresolvable complication of appearance and reality, "réalité voilée et dévoilée par les faits." And his usual ironies of event, like his ironies of statement we are here analyzing, have a complexity equal to that we have discovered in his quotation from Ronsard. That this has, literally, infinite extension, as a series of self-reflecting mirrors, this diagram will help make clear. Each bracket stands for an irony:

```
Ronsard says ⎫
Vesper        ⎬
             ⎭ artifice ⎫
Ronsard                ⎬
disbelieves            ⎭ Ronsard: ⎫
Vesper                   Stendhal  ⎬
                         quotes as ⎭ Stendhal  ⎫
Ronsard's ⎫              artifice    disbelieves ⎬
statement  ⎬                         the         ⎭ But the
artificial ⎭ reality ⎫    versus     (itself       Abbé Blanès'
                    ⎬               artificial)    predictions
But true ⎭           reality  statement    come true;
                     of prose Ronsard      though
Novel an artifice ⎫  of La    makes        Fabrice
with a reality    ⎬  Chartreuse about      is callow
(like the poem    ⎭  de Parme fate         to believe
of Ronsard)                                them
```

Since any bracket (the artifice-reality of Ronsard) may be identified with any other (Stendhal's belief-disbelief in astrology), and any pair of brackets in turn, the brackets, that is, the ironies, can be multiplied *ad infinitum*. Stendhal's quotation from Ronsard provides us explicitly with what all Stendhal's ironies of event imply, an infinite artifice and appearance of irony behind the reality of love.

This "infinite" irony of Stendhal reveals, in the events he narrates, a kind of contingency absolute enough to express itself without the reflexivity of a Sterne. It finds the secret life, not in the private, humdrum, pettifogging pettinesses of life in which Sterne deliberately, reflexively, bogs himself down, but in the great, situational, public events of politics and a career, in a love whose physical base, important and revelatory to Sterne, can fade so as to disappear almost entirely. The incongruities of life are basic to it, and Stendhal's sophisticate refines himself by recognizing them—not by rising above an occasionally ridiculous role but by glorying in the ridiculousness. What is odder, or more sensitive, than the terms on which Gina becomes Mosca's mistress? Prison makes Fabrice fall in love with Clélia Conti, insecurity traps Julien into desperate affection for a woman he has approached out of emulation for Napoleon. The ridicule incident to his falling off a horse before her window is the branch, itself incongruously nothing, on which crystallizes Lucien's grand passion for Madame de Chasteller.

Gide (*Journal des Faux Monnayeurs*) has noticed even in Stendhal's style the contingent discontinuity of events "chez Stendhal, jamais une phrase n'appelle la suivante, ni ne naît de la précédente. Chacune se tient perpendiculairement au fait ou à l'idée." Stendhal's famous style, then, does not operate in a void, but, like his irony, gains its force from the reality it expresses; his incongruities, like the style which narrates them, possess, as Gide says elsewhere of the style, "ce quelque chose d'alerte et de primesautier, de disconvenu, de subit et de nu qui nous ravit toujours à neuf dans son style."

Stendhal handles reality with the masterly agility of one who knows it inside out, so that both outside and inside are felt relative to one another, with the imaginative force of one whose love for life, for love, and for honesty is so all embracing that it can lay bare at a stroke all the intricate contingencies of a situation. A very situation, one Balzac would define as a maze of congruities, is delightfully incongruous: Octave, a millionaire polytechnique alumnus, in despair at impotence, runs off to Turkish Greece to commit suicide. His modesty and timidity, like that of all

Stendhal's heroes, remembers with excruciating exactness the incongruities as so far reaching that they transcend the certitude of Don Quixote's illusions, which Stendhal so admired, to mirror an affective life.

"The great truth in the whole connexion," James says, with much suggestion for the tightness of his own plots, ". . . is . . . that one never really chooses one's general range of vision—the experience from which ideas and themes and suggestions spring: this proves ever what it has *had* to be, this is one with the very turn one's life has taken; so that whatever it 'gives,' whatever it makes us feel and think of, we regard very much as imposed and inevitable." But Stendhal's plot, far from being "inevitable," is free at every point to go off in a multitude of directions. The contingent ironies of event, for the very close-knit multiplicity of their causes, need not have been at all as they were. In *De l'Amour* Stendhal cites the case of a girl who mistakenly identifies a young man seen in church with an Edouard who was her distant relative. Through the mistake she falls into *amour-passion* with the stranger. When the real Edouard arrives she is so far gone that it would have given her lifelong unhappiness to marry him. This *déraison d'amour* is of its essence; without such contingencies, crystallization could not have taken place. Had Fabrice not happened to be mistaken (itself ironically prophetical, in an almost Freudian sense) for Fabio Conti, so that his carriage was stopped along with Clélia's, had he not been imprisoned later in the infamous prison her father supervised so that he could watch her feed her birds daily, the great passion of his life would have been devoted to someone else, perhaps to his aunt; he might never have taken his later vow of silence.

Touch Stendhal's web of causality at any point, and one traces a bewilderingly complex tissue of threads, all related as ironies of event one to another. Why was Fabrice imprisoned in the first place? Because he had quarrelled with

and killed Giletti over another woman, an irony which gives
Clélia jealous pause about his love. The murder of a transient
plebeian, however, would not have been enough to imprison
him without the animosity of a prince who hated him because of the liberal sincerity which showed through his
fledgling Machiavellianism (as it did not through the more
experienced Mosca's). The prince hates Mosca, too, because he feels inferior to him, jealous of Mosca's, and of
Fabrice's, attraction for his aunt Gina. Each of these threads
leads us as well into a maze of ironies, all composed of
alertly observed traits of real life, love, politics, and court
intrigue.

But why did Fabrice kill Giletti in the first place? Because Giletti, ironically hurrying out of Parma to get Marietta away from Fabrice, saw him with a musket in the middle of the road and imagined Fabrice pursuing him; Fabrice
was, ironically, only chasing a lark he had shot down. Why
was he shooting larks? For diversion from supervising arche-
ological excavations. He was doing this, in turn, a little
because during his three years studying theology at Naples
he had developed an interest in archeology, but mostly to
prove, in a professedly Machiavellian way, his gratitude
to Mosca for getting him a bishopric; they were Mosca's
excavations, and he was making sure the workers, ironically,
did not abscond with the finds. "Un bon courtisan doit
flatter la passion dominante; hier vous témoigniez la crainte
que vos ouvriers de Sanguigna ne volent les fragments de
statues antiques . . . si vous voulez bien le permettre, j'irai
voir les ouvriers." Actually, though, this is only Fabrice's
professed reason. Ironically, in professing Machiavellian
gratitude, Fabrice is exhibiting the deeper Machiavellianism
of concealing his real purpose, which is to alleviate Mosca's
jealousy. At the beginning of the scene, Mosca has come in
abruptly and found Fabrice kissing his aunt.

Fabrice has the further purpose of separating himself
from Gina's importunacy. She has earlier dissuaded him

from going to the excavations, and immediately following his speech quoted above she tries unsuccessfully to change the subject. If he is putting her off why did he kiss her in the first place? Because, ironically, having just come from seesawing ironically between a visit to the archbishop and a visit to Marietta, he felt cold toward her; sensing his coldness, attracted to it as proof of his maturity, she threw herself into his arms; too inexperienced to reject her without offending her, he took pity on her, and his pity combined with his desire to counteract his coldness made him kiss her.

The multiple sequences of ironies of event we have begun to trace out—there are many more subtleties involved—cover only a few pages of the narrative. The novel generates contingencies throughout in a fine precision and on a vast scale Balzac appreciated and formulated when he called *La Chartreuse de Parme* a fifty by thirty canvas authentic in every detail.

Toward this thousandfold sequence of ironic events, Stendhal himself is ironic, with all the flash of a mirror conducted along a highway. ("Un roman: c'est un miroir qu'on promène le long d'un chemin.") His narrative is interlarded with his dexterous disclaimers of style. And he falsifies the very conditions of its composition when he says ironically that *La Chartreuse* was written in 1830 a thousand leagues from Paris (actually in the heart of Paris during 1838-9).

The charterhouse of the title, too, appears only on the last page of the novel. A disillusioned, refined Fabrice retires into a vow of silence after the death of Clélia, both for penance and, with ambiguous irony, to be alone with her memory. The oddness of this silence must be supposed from the title as qualifying the whole novel; the novel is about what obsesses Fabrice in his charterhouse, what one could read as an ironic love in his silent eyes, a knowledge all the more profound for being silent. The novel, too, implies by its title a silence only to be understood by "the happy few" to whom Stendhal dedicates it, oddly at the very end rather than as customarily next to the title page.

The silence of the charterhouse invades the book, as R. M. Adams points out;[4] all the most important causes are unexpressed, or *malentendus:* Fabrice's parentage, never once more than ironically hinted at by Stendhal; his ignorance that the decorated, wounded general who steals his horse at Waterloo is his real father; the darkness at the end in which he conducts his relations with Clélia; the duchess' feeling for him; Mosca's jealousy, Mosca's underlying liberalism which is never once explicitly mentioned, Mosca's poisoning of the prince—all only insinuated silently by Stendhal in the odd ironies of his narrative.

In the oddness of his irony Stendhal was able to invest with reality the trivial conventions of the picaresque novel; the footloose character moves in a freedom not completely arbitrary, as in Smollett (whose only fictional achievement is detached characterization and occasional portrayal of places); each event is linked with the past it rises surprisingly out of by all the causality of the plot. The plot's ironies of event are further reflected in the oddly gerrymandered states of Italy and Austrian territory, the spatial aspect of the clashing jealousies through which Fabrice must move.

"On gâte des sentiments si tendres à les raconter en détail," Stendhal says at the very end of the finished but unconcluded *Vie de Henri Brulard.* What he felt lacking was not detail, in spite of what he says, but a meaningful way of showing the hidden reality in appearances, of verbalizing the knowledge that his fiftieth birthday made him realize was aching for expression. He was to find this, as he had previously in *Le Rouge et le Noir* and *Armance,* through the ironies of event and narrative statement which would flashingly mirror the reality of his greatest novel.

[4] R. M. Adams, "Art as Insurrection: The Charterhouse of Parma," *The Hudson Review,* VI, Autumn, 1953.

The ironies of *La Chartreuse de Parme* redeem the tentative declarations of *Henri Brulard*.

Turning on a mere branch are the crystals of love, "mobiles et éblouissants." Infinitude, love, is the lovelier for refracting the finitudes of ironic events; Fabrice communicates with Clélia through a precious hole—a nothing—in his shutters; she is later the more ironically dazzling in her beauty at chapel, Stendhal says, because for eight months Fabrice has seen no one but jailers. (Fabrice's father had been the more powerfully in love with the Marchesa del Dongo because he has just completed the hard march over the Alps.) Love redoubles from arbitrary connection with the orange trees praised in *De l'Amour* and *La Chartreuse de Parme*, with Lamiel's green facial patch, with blacked shoelaces, holes in shutters, silk rescue cords, flashed messages, and sonnets inscribed in the margins of a complete Saint Jerome.

The patristic text was given Fabrice by Clélia's clerical uncle. It is one of our central, and oddest, ironies, that he is in orders out of political necessity, perhaps partly out of Mosca's jealousy. Mosca, in urging political necessity, gets Fabrice, he thinks, out of Gina's way by garbing him in the cloth. The violet stockings of Fabrice's office, oddly incongruous in a lover, are a further limit (he should not be making love at all) out of which the love rises deepened. Sublimating his passion for a married Clélia makes him the homiletic rage of Parma; she comes to hear him speak and leaves smitten enough to break religious law twice (in adultery with a priest), as well as her own vow to the Madonna not to see him, a further irony which shrouds their lovemaking in an intensifying darkness.[5] In all Sten-

---

[5] May we note in passing, as Valéry and Alain have suggested, that Stendhal is not fundamentally irreligious? Religion is an ironic device in his novels, not something true or false in itself. So that, like Proust, Joyce, James, and others who use religion for fictive ends, *inside his works* he is neutral toward it. If God is truth, the closer one is to truth the closer one would be to God. However

dhal's fictions, if not in *De l'Amour*, love is precisely the feeling a man and a woman feel when each senses in the other a sincere devotion to the reality of life beneath its appearances. However cynically they exploit these appearances, there is all the difference in the world between a Mosca and a Rassi in their Machiavellianism. Rassi could never understand, let alone experience, Mosca's love for Gina; Rassi exults in ruthlessness for its own sake, while Mosca acquiesces to it sensitively as a *faute de mieux*. The unenlightened, sensing what they have missed, hate none worse than the enlightened.

However infinite the sensitivity of a Mosca, a Fabrice, a Julien, an Abbesse de Castro, the very essence of its love's condition places it in a situation not only ironically finite but exacting. Fabrice's courtship takes place amid—and rises out of—death sentence, poisoning, slaughter. The political reality of this situation is so thoroughgoingly grim that Stendhal alone matches Dostoevsky in the ability to visualize its bottomless horror. On the level of authority, even the petty authority of Parma, politics embraces without blinking the coldest duplicities of intrigue and mendacious manipulation. On the level of force, even a Mosca will kill wholesale when necessary, as well as poison the prince. And the young prince, late a shy harmless amateur mineralogist, quickly assumes the hardness of his office in bargaining the life of Fabrice for the temporary usufruct of Gina's body. No matter that sometimes pusillanimous fear can inspire cruelties; these are no less harsh for arising

perilously irreligious Stendhal may have been in his real life, still his intellectual life, the attempt to get at social truth through created fictions, is religiously as well as literarily praiseworthy.

Further, as he says near the end of the final chapter, "Fabrice était trop amoureux et trop croyant pour avoir recours au suicide; il espérait retrouver Clélia dans un meilleur monde, mais il avait trop d'esprit pour ne pas sentir qu'il avait beaucoup à réparer." If "esprit," Stendhal's superlative quality, dictates atonement, in what way is Stendhal not a believer?

from fear; so, of the father of the beautiful Clélia: "Fabio Conti était un geôlier toujours inquiet, toujours malheureux, voyant toujours en songe quelqu'un de ses prisonniers lui échapper: il était abhorré de tout ce qui était dans la citadelle." (Fabio Conti was a jailer always nervous and unhappy, always imagining one of his prisoners escaping from him: he was abhorred by everyone in the citadel.) With an ironic acuteness nearly incredible in one who had not witnessed Belsen or read Kogon, Stendhal analyzes the effect of this cruelty on the minds of the prisoners: "Mais le malheur inspirant les mêmes résolutions à tous les hommes, les pauvres prisonniers, ceux-là même qui étaient enchaînés dans des cachots hauts de trois pieds, larges de trois pieds, et de huit pieds de longueur, et où ils ne pouvaient se tenir debout ou assis, tous les prisonniers, même ceux-là, dis-je, eurent l'idée de faire chanter à leurs frais un *Te Deum* lorsqu'ils surent que leur gouverneur était hors de danger. Deux ou trois de ces malheureux firent des sonnets en l'honneur de Fabio Conti. Oh! effet du malheur sur ces hommes!" (But misfortune inspires the same thoughts in all men, and the poor prisoners, even those chained in cells three feet high, three feet wide, and eight feet long, where they could neither sit nor stand—all the prisoners, even these, I say, got the idea of having a *Te Deum* sung at their own expense when they knew their governor was out of danger. Two or three of these wretches composed sonnets in honor of Fabio Conti. Oh, the effect of misfortune on these men!) And for those who wilfully malign the depths of a degradation heart-rending to the point of exclamation marks for Stendhal, he wishes, "Que celui qui les blâme soit conduit par sa destinée à passer un an dans un cachot haut de trois pieds, avec huit onces de pain par jour et jeûnant les vendredis!" (May he who blames them be led by his destiny to spend a year in a cell three feet high with eight ounces of bread a day and fasting on Fridays!)

Politics, he says in *Le Rouge et le Noir*, is a pistol shot at a concert. For Stendhal, in the phrase of Harry Levin, "the pistol shot is in the score." Pistol shot and concert are all but united when Clélia by singing a mock operatic aria informs the imprisoned Fabrice that he is about to be poisoned. No politics, no love. "Put thousands together less bad, but the cage less gay," Stendhal quotes, or pretends to quote, from Hobbes at the beginning of *Le Rouge et le Noir*. In politics there is the further irony that those who are sensitive enough to be adepts either have no heart for the cage, like Mosca, M. Leuwen, even Erneste-Ranuce IV, or are acting out of dedication to some romantic ideal, like Julien Sorel, who believes himself not consolidating a worldly position but aping Napoleon. The adept, then, seeks consolation from a blackness and pure appearance in politics which others either coldly and horribly stomach without flinching or blindly ignore; thereby he is thrown by his sensitivity into the reality of love with a woman who, by a corresponding disillusionment, is likewise seeking consolation. Madame de Rênal is turning to Julien from a brutally imperceptive, coldly canny husband; Mathilde de la Mole takes him up from boredom with the mechanically adroit associates of her own class.

A romantic idea makes a climber of Julien; a romantic ideal makes Mathilde leap the barriers of class; the child she becomes pregnant with is none the less real, the head she clutches in the ironically grotesque final scene none the less gory for her insane identification of it with a scarcely known ancestor. While Julien's ideal motivates in him an engaging finesse that has carried him from the seminary to the confidential service of the Marquis de la Mole, its otherworldliness, and its very frankness (two sides to the same idealism) brings him up abruptly against the hard realities of caste. His love for Mathilde has been artificial compared with what he feels for Madame de Rênal. Returning to the sincerity of that passion, a momentary jealousy has him fire a pistol shot at the "concert" of a mass she is hearing. It is, ironically, his return to the truth of his own feelings that causes his death.

In this novel, even more in *La Chartreuse de Parme*, the plot complicates a manifold ironic series of events which vivify and deepen the characters who act them out. The oddness of Stendhal's pyrotechnic ironies, coupling the most far-reaching truths of public life with the deepest private feelings, sets up the sharpest distinction between appearances and realities, at the same time leaving infinitely unresolvable the necessity of appearance to reality. Precisely where he is most splendidly clear Stendhal is most inscrutable, or, as Valéry puts it, speaking of Stendhal's method of writing. "Vérité et volonté de vérité forment ensemble un instable mélange où fermente une contradiction et d'où ne manque jamais de sortir une production falsifiée. *En littérature le vrai n'est pas concevable.* . . . Nous savons bien qu'on ne se dévoile que pour quelque effet." (Italics Valéry's.) Stendhal himself knew this in some way, or how could he have spoken of "réalité voilée et dévoilée par les faits"?

There is a reality, as well as an artificiality, in Stendhal's infinite irony, so much so that, as Valéry concludes the essay I have been quoting, "On n'en finirait plus avec Stendhal. Je ne vois pas de plus grande louange."

✠ IV ✠

HISTORY AS RHETORIC

BALZAC

Some novelists complicate the formal side of their art by using irony or the kind of irony toward their own fictiveness which we have called reflexivity. Another approach is a more direct frontal attack on reality itself. *U.S.A.* and *La Comédie Humaine* are crowded with social facts in such a way as to seem to rival history. The distinction between fiction and history, confused in early works like Dekker's *The Wonderfull Yeare 1603* and Defoe's *Journal of the Plague Year*, is exploited by Balzac and Dos Passos to relate the appearance of quasi-historical facts with the myth-like reality of a series of romance plots. Dos Passos' success is qualified by his pastiche style and also by too explicit an illustrative purpose; he tends merely to document how money debases people in a capitalist society. The very magnificence of Balzac's success, however, has kept his rhetorical substructure unexamined; critics admire either the concreteness of his exhibited reality or the grandeur of his vision without perceiving the fructifying interdependence of the two.

In particular, Balzac's ability—unequaled among novelists—to compass a diversity of places and people, added to his own professed documentary purpose, has often obscured both his transcendence of a mere programmatic realism and the uses to which he put historicizing detail. "J'ai mainte fois été étonné," said Baudelaire, "que la grande gloire de Balzac fût de passer pour un observateur; il m'avait toujours semblé que son principal mérite était d'être visionnaire. . . . Tous ses personnages sont doués de l'ardeur vitale dont il était animé lui-même. Toutes ses fictions sont aussi profondément colorées que les rêves."

"Tous les acteurs de sa Comédie," he continues, "sont plus âpres à la vie, plus actifs et rusés dans la lutte, plus patients dans le malheur, plus goulus dans la jouissance, plus angéliques dans le dévouement . . . que la comédie du vrai monde nous montre."

(I have often been astonished that Balzac's great glory was to pass for an observer. It has always seemed to me that his chief merit was that of being a visionary. . . . All his characters are gifted with the vital ardor by which he was himself animated. All his fictions are as deeply colored as dreams.

All the actors in his Comedy are more violent in life, more active and resourceful in struggle, more patient in misfortune, more gluttonous of enjoyment, more angelic of devotion, than the comedy of the real world shows us.)

The last statement is curious. What does Baudelaire mean by "la comédie du vrai monde"? Is fiction, Balzac's or anybody's, not a representation of the "vrai monde"? In what way, more than any other literary artifice, does Balzac's imaginary world exaggerate the real world it envisions?

Baudelaire specifies, "Bref, chacun chez Balzac, même les portières, a du génie . . . c'est bien Balzac lui-même." But if so, why would not an autobiography have served Balzac's purpose? Baudelaire here approaches a confusion of Balzac's life with the fiction it created, a confusion Balzac himself sometimes shared and which he parallels in his fruitful fusion of history with fiction. To justify the historicist, documentary bias in Balzac, Baudelaire is content to induce a kind of symmetry as principle; Balzac's passion for detail obliged him to use characters of mythical stature to "sauver la perspective de l'ensemble." And Baudelaire seems to pass over the use of history in fiction which the Romantics, with their peculiar faith in the meaning of history, were the first to create. I do not intend to carp at Baudelaire's signal insight. He made these remarks as a digression in an essay on Théophile Gautier and was not, perhaps, much concerned with how the documentation and the myths in Balzac arrive at a fictive unity. Yet it is surely a problem central to understanding Balzac.

Why do myths require the mode of facts? Why does Lear-Goriot need all the furniture of the *Restauration* and a legion of bits of lives whose own grand passion is played out in a related elsewhere? "What concern has the poet with so much arithmetic?" James asks of Balzac. "The contradiction is always before us."

Some call money the figure in Balzac's carpet. Balzac does think in terms of money. "The general money question," James says, "so loads him up and weighs him down that he moves through the human comedy, from beginning to end, very much in the fashion of a camel, the ship of the desert, surmounted with a cargo." The odiousness of avarice comes often before his eye: its pettiness in the robbery of César Birotteau's till by the *commis* who later becomes a great financier, its fraudulent cruelty in *La Maison Nucingen*'s treacherous manipulations, its Dantesque revelation in death, the disgusting end of even the philosophical Gobseck, who dies while the perishables he held for a fanatic point of speculation are decomposing horribly in an adjoining room.

Money in Balzac is real enough to put one off from human love, even from power. It is significantly Nucingen whom La Torpille, significantly the niece of Gobseck, leads by the nose for so long without according him the favors he exorbitantly buys. Nucingen's German accent, both the disguise and the underlying stark reality of power, also plates with impotence all his statements, as in the "Pape Satan, Pape Satan, aleppe" of Dante's Plutus. Mlle. Zéphirine in *Béatrix* hampers her power because she will not relinquish the necessary *louis* to have the cataracts removed from her blind eyes.

Still, to describe *La Comédie Humaine* through the centrality of money is only to trace a relation, leaving the important critical questions unanswered.

Money, for all the force of its omnipresent appearances, is controlled by a deeper, related, reality of which it is a figure: this deeper reality controls the individuation we find everywhere in Balzac, even among his usurers. "D'abord l'avare de province, le Père Grandet, . . . avare comme le tigre est cruel; puis Gobseck l'escompteur, le jésuite de l'or, n'en savourant que la puissance et dégustant les larmes du malheur, à savoir quel est leur cru; puis le baron de Nucingen, élevant les fraudes de l'argent à la hauteur de la Politique . . . la Parcimonie domestique, le vieil Hochon d'Issoudun, et de cet autre avare par esprit de famille, le petit La Baudraye de Sancerre. . . ." (First the miser of the provinces, Père Grandet, . . . avaricious as the tiger is cruel; then the discounter Gobseck, the Jesuit of gold, tasting only its power and savoring the tears of misery to ascertain their vintage; then Baron Nucingen, raising financial fraud to the level of politics . . . domestic parsimony, old Houchon of Issoudun, and that other miser by family spirit, little La Baudraye of Sancerre. . . .) "Les sentiments humains," Balzac says, "et surtout l'avarice, ont des nuances . . . diverses dans les divers milieux de notre société." (Human feelings, and above all avarice, have various nuances in the various environments of our society.) Money itself is a mystery, like love. It too, like the char-

acters in Balzac, is at once driven by grand passions and
calculated in exact, detailed evolutions. "Tout est le même
argent," says Nucingen. Every accountant a Midas, and
vice versa.

The reality of history in Balzac does not reside finally
in the appearances of the money it unfailingly uses. Not
for this did "his imagination achieve," as James says, "the
miracle of absolutely resolving itself into multifarious
knowledge. Since history proceeds by documents, he constructed, as he needed them, the documents too—fictive
sources that imitated the actual to the life. It was of course
a terrible business."

A terrible business indeed. For history already resembles fiction as a narrative of ordered facts. History takes on
itself the burden, and the limitation, of the existence of its
facts, while fiction assumes the glory of using only gratuitous facts, whether or not all or some or similar happened. History realizes its themes through the facts it as-
sembles and orders, while fiction brings about a simultane-
ous verbal vision of the necessary interrelation of theme
and facts through the gratuitousness it accepts as an exclu-
sive task.

History can invent verbalizations of political forces on
a given occasion: the speeches of Thucydides do this. It
can introduce a primitive fiction in the body of its narrative, in the manner of the anecdotes of Herodotus. With
Thucydides, we assume that the forces actually played as
the invented speeches demonstrate; Herodotus intends the
tales only to describe how the mores of the Egyptians or
the Persians actually operated; he does not compose them
into a vision of appearances and realities, the end of fiction.
Free in its choice of material, fiction as well as history can
utilize facts which happen to be true. Melville uses whaling
lore, Joyce geographical and historical facts. The events in
Henry Miller's *The Tropic of Cancer* all happened, the
author is proud to tell us; which is to say that he took as

one of his fictive limitations the historical condition; but gratuitously, as fiction always does, not of necessity, as a historian must. "J'ai mieux fait que l'historien," says Balzac. "Je suis plus libre."

As history lays itself open perpetually at every step to the question, "Did it really happen so?" philosophy lays itself open to the perpetual necessity of proof and defense against any possible formal denial; it must hedge itself in with a reasoned explanation at every step. Poetry says, gratuitously, among other things, what philosophy tries to explain by extension and defense, and this gratuitousness is its burden.

Philosophy is to poetry as history is to fiction.

Poetry can be philosophic, using some philosophical question as its theme, like Lucretius, or as its meaning, like Heraclitus. It can use a philosophical device as part of its artifice, as Donne uses logic. It can treat philosophically the theme of its own nature, as Heidegger shows Hoelderlin does.

Fiction parallels all these uses by employing history, its counterpart, as device or theme. Almost always history is a theme when used in fiction, not a device. In *War and Peace* the integrated historical parts of the novel constitute an insight into fictional relations in history, rather than a use of history as a device to produce fictional insights, Balzac's practice. Tolstoi's result, his theme, is, among much else, an insight into history, while Balzac's result is scarcely more historical than Dickens', though he achieves it by the gigantic labor of writing as if his theme were historical. We get a wonderful picture of the period in him, but we get that in any novelist.

Balzac mimics the discourse of history. All the facts he narrates are told as if told by an historian. He begins his work with a quasi-scholarly preface. His references to other writers, even novelists, often have the air of a scholarly citation, and he permits himself veritable opuscules of sociology to define his characters, as well as to describe their dwellings, their clothes, their incomes. "L'archéologue du mobilier social," he calls himself, "le nomenclateur des professions, l'enregistreur du bien et du mal."

History essays complete description, and Balzac, writing his "histoire du coeur humain," approaches the romantic error that we can wholly perceive an immanent order in history. In imitating the *parti pris* of history, Balzac lends to his work by artifice a degree of conviction it must earn, as he suggests. History is given this conviction to start with. *La Comédie Humaine*'s earning is realized through what it pretends to give itself, and Balzac's fiction succeeds by a serious reflexive rhetoric which he uses directly and which comic novelists like Sterne, whom he admired, use as an assertedly self-conscious ironic device. While Sterne and Gogol pretend nonsense, Balzac pretends certitude, and the pretense serves to strike a unifying tone.

"What is the historic sense after all," James asks of Balzac, "but animated, but impassioned knowledge seeking to enlarge itself?" In the fictive world of *La Comédie Humaine*, as in James, to recreate the past as a fictive history has the effect of at once generalizing and impassioning the life of a society by making it fixed, and even legendary. A vast single reality is felt to underlie the past's manifold appearances. Balzac fuses the distinction, as Dante makes an equation, between mythological and historical beings. Ulysses in Dante has the same status as Guido di Montefeltro; Goriot's historicity is his myth, as his myth is buried in his history.

The events in fiction, as rendered in a sequence of time necessarily past if capable of narration, are anyway always an hypostatized search of the past, like written history. The novel which takes as its theme the search of the past is consistently also the novel about the final meaning of art, including novels, and about the process of creating them in a life: *A la Recherche du Temps Perdu*.

Balzac's history is not Proust's; his history does not

speak of itself as *fictively* historical, any more than it asserts the imaginative coexistence of its different epochs, as does *Finnegans Wake*. The lives of his characters proceed in the blocked-off rooms of the separate novels unpredictably, resurgently. Unlike Proust's novel, where the lines of sequence are a simple evolution of the beginning, or Joyce's, where they are also a reassertion of the beginning, the time of events in Balzac's novel is deserted by the compulsions of other events, as the Maison Vauquer is deserted by the compulsions of its transients. "Le char de la civilisation, semblable à celui de l'idole de Jaggernat, à peine retardé par un coeur moins facile à broyer que les autres et qui enraye sa roue, l'a brisé bientôt et continue sa marche glorieuse." "L'histoire vieillissait promptement, constamment mûrie par des intérêts nouveaux et ardents." And, "la nature sociale, de même que la nature elle-même, est une grande oublieuse." (The chariot of civilization, like that of the idol of Juggernaut, scarcely held up by a heart less easily crushed than the others, a heart clogging its wheel, soon breaks that one and continues its glorious progress. History ages promptly, constantly ripened by new and ardent interests. Social nature, like nature itself, is a great forgetter.) But if social nature forgets her past, Balzac, setting himself the task of a fictional historian, tries to remember it, to recreate it by using the historiographer's approach as the central rhetorical device of his vast fiction.

Balzac's plots, as Baudelaire said of his personages, have mythical stature; not that they relate to a primitive spirit, but that their action is archetypal, more than fictional in the sense that the work of James or Flaubert or Jane Austen or Proust or Joyce (even as a mythographer) is purely fictional. One could, of course, find a sacrifice ritual in *Wings of the Dove* (doves, we remember are traditional sacrificial birds), the Queen of the Dead in *Madame Bovary*, a quest in any of Jane Austen's novels (or in almost any novel, according to Lionel Trilling). Balzac's work is directly, more manifestly, archetypal. His plots turn the passion generated by his characters into mythical types: Madame Graslin is repentant sin, Julie d'Aiglemont, disillusion, de Rubempré, weak genius, Vautrin, Mephistopheles, Thadée Paz, devotion, Abbé Birotteau, flouted virtue, César Birotteau, tottering ambition, Père Goriot, the object of filial ingratitude. "C'était la Force et la Faiblesse de la femme dans tous leurs développements, une parfaite antithèse," Balzac says of two women in *Béatrix*. Eugénie Grandet is love unrequited, a Danae imprisoned by a cruel father who none the less receives her shower of gold from heaven, not only her inexhaustible treasures of love but real gold in the form of an unexpected inheritance.

In one sense the power and passion generated in Balzac's plots are mythical, because, like the figures in a myth, the characters of Balzac embody as well as seek their desire. They are, says Béguin, "Mythologie . . . par ce que les passions . . . [ont] pris forme et réalité de personnes différentes."

Among components of the novel, Northrop Frye specifies (*The Anatomy of Criticism*) "fiction," the conventional novel of social events and character development, and "romance," as Hawthorne called his novels romances, plots that work out the oppositions of simple, undeveloping characters. Romances have been called allegories and allegories myths. Without trying to define such basic concepts in literature as allegory and myth, we may say that Balzac's novels are both romances, by virtue of their myths, and fictions.

The plots of Hawthorne and Melville involve characters who are, if not abstractions, at least singly motivated and predictable, existing in a closed world. We can foresee the death of the judge in *The House of the Seven Gables*, of Ahab in *Moby Dick*, of Melville's Pierre. The Maule's curse in Balzac's *L'Interdiction* comes as a surprise; in Haw-

thorne the curse begins the novel. In Balzac, both the judge
and the defendant resemble Hawthorne's daguerreotypist:
the "good" of the romance is thwarted by the complications
of a fictive intrigue involving the ambition of men in high
places, the love affair of the plaintiff with Rastignac, the
accidental relation of Judge Popinot to Bianchon, who is
accidentally the friend of Rastignac, and so forth. These
complications and accidents are fiction, not romance or
myth. There are the further fictions of the scholarly Chinese
history and the live, ugly Huguenot beneficiary. In Balzac's
tale, good is good, evil evil, as in romance. They work
themselves out with evolutions proper to fiction. Balzac's
fictive facts, then, not only document his work with appearances; they qualify, individuate, and even deflect, the
reality of his romance plots.

Balzac limits a single episode or even novel to romance.
His characters are not complex in motive or action, only in
relation. They are strong or weak, good or evil, lucky or
unlucky, rich or poor, wise or foolish. A change of heart
is always a strong reversal (*L'Envers de l'Histoire Contemporaine, Le Médecin de Campagne, Le Curé de Village,
Un Début dans la Vie*). Balzac's people are never transformed into a revelation of their earlier selves, like Dmitri
Karamazov or the major characters in *War and Peace* and
Anna Karenina. History, the sequences of events in fictive
time, merely entangles them desperately. In *Béatrix*, experienced women of the world become—and act—as virgins
before Calyste. Lovers in Balzac do not debase a woman
qualitatively, as in Middleton, *Anna Karenina, Madame
Bovary;* nor does marriage alter her by fusion with another
person, though it compromise and check her for life, as in
La Maison du Chat-qui-pelote. It is impassioned knowledge
that brings the adulterous wives in *La Femme de Trente
Ans* and *Le Curé de Village* to repent, a knowledge brought
about not by an inner savor of evil, like Anna Karenina's
knowledge, but by the disasters which overtake daughter

and lover as a result of their sin. The right, strange fictive combinations can restore her virginity to the Princesse de Cadignan after nearly twenty years of dissolute life. The romances Balzac's characters work out constitute a fiction in which they act, the total novel of *La Comédie Humaine*. Just as Myshkin's complexity in *The Idiot* and Stavrogin's in *The Possessed* come from the apparent contradictions (but deep fictive insight) of their successive appearances, so Balzac's characters are sometimes fictively[1] complex *in toto* while "romantically" simple in an individual episode or novel.

Mauriac calls *Le Père Goriot* the "rond-point" of *La Comédie Humaine*. Of what city is it the *rond-point?* How does Balzac's work differ from a mere extensive accumulation of recurring characters like Romains' *Hommes de Bonne Volonté*, of an unrealized multiple fiction like Zola's Rougon-Macquart series, where the individual novels are successful but do not compose into a qualitatively higher order? Nana in *L'Assommoir* contains potentially the Nana of the novel which bears her name, but these novels do not combine to form a greater novel. They simply reassert the disintegrating force of the sexual energy which is Zola's theme. But sex in Balzac is only one form of the energy of destiny. Sexual love can kill an Esther, transform a Princesse de Cadignan, console a Lambert. It interacts with other forces in a greater fictional unity, and Balzac's *Nana*, *Splendeurs et Misères des Courtisanes*, leads its many themes be-

---

[1] It is significant that Balzac conceived very late what are perhaps his most purely fictional novels, *Le Cousin Pons* and *La Cousine Bette*, which were not included in the catalog of 1845, three years before his death. One can imagine a possible Balzac living to complete *La Comédie Humaine* at, say, sixty, and rivaling by different means the precision of a Flaubert who would then be his contemporary.

sides sex back to a central order. Balzac had such a larger central order in mind, or his constant willingness to digress, as in the five thousand word treatise about the Faubourg Saint Germain in *La Duchesse de Langeais,* would overbalance that short fiction if read, contrary to Balzac's intention, separately. When Rastignac surveys Paris from the heights of Père Lachaise and makes his famous statement of defiance, "A nous deux maintenant," this decision would be a poor conclusion to *Père Goriot* itself. We must complete Rastignac's statement by his successive career in *La Comédie Humaine,* as he gets progressively involved in that expanding universe of Balzacian fact.

James gave Balzac "the appetite of an ogre . . . for facts." Of a hydra, rather. A hydra with hydropsy, if facts can be fancied as suspended in water. "Mais Paris est un véritable océan. Jetez-y la sonde, vous n'en connaîtrez jamais la profondeur . . . quelque soin que vous mettiez à le parcourir, à le décrire; quelque nombreux et intéressés que soient les explorateurs de cette mer, il s'y rencontrera toujours un lieu vierge, un antre inconnu, des fleurs, des perles, des monstres, quelque chose d'inouï, oublié par les plongeurs littéraires." (But Paris is a veritable ocean. Throw the plummet into it; you will never know its depth . . . no matter what care you take to traverse and describe it, no matter how numerous and devoted the explorers are of this sea, there is always met along with these a virgin spot, an unknown cave, flowers, pearls, monsters, something unheard of, forgotten by the literary divers.) It is in a unified, imaginary sea of hunger that *La Torpille* (the rayfish) can sting victims, afflicted herself by a hunger that binds her unwittingly to Vautrin and finally kills her.

Hunger is multiform in Balzac. The hunger of Rastignac rejects the satiation proffered by the hunger of Vautrin, which the hunger of de Rubempré seizes. All these hungers are played out among oblivious other hungers which draw them, interact, give them being—hungers not only for money, love, honor, comfort, filial gratitude, meta-physical answers, glory, realization, but for fulfillment in a world of facts we call Balzac's world.

In Balzac knowledge is power and people are continu-ally reciting the past as parables which will inform others of a deeper reality than they have encountered, in little series like *Echantillons de Causerie Française*, or in such entire novels, cast in parable frame, as *Gobseck, Les Pay-sans, Drame au Bord de la Mer, Le Médecin de Campagne, Le Colonel Chabert, Le Lys dan la Vallée*. But one charac-ter cannot compass the expanse of the Balzacian world, and while his knowledge is a power to master it, his ignorance makes him perforce a "comédien sans le savoir." Power, however, in Balzac's giant, iron-willed characters, cannot only become knowledge but overcome the ignorance of it-self and others. The power of Rosalie de Watteville's devo-tion to Albert Savarus, of Pons' desire for comfortable ac-ceptance, of Bette's meddling, of Eugénie Grandet's or Goriot's love, of Louis Lambert's insights, battles not only against odds and opposition (a form of recognition), but against a void of silence, an indifference, a lack of cogni-zance on the part of the society which, with all these char-acters, seeming their most implacable enemy, becomes their strongest ally by a process analogous to that through which reality pervades history's appearances, enabling them to become not what they wanted (for example, the wife of Albert Savarus), but a fulfillment of what they were bound to be (for example, the founder of a Trappist nunnery). The force of each will is deflected by all the other wills, and this deflection, unperceived by the character, is the "comedy" of *La Comédie Humaine*.

Comedy usually presents its characters and action against a norm of virtue or wisdom. The norm in *La Comé-die Humaine* is the classificatory scheme wherein all the characters are located and implicitly related to one another. The tragedy of one incident, of one novel, becomes comic as soon as it is set off against another incident, beginning the analogy which produces a norm of social knowledge, one motif in all comedy. Every character thus finds a specific reality within the framework of a vast historical matrix of appearances.

Balzac's plots, within each of his novels, have a vertical density, an intricate pattern of timing and doubling the nexus of causes, which he learned from Walter Scott. The details of this causal intricacy, however, are not determined by mere narrator's tricks, as in Walter Scott, but, on Balzac's principle of analogy, the horizontal or lateral incursion of characters from other novels. In his excellent map of Balzac's ideas, E. R. Curtius stresses the importance of will to this author. The intensity of a Balzac character's will, and the unique shape that the will's action takes, arises from the lateral pressure of the two thousand other characters who are related to him by myriad strands within this quasi-historical fictional world.

From the *Odyssey* on, writers have juxtaposed characters with different pasts to extend reference and enrich tone. It is the ex-lover of Calypso who stands foul from the sea before Nausicaa, though she knows it not. The commander "of many wiles" knows without being told that the young girl facing him is anxious for a husband (we learned it as she got up that morning at the beginning of the book). He plays on that anxiety without intending, we know from his past, to allay it. A range of ironies serves social insight here, as later in Odysseus' many encounters with Penelope and others before he reveals his identity.

The plot line of the one long novel which includes *Illusions Perdues* and *Splendeurs et Misères des Courtisanes* could stand by itself as a rigorously evolved fiction. But its true range of irony and richness of tone are only perceived when its relations to the rest of *La Comédie Humaine* are realized; otherwise it is as if we read about Odysseus and Nausicaa without knowing his long history or seeing her that morning. The magnitude of the illusions that Lucien de Rubempré gradually loses, the scale of the *splendeurs* and *misères*, derives from the gamut of wills Balzac has compounded with this plot from the rest of the *Comédie*. Let Lucien move from drawing room to tavern, from government office to opera, from publisher's suite to prison; he is accompanied at every step by nuclei of others who bear the stigmata of related chapters in this giant novel. It is the Marquise d'Espard, the angel of cruelty and hypocrisy from *L'Interdiction*, who persuades Madame de Bargeton to drop the Lucien she has fled with to Paris. The whole *Comédie* has been at work forming the hauteur that draws love away from Lucien, the hauteur which is itself destined to become an implacable hate working behind the scenes for his later condemnation. It is the Daniel d'Arthez of *Les Secrets de la Princesse de Cadignan* (where it is the Marquise d'Espard who introduces the lovers!) who fortifies him for literary combat, as it is the Coralie of *Une Fille d'Eve* who seduces him, along with the Blondet and the Lousteau of a dozen novels. Lousteau, indeed, has in the *Muse de Département*, the muse with whom he too runs away to Paris, his own disillusioning Madame de Bargeton. And Blondet has elsewhere his own liaison with a countess (though they are protected by the Marquise d'Espard). It is the Vautrin of *Père Goriot*, disguised, who dissuades Lucien from suicidal desires and brings him back as his protégé to Paris and a later suicide. When Vautrin, in his "dernière incarnation," trades his marshalship in crime for a high office in the police, it is the wily Camusot of *Cousin Pons* and other novels that he outwits—the very Camusot whom Lucien had supplanted in the affections of Coralie, and who had extracted the confession that led him to suicide. And it is with the great, disillusioned Granville of, among others, *Une Double Famille*, that he bargains.

Rastignac, the Nucingens, de Marsay, also recombine here as elsewhere. It takes the full complexities of the society and its institutions—law, finance, literature, demimonde, nobility—not only to overcome Lucien but to give the measure of his illusion. Balzac's incredibly unremitting concentration on this novel for a period of twenty years would have been wasted if he had not managed, as he does, to make these multiple recurrences comment on each other tonally.

Disillusion is the key feeling in the whole of *La Comédie Humaine* as in *Illusions Perdues;* it is shared by everybody from the street musician Gambara to the provincial philanthropist Madame de Graslin, from the famous Colonel Chabert to the lowest of the convicts whom Vautrin has at his beck and call. Horace Bianchon, de Marsay, Rastignac, La Duchesse de Langeais—all are alike in being disillusioned, but the note of disillusion is individuated for each in the chapter which he dominates. The whole is a polyphony of disillusions which orchestrates and counterpoints each single disillusion.

The reader alone is possessed of the total reality which charges this novel. No character can know enough to get behind the appearances that must delude Lucien or anybody. Disillusion in Balzac amounts to consciousness of the necessary deflection of any will, however titanic. Even the superhuman omniscience of a Jacques Collin must succumb to the deflection his necessary ignorance entails. Not only Gazonal in the tale of that name, but everyone, is a "comédien sans le savoir."

Illusion is individual, reality social; but society is made up of individuals' inner lives; the *comédie* comes not only from the typifying events of a comic drama, but, as in all fiction, from the indissoluble relation of illusion and reality.

The characters related and contrasted on this vast analogical scale are, then, not abstractions, either the mythical archetypes Baudelaire attributes to Balzac or the simple sociological types Balzac's historian's rhetoric committed him sometimes to calling them. They are fictions, individualized by their own actions, by the reactions of analogical other characters, and by their own possessions. "Ainsi l'oeuvre à faire devait avoir une triple forme: les hommes, les femmes et les choses, c'est-à-dire les personnes et la représentation matérielle qu'ils donnent de leur pensée; enfin l'homme et la vie." The perpetual categorizing of *La Comédie Humaine* relates the enumerated details for which Balzac is celebrated to the mythological passions of his characters. "Enfin," he says of Madame Vauquer, "toute sa personne explique la pension comme la pension implique sa personne." Scenic descriptions in Balzac are a dimension of the characters they define; every Balzacian house bears its owner's imprint existentially. To Balzac the action was immanent in the physical scene, as Lubbock (*The Craft of Fiction*) demonstrates of Eugénie Grandet, "the generalized picture . . . supporting the play of action," "the pictorial impression . . . [to] speed the work of drama."

Places become attributes of characters, not mere ballast, as Baudelaire thought, but extension and hieroglyph of their uniqueness, of fictive status. Provins renders the suffering of Pierrette drier and crueler than it could have been in the Brittany she came from. The sea and the rude Breton village render the father in *Drame au Bord de la Mer* more desolate, justifying the tale's long introduction; the Breton scene is set off against the effete, saccharine, unattaining life of the Parisians who observe it, to whose heads the tragedy painfully goes. It is off the rocks of this Breton sea that the father drowns his disgraced beloved son by tying a rock around his neck—rock and water unlikely for that use elsewhere in France by other folkways, if not unavailable. "Les particularités de cette scène pleine d'observations et de couleurs locales ne peuvent être appréciées qu'entre les Buttes de Montmartre et les hauteurs de Montrouge," Balzac states at the beginning of *Père Goriot*. "La rue Neuve-Sainte Geneviève surtout est comme un cadre de bronze, le seul qui convienne à ce récit, auquel on ne saurait trop préparer l'intelligence par des couleurs brunes, par des idées graves."

People are rooted in a scene, and a change of place, unlike the shifts in *L'Education Sentimentale* or Stendhal's novels, is either a fleeting tour, like Béatrix' trip to Italy, or permanent for life, like Pierrette's move from Brittany to Provins, or the engineer's move to Limoges in *Le Curé de Village*. A house, a place, are appearances that fix and individualize a character's reality in time by exact, gusty strokes which suggest those of a painting by Delacroix (*La Comédie Humaine*'s Joseph Bridau). The poetry of these details is not deciphered by tropes of language but rendered whole by its relation to the character. Scene in Balzac, like dialog in Dostoevsky and narrative irony in Stendhal, helps to give the characters their unique fictional being.

There was a possible Balzac—of whom Louis Lambert is the aborted counterpart—the philosopher of the will, or even a mere writer of romances like *Les Chouans*, the first novel he signed with his own name. His work might have taken the form of the Heraclitean aphorisms which intersperse *La Physiologie du Mariage* and conclude *Louis Lambert*, or of treatises like those that comprise the "Etudes Analytiques," where illustrative anecdotes are built around a handful of characters. These characters are putative, Caroline, Adolphe, Madame Fischtaminel, and others, the inverse of the fictively actual characters elsewhere in *La Comédie Humaine*. The historical *parti pris*, in the economy of his imagination, deflected Balzac from his earlier philosophical vein, saving him, as it were, for fiction, one whose glory is all the more real for the details of appearance it encompasses. The unparalleled lateral extent of his fiction, which the rhetoric of the historical *parti pris*[2] allows,—as a

[2] It ought to be noted that the Balzac who called for the medical aid of his own invented Doctor Bianchon on his deathbed would not agree with the view presented here of his history as a formal narrative device. "L'histoire est au rang des sciences," he says. "Car c'est la volonté de Dieu qui s'exécute, c'est sa pensée qui se réalise." When he begins his *Avant-propos* by saying, "Cette idée vint d'une comparaison entre l'Humanité et l'Animalité," he means *animalité*

researcher he may cover everything—creates, like the fabulous hydraulic machine in *La Peau de Chagrin,* an unparalleled concentration, in which the range of documented facts is made to serve a related depth of reality.

in the special sense of biological principles, the *unité de composition* which was expressed in the theories of Cuvier and Geoffrey St. Hilaire, to whom he dedicated *Le Père Goriot.* St. Hilaire's four principles of analogy could well serve as a résumé of the principles of character relations in *La Comédie Humaine:* the principles of elective affinities, of unequal development among creatures, of fixity of connections, and of a balance among organs whereby one hypertrophies when another atrophies.

V

THE LANGUAGE OF FICTION

While the poem sets our organism directly into play and
has, with respect to song, a limit which is an exercise of
connection exact and consistent among the hearing, the form
of the voice, and articulated expression—the novel wants to
excite and maintain in us that general and irregular waiting
which is our waiting for real events: the art of the narrator
imitates their bizarre deductive connection or their ordinary
sequences. And while the world of the poem is essentially
closed and complete in itself, being the pure system of the
ornaments and accidents of language, the universe of the
novel, even of a novel in fantasy, binds itself to the real
world, as an optical illusion accommodates itself to the tan-
gible things among which a spectator comes and goes.

The appearance of "life" and of "truth," which is the
object of the calculations and ambitions of the novelist, depends on the incessant introduction of *observations* [Italics
Valéry's]—that is, on recognizable elements which he incorporates in his design. A web of veritable and arbitrary
details relates the real existence of the reader to the feigned
existence of the personnages.

Valéry (on Proust)[1]

The basic talent of the novelist is to observe social behavior:
the way a person furnishes his house or makes love or reacts
to death or folds an envelope or constructs his sentences or
plans his career. How penetrating of Balzac to see that it is
the macaroni manufacturer whose simplicity would be open

---

[1] Translated from the Pléiade edition of Valéry, Vol. I (Paris:
Gallimard, 1958). Quoted with the permission of the publisher.

to the full anguish which assails Père Goriot! It is a verifiable observation that wholesalers of foodstuffs tend to be more devoted family men than, say, the public functionaries of *Les Employés;* and they tend to be simpler minded, than, say, petty financiers like Hulot of *La Cousine Bette,* who deal more abstractly in their commerce. How true, as James observes, that revolutionaries like M. Poupin tend to enter the "literary" trades, printing and bookbinding! How well-drawn is the mysterious connection Tolstoi makes for Prince Andrey between an early noble upbringing and an intense religious idealism—a connection observable, among countless examples, in the life of St. Francis.

It is above all, and first, on the fidelity and depth of such observations, insight by insight and in the total insight of the plot, that we should judge the merit of novels. We quite rightly ask first of them that they make explicit a reality we had already found implicit, not a poem's reality of rhythms and "correspondences," not a play's ritual, almost musical, reality of abstracted emotions, but the tapestry of hidden meaning, thread by thread, in the appearances of everyday.

So long as a novelist observes well, he may put his observations together in a clumsy and blundering style, like Dreiser or, among contemporary writers, James Jones and Jerome Weidman. Let a poem be shoddy in language and rhythm, and you have nothing: the poem is first its verbal artifice; but a good novel may be ill-written, a poor one well-written.

Imperfect control of language may imperil a novelist. Still, the special relation of language in a novel to the observation it recounts makes it possible for a fine novel to be clumsily, tastelessly, and flatly written. One such novel, whose style (and sentiment) has set many critics' teeth on edge, is James Jones' first (and so far only good) novel, *From Here to Eternity.* Here is a random passage from that work:

Prewitt was relieved to find Holmes was not around when they got back the second time. Paluso was relieved too. He released Prewitt quickly and took off for the PX, to be out of sight. Neither one of them understood that it was over. Prew limped upstairs and unmade the pack and put the stuff away and showered and changed to clean clothes and stretched out on his bunk, and waited for the OD or the Sergeant of the Guard. When they had not come for him by chowtime, he knew then they were not coming. He had been waiting for an hour and a half.

When the chow whistle blew, he knew something had interposed itself between himself and fate. The only possible answer was the Warden, who had seen fit to take a hand for one of those obscure screwy reasons of his own. I don't know what the hell business it is of his, he thought angrily, as he limped downstairs for chow. Why can't he keep his big nose out of things? [2]

Here we find no vestige of redeeming sparkle in the clumsy style, as we do in Dreiser or Weidman. There is no rhythm or grace to the movement, not even a felt personality. The whole operates at some stunned and colorless middle distance between colloquial speech ("was not around," "took off," "the stuff," "obscure screwy reasons," "what the hell," "keep his big nose out") and the impersonal prose of office reports; and yet Jones's language lacks both the verve of live speech and the crisp objectivity of an official document. Lost in so much blue mud are such occasional small diamonds of verbal use as the change from Prewitt to Prew in the first paragraph when the main character ceases to be an official object of punishment and becomes once more a nicknamed member of the company.

One suspects, too, that at times the individual details (here the shower and so on) are not only drab, but also have no fictive force underlying their documentative presentation. And this suspicion is confirmed by the monstrous accumulation of stultified detail in *Some Came Running*.

[2] Reprinted with the permission of the publishers, Charles Scribner's Sons, New York.

Still, in spite of all this, *From Here to Eternity* is a magnificent novel, extraordinary in the depth of its human understanding and its vast scope of relations. Prewitt's attitude as he returns from his second punitive march is well observed and fictively realized, both in itself and as one of a large and fine sequence of moments in his developing awareness and performance of his human role. This awareness is far too complex to be ticked off simply as "protest," and Jones has kept it in a true perspective throughout by bringing it into changing relation with other, equally complex, people. Captain Holmes's anger at Prewitt, well observed and created, has been managed by Milt Warden so that he drops his intended court-martial. It is deeply in character that Prewitt could not know this and yet sense it enough to feel first relief, then anger as he correctly and characteristically guesses whom he has to thank. His relief would be shared by Corporal Paluso, one of the host of minor characters this novel presents with unfailing differentiation and insight. Paluso, in a well observed sequence, first ragged Prewitt that morning, then embarrassedly directed the first punitive hike, then followed through resignedly for the second; here, at last, he washes his hands quickly of Prewitt and disappears.

For all its lack of color, the language carries along insight by insight this fine process of character relations, and these notes of observation, ringing true through the mutes of clumsy style, combine to present a solid and impressive novelistic symphony.

Not only the observed details of a good novel should be thus true to life. The plot itself must conform, in its temporal rhythm, its social relations, its causality, authentically to life; the plot of a novel, more than the plot of a drama, must have a close verisimilitude. Even the romancer, who seems to work with a wholly metaphorical plot, begins with observation: Ahab is erected on the sweeping observation of the way old men with power conduct themselves under the sway of *idées fixes;* Joseph K is constructed from observing the typical reactions of modern metropolitan functionaries who are sensitive to the frustrating paradoxes of their existence.

His particular relation to reality saddles the novelist with a compulsion to document and verify. Even Proust, for all his belief in imagination's primacy, checked his dress fashions for accuracy. Jane Austen would not put hedgerows in a Northamptonshire that had none. The magic of words has its effect, too, and a documentative reality is felt to reside in the very names given to characters; otherwise why have so many great novelists tinkered elaborately in evolving names for their people? And these names by no means always have some buried pun in them from their own language (Christopher Newman) or another (Swann).

So, for Stendhal the novel is a mirror conducted along a highway. At each point of a novel, in each sentence, a suasive and economical clarity is felt to inhere. Partly this mirrorlike clarity derives from the common speech on which nearly every novelist bases his style; but even if we say of Jane Austen and Proust that they do something more with prose than merely to heighten the speech of acutely intelligent people, their prose is, and must be, less stylized than that of Plato or Milton. For the clearness of fictional language is produced mostly by the processive reality it allows itself as directly as possible to mirror.

In an observational statement of narrative, the words refer not to other words, other references, but to referents in reality. "They used to kiss," refers directly to (imagined) real people performing a real act. This must be an observation as well as a fact for it to take a justifiable place, as it does, in a short story by Joyce. Not only must people really kiss; there must be meaning in these two kissing at all at this particular past time of the narrative.

While in a novel one statement points singly to its object, in poetry the words themselves interact, both musically and logically. "I wandered lonely as a cloud" is not a single flash of observation. The word "lonely" is identified first with the word "cloud" before their constellation is referred to a referent in reality. (There may be no real cloud overhead in the poem.) And, further, the referent, a real "lonely-as-a-cloud" emotional state, goes on to make "wandered" almost analogical. "Wandered" means here in context, even more than the literal fact of walked aimlessly (as "wandered" would mean in narrative), walked in such a way as to lay one open to analogical correspondences like that between the feeling of loneliness and some supposed cloud. The poem builds, laterally, analogs; "cloud" defines "lonely" by analogy, both define "wandered," and so on. In a poem, abstractions too are often defined by other abstractions: "Th' expense of spirit in a waste of shame/ Is lust in action." A statement in a novel, even one composed of such moral abstractions with some other bearing, works first to record an item of social process.

From Madame de la Fayette to Gide, from Defoe to James, the moral observation does the main work of keeping the novel going. And yet these moral statements, by being brought to bear on the fine process of a social situation, resist the abstract and structured function such statements perform in plays from Sophocles to Ibsen. Moll Flanders, in the following passage, uses psychological generalizations to draw in the fine lines of a husband's character (the husband himself only one of a series of incidents to her, indiscriminate and yet fictively distinguished):

> My husband, to give him his due, was a man of infinite good nature, but he was no fool; and finding his income not suited to the manner of living which he had intended, if I had brought him what he expected, and being under a

disappointment in his return of his plantations in Virginia, he discovered many times his inclination of going over to Virginia to live upon his own; and often would be magnifying the way of living there, how cheap, how plentiful, how pleasant, and the like.

I began presently to understand his meaning, and I took him up very plainly one morning, and told him that I did so. . . .

Defoe has observed how males act with females, how indirect husbands can be with their wives, how direct the wives can be in return with them, how a wife may know her place even when it is shifting and count her blessings even when they are short-lived. His observations make up the integrity of *Moll Flanders* and lift it above ordinary rogues' narratives, also above the sort of document which records the unconscious values of a mercantile society (for which our critics have recently been reading it), establishing it firmly as fiction. The observations alone make it a novel, and not the well-managed common style, Defoe's clever notion of a criminal with middle class values, his honesty as an author, or any of the other contributory virtues of the work. Such virtues would themselves probably not exist without the guidance of the observational insight.

Observation must underlie the statements of a novel, or it will ring false no matter what its skill of style and complexity of structure. *Ulysses'* complexity acts to coordinate what are fundamentally observations of social process, as in this passage:

> With a keep quiet relief, his eyes took note: this is street here middle of the day Bob Doran's bottle shoulders. On his annual bend, M'Coy said. They drink in order to say or do something of *cherchez la femme*. Up in the Coombe with chummies and streetwalkers and then the rest of the year as sober as a judge.
>
> Yes. Thought so. Sloping into the Empire. Gone. Plain soda would do him good. Where Pat Kinsella had his Harp theatre before Whitbred ran the Queen's. Broth of a boy.

Dion Boucicault business with his harvest moon face in a poky bonnet.

Bloom, observing another, is himself observed, his mind characterized by what it throws up, and the mind in general characterized by the meandering sequence of its thoughts. The time of day, the place in Dublin, the changing face of the city, the sexual interest, the commercial interest, all do double duty to sketch in both Bloom and Bloom's newsday and private world. The *Odyssey* has really little to do with all this; precisely Joyce's ironic point in the title. We may read *Ulysses* as a poem; we do so not first to hear the inter-echoing rings of the words but to learn how the observations comment on each other. Each of these sentences gives a fictional insight related with a clarity initially as simple as Defoe's to a social process it is presenting.

The novelist's need to flesh out reality may also lead him to furnish some of his observations in the form of documentations. Joyce wants to recreate as much as possible of a real city's sights and sounds as taken into the consciousness of Bloom, Stephen, and Molly. Documentations can exist on as vast a scale as Balzac's, or as narrow as that of William Sansom, who documents places as part of some of the observations of his stories. Historical novelists tend to use documentative statements—for obvious reasons. Traces of documentation can be found in nearly any novel. In fact, one might define the normal statement of fiction as an observation with both moral and documentative overtones.

Again, when Joyce and Flaubert use detail metaphorically, they do so by way of observing process, and not in order to build the tight little world which metaphors can make of a poem. The fly that Allen Tate (*On the Limits of Poetry*) finds so symbolic in *The Idiot*, as it buzzes over the dead Nastasya, is first of all a real fly in a real room, seen as an item of one processive moment which also includes bottles of Zhdanov's fluid and some American leather.

When in a poem Emily Dickinson calls death an "exploit," she is making a prediction of an analogical type. In calling it a "white exploit," she is making a further analogy, a metaphorical statement about the exploit. The immediacy is so superb that it dazzles, "White exploit!" What a surprise! We had traditionally thought of death as dark. A reference to heaven is suggested in "white," but the white is too in-definite and general to be merely what it is partly, an attri-bute of the light with which heaven is supposedly filled. How, too, can an exploit have a color? To call death an ex-ploit is a surprising conjunction, a white exploit another surprise. Many, if not all, poems are tissues of such sur-prises: their series of rhythmic statements make up worlds from series of analogical correspondences.

As a novel's individual statements must be observed, so the connections from statement to statement must be al-lowed to meander along. These connections must rise from the presented process and not get so stiff a structure as would be given by narrative in another form, such as the *Odyssey* or *Hero and Leander*; as prose with some other purpose, *The Republic* or *The Ecclesiastical Polity*.

Poetry, like philosophy, orders the world, mainly by analogical identification, into an order ideally both concrete and abstract. Fiction, though, is like history, and it com-bines its usually observational statements on the base of a narrative line. In fiction one statement is not a surprise or a revelation of another, as in poetry; it is merely in sequence; and of a long series of such unsurprising, rather repetitive, statements, each a flash of observation, is the novel com-posed. Fiction can deal with change, but from chapter to chapter, rarely from sentence to sentence. By this accretion of resembling insights a novel unfolds what Paul Goodman calls its "full expansion of slowly maturing sequences."

How the meaning of fiction rises from a sequence of similar observations may be seen in a passage from Tolstoi's *Ivan Ilych:*

All this was just what Ivan Ilych had himself brilliantly accomplished a thousand times in dealing with men on trial. The doctor summed up just as brilliantly, looking over his spectacles triumphantly and even gaily at the accused. From the doctor's summing up Ivan Ilych concluded that things were bad, but that for the doctor, and perhaps for everybody else, it was a matter of indifference, though for him it was bad. And this conclusion struck him painfully, arousing in him a great feeling of pity for himself and of bitterness towards the doctor's indifference to a matter of such importance.

He said nothing of this, but rose, placed the doctor's fee on the table, and remarked with a sigh: "We sick people probably often put inappropriate questions. But tell me, in general, is this complaint dangerous or not? . . ."

The doctor looked at him sternly over his spectacles with one eye, as if to say: "Prisoner, if you will not keep to the questions put to you, I shall be obliged to have you removed from the court."

"I have already told you what I consider necessary and proper. The analysis may show something more." And the doctor bowed.

Ivan Ilych went out slowly, seated himself disconsolately on his sledge, and drove home. All the way home he was going over what the doctor had said, trying to translate those complicated, obscure, scientific phrases into plain language and find in them an answer to the question: "Is my condition bad? Is it very bad? Or is there as yet nothing much wrong?" And it seemed to him that the meaning of what the doctor had said was that it was very bad. Everything in the streets seemed depressing. The cabmen, the houses, the passers-by, and the shops, were dismal. His ache, this dull, gnawing ache that never ceased for a moment, seemed to have acquired a new and more serious significance from the doctor's dubious remarks. Ivan Ilych now watched it with a new and oppressive feeling.

He reached home and began to tell his wife about it. She listened, but in the middle of his account his daughter came in with her hat on, ready to go out with her mother. She sat down reluctantly to listen to this tedious story, but could not stand it long, and her mother too did not hear him to the end.

Something is narrated that has happened to Ivan Ilych: he has got serious, disturbing advice from the doctor, and his outlook has changed. The change is presented as part of, and identical with, a series of observations: the brilliant indifference of the doctor, the politely glazed-over dismay of Ilych, his consequent coloring the very scene about him ("Everything in the streets seemed depressing"), the further blow of the hard core of human selfishness underneath the perfunctory solicitude of his family. The progress of the narrative goes hand in hand with the analysis: act and analysis of act, indeed, are given at one stroke; and by showing Ilych's realization that he himself "a thousand times," had acted like the doctor, Tolstoi's insight can tie in the fine social context of Ilych's death with the generalized plot of his life. Here Ilych only seems to stand for all men. These analyses, the separate statements, down to the doctor's manner of looking sternly with one eye over his spectacles, Ilych's matter-of-fact bestowal of the fee, his polite insistence, his daughter's rhythm and attitude of entry, are all similar Tolstoian insights.

In these six paragraphs of narrative no one paragraph qualifies or changes the others, as stanzas might in a poem or sections in a philosophical work; the combination proceeds by the accretion of similar observations, flashes of such commanding generality that they seem real and that Tolstoi has been praised for rendering life itself, as if he had done so in a way unlike any other novelist's.

The plot is all the time progressing through these similar details of observation, and there is an obscure rhythm of process here, as in the whole story, a sort of dizzying spiral in these six paragraphs rising out of what had earlier in the story seemed an endless metronomic progression. Metronome, in mortal life, dizzies into Ilych's "dull ache." The rhythm is unique for this story (or for any successful story); it expresses the life feeling of the story. This rhythm, however, I mean as a metaphor for the pace of the story, for the relation of parts to the whole in time (narrative is temporal); it is not the same as what it rises out of, and loosely coincides with, the prose rhythm of the words. The rhythm is that of narrative time in fiction, not of sound structure, as in poetry. The novelist has a "voice," like a poet, but it does not sound to the same end, except when the sophisticated novelist, from Flaubert on, deliberately harnesses poetic rhythms.

Fiction can compose its observations out of statements that are, in themselves, analogies of preconceived abstractions. When Flaubert compares torn fragments of a letter to butterflies, or when he merely presents the crow of a cock in a barnyard to get at something of the lonely anxiety Charles feels, he is using analogies as a means of social observation. When Tolstoi has Anna Karenina lower her eyelids toward the end, this is both an observed fact and a metaphor of shutting out reality's moral light. When Jane Austen says "Marianne was sensible," she is using a preconceived abstraction to make a genuine observation.

This may seem a quibble, but prose which is simply analogical cannot conceivably be fictive; it would be prose poetry, like the last chapter of *Ecclesiastes*. And imaginative prose which used mostly abstractions would be pure romance, like the *Morte d'Arthur*. The special relation of fiction to the process of reality demands that its statements have an observational side. In *The Tale of Genji*, the dialog is not observed, even though elaborately ceremonious people might also conform to the abstract norm governing it; this dialog refers univocally to an ideal system—one expressed in the love poems of the period, which it occasionally quotes.

While in almost all poetry we are aware of the presence of convention, in fiction we are aware of it never so powerfully and sometimes not at all. There is no fictive diction that corresponds to a poetic diction. The prose of ordinary life which is the normal narrative mode for fiction lends, and borrows, for its observations a feeling of the reality which I believe to be the characteristic emotion of fiction. What we feel in fiction is a succession of shocks, flashes of observation which relate us to reality.

The secret lives of characters are revealed by the observations describing them. It is we and Tolstoi, not Ivan Ilych, who are aware of the meaning of his feelings; he has them mutely. Charles Bovary is surrounded by mute metaphors. In poetry, contrastingly, everything is present, spoken, public (not secret) in the voice and persona of the poet; and in drama one or more characters are in some sense aware of all the meaning present, since that meaning resides totally in speeches made by the characters.

Of course, no matter how seemingly documentary the observations in fiction may be, they are still fictive, part of an artifice, and their make-believe is inseparable from their meaning, their illusion from their reality: "Even if it were described to me in minute detail," Maurice Blanchot says (in *La Part du Feu*)[3] of fictional language, ". . . even if I penetrated marvelously the whole mechanism of administration in the castle, I would always remain more or less conscious of the little I knew, for this poverty is the essence of fiction: that essence consists in rendering present to me just that which makes it unreal—accessible to reading alone, inaccessible to my existence; and no richness of imagination, no exactness of observation, could correct such an indigence, so long as this indigence is always implied by fiction and always posited and attained by it through a content as dense or as close to the real as it permits itself." The reality to which the observations of fiction relate is inseparable from the artifice into which they compose, the fact that each is selected out in a relative *pauvreté* compared to the richness of one's existence. But it is this richness and this existence that the expansive observations of fiction can render as no other art form can.

[3] (Paris: Gallimard, 1949.) Quoted with the permission of the publishers.

⚕ VI ⚕

THE RICHES OF DETACHMENT

FLAUBERT

Flaubert is so meticulous of his language that a constant distance is felt to exist between him as the observing novelist and the observations he recounts. The observing novelist is detached, and through his detachment he is able to make each statement of his narrative do double duty, as the sort of observation that may be found in any novel and as the sort of analogy we expect to find in poetry.

Flaubert's detachment as the narrator in *Madame Bovary*, carefully sustained, creates between his style and Emma's feelings an irony which is not an irony in the usual sense. When Flaubert says of her girlhood, "Comme c'était loin tout cela! Comme c'était loin!" he means exactly what he says, not the contrary. The succinctness of the phrase, its repetition, the contrast between the outburst of these exclamation points and the moderation of the rest of the context, all imply that the exclamation is Emma's, not Flaubert's, though his perfect control has not quite slipped into indirect discourse. This control governs the mediation between what appears to Emma and the hidden reality behind it.

Flaubert's irony is infused into his style, unassertive and pervasive. It is curiously serious in its generality and has so little ironic tone that it might pass unnoticed, as

Stendhal's irony or Jane Austen's could never do. This irony is an irony of point of view, ironic in that it has the whole novel qualify Emma. Flaubert's irony differs in its detachment from, say, Jane Austen's. Her irony sets up directly, with no more than intermittent detachment, the contrasting ideas through which the man and the woman of both sense and sensibility can find each other. Jane Austen has a spokesman in all her novels, but Flaubert could not have one in his without violating their essential condition. His detachment is pivotal to *Madame Bovary*. It is almost the initial conception of the novel.

For the first time in the history of fiction point of view is used thematically. What we know about Madame Bovary we know through, and by means of, the fact that Flaubert has indicated in his style a consciousness of his, and our, distance from her. We cannot talk about point of view in Flaubert without talking about the meaning of his novel, because that meaning resides in the discrepancy between appearance and reality which the narrator's detachment keeps taut. To speak of Jane Austen's point of view, or Stendhal's, comparing as Bardèche does the technique of Balzac to the *rosace* method of Proust, is off the subject; we can never ascertain what *Emma* or *La Chartreuse de Parme* or *Illusions Perdues* mean by discussing point of view, whereas for Flaubert it is at the heart of the subject; the novelist has reflexively identified the subject with it.

Point of view in fiction, like perspective in easel painting, is always necessarily present. Only from the Renaissance on is the painter conscious of perspective as a thematic element in the painting, and only after Flaubert does point of view become thematic in fiction. By introducing conscious perspective, Flaubert changed both fiction and its perspective; the novel, stating itself conscious of being a novel, would then perform a new range of imaginative tasks.

How this perspective works in Flaubert may be seen

in a passage taken at random from *L'Education Sentimentale.*

> Mais la causerie surtout amusait Frédéric. Son goût pour les voyages fut caressé par Dittmer, qui parla de l'Orient; il assouvit sa curiosité des choses du théâtre en écoutant Rosenwald causer de l'Opéra; et l'existence atroce de la bohême lui parut drôle, à travers la gaieté d'Hussonet, lequel narra, d'une manière pittoresque, comment il avait passé tout un hiver, n'ayant pour nourriture que du fromage de Hollande. Puis une discussion entre Lovarias et Burieu, sur l'école florentine, lui révéla des chefs-d'oeuvre, lui ouvrit des horizons, et il eut mal à contenir son enthousiasme quand Pellerin s'écria:
> —Laissez-moi tranquille avec votre hideuse réalité!

> (But the conversation above all pleased Frédéric. His taste for travel was titillated by Dittmer, who spoke of the Orient; he satisfied his curiosity in theatrical matters as he heard Rosenwald go on about the opera; and the atrocious existence of Bohemia seemed funny to him through the gaiety of Hussonet, who told picturesquely how he spent a whole winter with nothing to eat but Dutch cheese. Then a discussion between Lovarias and Burieu, about the Florentine school, revealed masterpieces, opened horizons, for him; and he could hardly contain his enthusiasm when Pellerin exclaimed, "Leave me alone with your hideous reality!")

In any novel each detail flows in with the others, forming that unity in the work by virtue of which alone any single detail is significant. In Flaubert the novelist's consciousness of this process is rendered ironically as part of the theme. The phrases in the passage above take their hard, definite, summary quality from Flaubert's stylized consciousness of each detail's signification. These disparate, denotative phrases are far from the thinness of an ordinary reporter's narrative, which they seem to imitate. The disparateness of the facts is conscious, carefully preserved as an element in style; for example, by the grammatically otiose commas in "Burieu, sur l'école florentine, lui révéla." Flaubert means each statement to be a conscious, objectified summary of Frédéric's character, as well as a narrative unit. The self-conscious definition fixes—spatializes, as it were— the necessarily unfixed temporally successive events in life. Impressionist literature, as in Mallarmé and Flaubert, makes a temporal art spatial just as impressionist painting makes a spatial art represent a temporal moment. Flaubert, by the artful detachment of his representation, deepens the succession of fictional events by realizing a contrast between their appearance of represented fixity and their reality of actual flow, just as Cézanne deepens a represented landscape by composing its spaces and colors, "flowing" to an impressionist, in abstract fixity on a canvas. This is what Proust sensed when he said of Flaubert's style, "A man who by his entirely new use of the past definite, the past indefinite, the present participle, and of certain pronouns and prepositions, renewed our vision of things almost as much as Kant did with his categories, his theories of knowledge and of the reality of the exterior world."

Here and throughout, Flaubert is saying, "Frédéric is young now; he will grow old, as we all must. His *éducation* is a permanent thing, as my style renders it, and he can never lose the knowledge he thus accumulates; though, unlike the overseeing novelist, he might not recall the details. His life, the lives of the other characters as well, is nothing but a succession of such lessons, whose sum defines the limit of life in this novel. Frédéric will be true to himself, repeat himself, act out unforeseen phases with a foreseen cast of people, the ones we have given him at the very outset." The reality Frédéric evades, like the *raté* who finds it *hideuse*, will have become identical with the disparate appearances that are silently and secretly "educating" his missed life.

Flaubert, then, is a trouvère, as Allen Tate calls him (*On the Limits of Poetry*). He has found a way for fiction to use thematically the point of view always necessarily present in a novel, a way more searching than the arbitrary first person of a Defoe or the omniscient authorship of a

Thackeray, a way that, linked with reflexivity, would likewise liberate reflexivity from the necessity of talking about
itself. Fiction, starting afresh with the fact of itself as fiction, is given by Flaubert a whole range of double views
we are not yet done exploiting.

Flaubert's perspective controls economically his use of sensuous detail in such a way as to make each detail a metaphorical correlative of the action. Not only is the love song
of the blind man outside the dying Emma's window a metaphor, not only the bleating animals and fulsome oratory
amid which Rodolphe courts Emma at the *Comices Agri-
coles*. Through the sense of the novel as a novel, every last
detail of his narrative is made to do double duty, as observed
detail and as correlative of the action. Consistently, critics
like Martin Turnell (*The Novel in France*) can read allegories of meaning into the three parts of the schoolboy
Charles's hat. When Charles's horse stumbles in the ruts that
have become deeper, we are invited by the detachment of
the style to say that he has got in deeper metaphorically.
His emotions, too, are symbolized by the watchdogs barking
and tugging at their chains as he arrives in the Rouaults'
barnyard. The five or six peacocks mingling with chickens
and turkeys atop the dunghill, the soiled fleece of the fat
sheep, are metaphors of his later feelings, of Emma's. Emma's sensuousness, her appeal for Charles, are at once revealed and symbolized by her throwing back her head and
licking "drop by drop" the liquor out of the bottom of a
glass. *Madame Bovary* is composed of thousands of such
sensuous details which are at once observation, point for
point, in that they represent the observed reality Flaubert
so anxiously sought for his narrative, and also analogies in
the meaning his detachment intends them to have. Thus
every concrete appearance hides and figures a psychological

reality; appearance is sealed off from reality in the character's unconsciousness to become the more united through the secret life of feelings that the narrator's detachment is unremittingly etching in.

Tate cites this passage to illustrate Flaubert's use of metaphorical correlatives:

> Les ardoises laissaient tomber d'aplomb une chaleur lourde qui lui serrait les tempes et l'étouffait; elle se traîna jusqu'à la mansarde close dont elle tira le verrou, et la lumière éblouissante jaillit d'un bond.
>
> En face, par-dessus les toits, la pleine campagne s'étalait à perte de vue. En bas, sous elle, la place du village était vide; les cailloux du trottoir scintillaient, les girouettes des maisons se tenaient immobiles; au coin de la rue, il partait d'un étage inférieur une sorte de ronflement à modulations stridentes. C'était Binet qui tournait.

> (There the roof slates were throwing down a heat that was all but unbearable; it pressed on her so that she could scarcely breathe. She dragged herself over to the dormer, whose shutters were closed; she pulled back the bolt, and the dazzling sunlight poured in.
>
> Out beyond the roof-tops, the open countryside stretched as far as eye could see. Below her the village square was empty; the stone sidewalk glittered; the weather vanes on the houses stood motionless. From the lower floor of a house at the corner came a whirring noise with strident changes of tone: Binet was at his lathe.)

"Here," Tate says, "using this mechanic's tool, Flaubert gives us a direct *impression* of Emma's sensation at a particular moment (which not even the drama could accomplish), and thus by rendering audible to us what Emma alone could hear he charged the entire scene with actuality. As Emma goes to the window she merely notes that Binet's lathe is turning—'C'était Binet qui tournait.' Then she looks down at the street which seems to rise toward her—'Allons! Allons!' she whispers, because she cannot find the will to jump. We have had rendered to us visually the shock of violent suicide. . . . The humming vertigo that draws the street toward her is rendered audible to us by the correlative sound of the lathe." Not only the lathe is a metaphor: the heavy heat of the tiles morally as well as physically grips her temples and stifles her. What the light dazzles is a moral darkness ensconced in her physical solitude. There is no end to the physical countryside, nor to the moral monotony she feels. The real emptiness of the village square reflects her condition: she is alone because she feels so, and also because no one knows of her love. No one, that is, except perhaps Binet, whose lathe, then, is metaphorically heard. For Binet stood present hunting in the fields when Emma first ran early one morning to Rodolphe; he embarrassed her shortly thereafter by (with ironic correlatives) ordering some acid to clean his hunting equipment. It will later be from Binet's point of view that we watch her rush around desperately seeking some means of salvaging her home from foreclosure.

Binet, like the metaphors, is pictorial. Indeed all characters in *Madame Bovary* seem so much so that the expression "pictorial made dramatic and dramatic made pictorial," Lubbock's characterization of the novel (*The Craft of Fiction*), almost does not go far enough. There is a curious passivity about all the characters in this village, a passivity not unlike that of Flaubert himself ("Madame Bovary, c'est moi"). Madame Bovary, and all the minor characters, either passively register—or worse, like Homais, fail to register— the thousands of impressions, of metaphorical details, that Flaubert's style rains on them. The revisions we may inspect in Flaubert's *ébauches* of *Madame Bovary* show that by and large his writing evolved through a progressive inspissation of these metaphors; he weeded out nonmetaphorical details and kept the details from being too explicit—and therefore not detached enough to strengthen the underlying reality. Binet may see, but he cannot know; he is himself known by the narrator, whose detachment keeps him from knowing.

The secret dissolution of Madame Bovary, no less than

the secret crumbling of her husband, takes place passively
in feeling rather than in action. Her love affairs, his desperate clubfoot cure, her suicide, his sinking into death, con-
cretize the feelings her reactions are metamorphosing. And
the foreclosure of bankruptcy only confirms what it is a
metaphor of, how far the feelings had gone. Their money
has been drained out to satisfy the importunacy of her vague
impressionistic desires. That Homais, the unfeeling man incarnate, should receive the Legion of Honor in the last sentence of the narrative, is a crowning and particularly appropriate irony; what the irony crowns is that the welter of
feelings, represented by the stream of analogical detail, has
drowned those who are most sensitive to it. Appearances
have hardened into a hideous reality.

Madame Bovary has been called a religious novel, and surely
what undoes Emma in the novel is a kind of mortal sin.
After Rodolphe her soul has still enough balance not to be
drawn down by the vertigo of the lathe, but after the deprivation of Léon she can submit to the horribly inky taste
of arsenic. The appearances she has submitted to have left
a residuum of gritty reality. The song of the blind man calls
her back to a life of the whole sentiments, a life now as lost
to her through the suicide that culminates her sin as the visible world is lost to him. He sings of a lost love, of a love
that in the song is already lost.

Her first seduction takes place on the autumn leaves, and
Flaubert describes it in terms of the lengthening shadows of
twilight, the patches of light on the leaves; a vague prolonged cry on the horizon is expressly denoted as resembling her feelings "like music." The second seduction, by
deliberate contrast, takes place in a black fiacre rattling
around Rouen after a tour of the cathedral. Out of the
fiacre float into the air the torn up pieces of the letter re-

fusing the Léon she has acquiesced to "like white butter-flies," the ironic simile echoing the "black butterflies" of the ashes at the back of the stove where she has long ago burned her wedding bouquet.

Here the secret history of the soul takes place in the feelings. Before her first seduction Emma reaches out to the Church, but an insensitive Abbé Bournisien, counterpart to the pigheaded Homais with whom he later argues, repulses her. His moral categories are a mere appearance which uncharitably refuse to face the reality of the environment-drenched feelings Emma is struggling to account for. "Emma Bovary's poor adventures are a tragedy," Henry James says, "for the very reason that in a world unsuspecting, unassisting, unconsoling, she has herself to distil the rich and the rare."

If we ask why Emma was seduced, we find not actions but feelings, impressions concretized in the details of the narrative. Rodolphe's gentility calls up in her a memory of her flood of impressions at the Vaubyessard dinner party. The sensation of having lost the too timid Léon makes her more willing to listen to another. But finally she needs the seduction, the abandonment (*abandonner* is Flaubert's usual verb for sexual seduction), to enjoy the luxuries she has already been buying from Lheureux; refusing to go riding with Rodolphe out of decorous fear and moral soundness, her reserve is broken down by a new riding costume she has just bought. "L'amazone la décida," Flaubert says. She goes riding because of the luxurious jodhpurs; she is seduced because she goes riding.[1]

Another reason she succumbs is the presence of what she thinks is Charles's revolting insensitivity. This is ironic for her past; she thought him not insensitive when he res-

[1] In *l'amazone*, the particular riding costume, reside additional suggestions of transvestism, loss of one breast, Orientalism (the Amazons lived in the Near East), and perhaps even the metaphorical parallel of Theseus' abandonment of the Amazon Queen Hippolyta.

cued her from the farm by marrying her. And it is ironic
for his mute sufferings, easily as sensitive as hers to the
stream of feeling. The sensitivity achingly present in the
first scene of the novel, where his schoolfellows tease him,
stakes its whole life on love for Madame Bovary. Hers
is a true marriage, then, and only with her husband, by
facing the clumsy physique and commonplace mind which
house the delicacy of his spirit, could she reach the good life
she perversely allows herself to feel him stifling out of her.
The title, *Madame Bovary*, is significant. *Anna Karenina*,
but not *Emma Bovary*, because Charles is not the stultified
Karenin Emma thinks him. She is his true wife, and her
tragic flaw is in not recognizing it.

Significant, too, is what many critics have pointed out,
that Charles surrounds Emma at the beginning and at the
end of the novel. The pathos of this passive "bourgeois
tragedy" is his as much as hers. We measure the effect of
her sin by the depth of his sadness much more than by the
brief mention of her daughter's later life as a factory
worker. Ugly he is, and ugly to her damnation she finds
him, not knowing, not willing to let her feelings know, as
Flaubert says of Charles's hat at the beginning of the narrative, that "la laideur muette a des profondeurs d'expression
comme le visage d'un imbécile." Charles's mute suffering is
deep enough to kill him; he is completely the husband of a
woman who perversely would not see his sensitivity.

In this novel the secret life accretes through a stream
of sensation diffused in the physical environment; the characters themselves as well are presented almost as undevel-
oped images. Charles is defined, and Flaubert's detachment
is aware of it, by his professional mediocrity and physical
clumsiness; Emma by her purchases, reading, and music;
Homais by his quack science; Rodolphe by his hunting;
Léon by his poetry and law. But these characters are fixed
in a kind of everyday reality which their feelings must admit, if, unlike Homais, they have feelings. The actual in-

dividualized town is the background against which Emma operates, and, while insensitive, it has a reality her romantic illusions will not recognize.

Flaubert's detachment, again, renders the reality of the town. He fixes each detail of town or of metaphorized feeling with a series of *mots justes*. The division in Flaubert's own spirit between romantic feeling and documentary accuracy was united in the style: each *mot juste* picks up a fact as with a pair of laboratory tweezers. His self-conscious detachment, present in every *mot juste*, draws the distinction between Emma's impression of the town's appearance, a kind of reality, and the everyday reality she does not realize is interacting with her impression. The possible synthesis of the romantic and the real is nowhere present in the novel but everywhere present in the narrator, so that, like Proust, Flaubert has a kind of health in his description of sickness.

How such impressionistic feelings jell into sentiments, then petrify into lifelong *idées fixes* is the subject of Flaubert's next French novel, his greatest, *L'Education Sentimentale*. Only the detached narrator, again, is aware of how the sentiments are educated. Metaphors are subordinated in this narrative, and the details have not so much lost as buried the analogical implications so prominent in *Madame Bovary*:

> —Mais oui, je l'aime, . . . je l'aime!
> Il lui semblait descendre dans quelque chose de profond qui n'en finissait plus. La pendule sonna trois heures. Elle écouta les vibrations du timbre mourir.—Et elle restait au bord de son fauteuil, les prunelles fixes, et souriant toujours.
> La même après-midi, au même moment, Frédéric et Mlle Louise se promenaient dans le jardin que M. Roque possédait au bout de l'île.

(Yes, I love him, I love him!

He seemed to go down in something deep that never ended. The clock struck three. She heard the vibrations of the bell die. She stayed on the edge of her chair, pupils fixed, smiling the whole time.

The same afternoon, at the same moment, Frédéric and Mlle. Louise were walking in the garden M. Roque owned at the end of the island.)

The impressions of Madame Arnoux here are summarized by each phrase of the narrative, rather than rendered by sensual correlatives. Even the sensual details carry a significance which has been generalized out of metaphor. The dying fall of the clock's vibrations, beginning as metaphor, leaves metaphor behind to stand in fixed self-consciousness of itself as an item of sentimental education. Madame Arnoux becomes defined as she changes, in the impressions of event after event, till she here finally recognizes—ironically because Deslauriers, led by his own impressions, has just accosted her—that she loves Frédéric. What she recognizes is the eroding effect of the impressions she has been subject to. The love she admits will bring her, at last, into Frédéric's bedroom, shockingly to unveil white hair, then to cut off a long lock "brutally at the root" before leaving him forever. It is Flaubert's detachment that gives its intensity and definiteness to this powerful late scene of the novel: into that act of farewell has gone the whole sequence of events, rendered inexorable by the analytical hardness of Flaubert's style. The detachment makes the separate generalized impressions cumulative, makes of sentimental experiences a sentimental education.

It is an education doomed to failure in a world fragmented into a babel of *idées fixes*. Frédéric, as this passage ironically says, is courting Louise at the very moment his idol, Madame Arnoux, realizes her love for him; but his affairs with Madame Dambreuse and Rosanette will undermine his chances to marry the provincial heiress who adores him, as the impressions of the noblewoman Dambreuse and the courtesan Rosanette undermine each other. Louise, too, will be fragmented; she will marry a disillusioned Deslauriers instead of her idol, Frédéric, and find him so rough that she will run away with a singer.

Among the women in Frédéric's life—Louise, Rosanette, Madame Arnoux, Madame Dambreuse—no unity. So among his impressions of the men. Devotion to Deslauriers undoes a career with M. Dambreuse, as does lending to M. Arnoux, which also estranges him from Deslauriers. And Deslauriers' own friendship with Sénécal masks and motivates a fatal separation from Frédéric.

The irritations of these *idées fixes*, coming to a head in the 1848 Revolution, which reveals and changes them all, complicate in rapprochements and contrasts of penetrating scope. The "laboured" qualities of this novel, the "leak in its stored sadness," which made James think it a failure, actually add to its success. The fixed hardness of style categorizes into reality the peculiar appearances of a world in which Frédéric, for example, can leave Madame Dambreuse to jostle Deslauriers on the streets of a Paris perhaps actually too large to make such accidental encounters likely: the hard style gives the plot the fixedness of a parable without taking away the observed complexity of a novel.

Frédéric is the center of these inexorable destinies, where the fanaticism of a Sénécal executes the unique idealism of a Dussardier in the name of the life of the Republic, where even religion estranges Arnoux from his old friends, where the timidity of a Cisy meets the same petrifaction as the Machiavellianism of a Martinon. A man without qualities, Frédéric's nerves have been rendered by Flaubert as taking in the cumulative experiences of the several destinies. Their disintegration culminates in his leaving the Revolution for a spell at Fontainebleau with Rosanette. Having fixed Frédéric's education in the hardness of his style, Flau-

bert can sweep to his conclusion and summarize by implication the cumulative effect of twenty years in the famous
narrative which succeeds the execution of Dussardier:

> Il voyagea.
> Il connut la mélancolie des paquebots, les froids réveils
> sous la tente, l'étourdissement des paysages et des ruines,
> l'amertume des sympathies interrompues.
> Il revint.
> Il fréquenta le monde, et il eut d'autres amours encore.
> Mais le souvenir continuel du premier les lui rendait insipides;
> et puis la véhémence du désir, la fleur même de la sensa-
> tion était perdue. Ses ambitions d'esprit avaient également
> diminué. Des années passèrent; et il supportait le désoeuvre-
> ment de son intelligence et l'inertie de son coeur.

> (He travelled.
> He knew the sadness of liners, the cold wakings under
> a tent, the stultification of landscapes and ruins, the bitter-
> ness of sympathies which are interrupted.
> He returned.
> He frequented the world, and he had still other loves.
> But the continual remembrance of the first made them in-
> sipid; besides, the vehemence of desire, the very crest of
> the sensation, was lost. His intellectual ambitions had les-
> sened to the same degree. Years passed; and he put up with
> the idleness of his intelligence and the inertness of his heart.)

The disintegrating *coup de grâce* of the sentiments is implied through the detached style, here so powerfully fore-
shortened.

Deslauriers, too, has gone from infatuation with Plato
through political disillusionment to a glorification of adolescent caterwauling, what he calls "the best we've had" in
the last sentence of the novel. His own decline parallels the
rigorous disillusionment of Frédéric. His life, like his
friend's, like everyone's, is that he has not lived; his ironies
of event are ironies of impression, "sentiments"; all his feelings have found no action but the frustrating contrast of
opposed feelings.

There are two sides to Flaubert's artistic mind: a romantic devotion to impressions, embodied in his mastery of the analogical detail, and a realistic, almost scientific, documentation expressed in the detachment of his style and in his care to verify the facts of his narrative. In *Madame Bovary* and *L'Education Sentimentale* he achieved two distinct fusions of the romantic and the realistic. And once again he was to succeed at such a fusion. The observed authenticity of Félicité's feelings in *Un Coeur Simple* redeems for the sharpest poignancy the story's most banal analogy, that a stuffed parrot symbolizes the dove of the Holy Spirit. The very banality is transformed into insight through the power of the detached style to charge, here and throughout, the simple life with a profundity of religious pathos.

Flaubert's romanticism and his realism may be seen as the two faces of the same coin. The romantic devotes himself to documentation because he feels an implicit order in facts; given the facts, the order is present. The realist is a romantic, and vice versa. It is hard, by the very union of the two views, for the romantic-realistic Janus head of Flaubert's vision to center unambiguously on a fictional object; and we have a record of this difficulty in the anguish Flaubert felt tortured by in the process of writing, his vacillation between Promethean struggles with words and disgust with his subject matter, between dissipating emotional memories and stagnating researches through all the manuals of his time.

The documentation not of the felt present but of a romanticized past fails twice in the stillborn *Salammbô*, in the platitudinous, occasionally poetical *Tentation de Saint Antoine*. Valéry finds the latter redeemed only in its intention and in fragments; and of both James perceptively says, ". . . what are all these, inviting because queer, but a confession of supreme impatience with the actual and the near, often queer enough too, no doubt, but not consolingly, not transcendentally?" The historical novel, as practised by Flaubert and others, possesses the radical defect of a form which makes nearly impossible the use of the novelist's basic material, direct observation of life, beyond the truism that life seems alike in all periods. Flaubert's consummate stylistic tact succeeded only twice, in *La Légende de St. Julien l'Hospitalier* and in *Hérodias*, in making minor fiction by impregnating history with feeling.

For his romantic side, the pitfall of the imagined past; for his realistic, the pitfall of documentation. *Bouvard et Pécuchet* is an achievement, but not one of a scope justifiable for Flaubert in the decade following *L'Education Sentimentale*. Subservience to the actual and the near betrayed him into platitude of an encyclopedic magnificence but of an insight shallower than that which penetrated his two best novels. Concurrently, and consequentially, the irony of his detachment ossifies, limiting the means of the fiction by its muscle-bound progressions. The attempt fails to give narrated fact the summary significance it achieved in *L'Education Sentimentale* through the sentiments of the diversified characters. The inhabitants of the village where Bouvard and Pécuchet retire are mere shells compared to such secondary figures in the Parisian novel as Mlle. Vatnaz or Regimbard; Bouvard and Pécuchet, well distinguished and well portrayed, are pitiful beside Emma and Frédéric. Swollen appearances, shrunken realities. All the substance of diverse feelings with which Flaubert's genius peopled the worlds of the earlier novels is petrified and lost in the documentation of half-baked farming techniques. Instead of people's actions we find the description of skills debased into hobbies, so that the narrating irony, as James says, "is made as dry as sand and as heavy as lead."

Flaubert's heroic effort to render the horror and banality of the urban mind's shallow pluralism meets with partial success; but plot must support documentation. Fuller success for this particular vision of the modern city had to await the masterly plots of *Voyage au Bout de la Nuit* and *Mort à Credit*.

There is, at the same time, a heroism in Flaubert's sedulous confrontation of the actual; and his labors were not lost; they got a poetic robustness and a definitive force into a style that might have been as limpid as Verlaine's or Colette's, had that unremitting patience not given it sculptural shape. Céline's style derives ultimately from Flaubert's, as does nearly all of modern fiction.

James was implicitly acknowledging a debt when he said of the novelist, writing about Flaubert, "The more he feels his subject the more he *can* render it—that is the first way. The more he renders it the more he *can* feel it—that is the second way. This second way was unmistakably Flaubert's." And unmistakably the way of most novelists thereafter, including James himself. The imaginative achievement of *Madame Bovary* and *L'Education Sentimentale* is great enough to exceed Flaubert's technical endowment of modern fiction with a point of view and with a consequent analogical method, both of which have proved almost the sole voices of its intellect and its sensibility.

☙ VII ☙

THE SPECIALIZING SENSIBILITY

The answer to all questions of life and death, "the absolute solution," was written all over the world he had known: it was like a traveller realising that the wild country he surveys is not an accidental assembly of natural phenomena, but the page in a book where these mountains and forests and fields and rivers are disposed in such a way as to form a coherent sentence; the vowel of a lake fusing with the consonant of a sibilant slope; the windings of a road writing its message in a round hand, as clear as that of one's father; trees conversing in dumb-show, making sense to one who has learnt the gestures of their language. . . . Thus the traveller spells the landscape and its sense is disclosed, and likewise, the intricate pattern of human life turns out to be monogrammatic, now quite clear to the inner eye disentangling the interwoven letters. And the word, the meaning which appears is astounding in its simplicity: the greatest surprise being perhaps that in the course of one's earthly existence, with one's brain encompassed by an iron ring, by the close-fitting dream of one's own personality—one had not made by chance that simple mental jerk, which would have set free imprisoned thought and granted it the great understanding. Now the puzzle was solved. "And as the meaning of all things shone through their shapes, many ideas and events which had seemed of the utmost importance dwindled not to insignificance, for nothing could be insignificant now, but to the same size which other ideas and events, once denied any importance, now attained." Thus, such shining giants of our brain as science, art or religion fell out of the familiar scheme of their classification, and joining hands, were mixed and joyfully levelled. Thus, a cherry stone and its tiny shadow which lay on the painted wood of a tired bench, or a bit of torn paper, or any other such trifle out of millions and millions of trifles grew to a wonderful size. Remodelled and recombined, the world yielded its sense to the soul as naturally as both breathed.

Vladimir Nabokov[1]

Once Flaubert had invented a detachment in style that could render feeling without discussing it, any novelist could develop, while remaining objective, a richly documented presentation of the areas of feeling in which his own sensibility specialized.

Flaubert introduced into fiction a pointed, metaphoric use of details from the physical world, chairs and boats and trees and carriages. So thoroughly did this change the texture of the novel that narrative has come to consist far more of statements about things, or about minute physical actions, than of moral descriptions. Here, for example, is the beginning of a chapter by Jane Austen:

> Emma could not feel a doubt of having given Harriet's fancy a proper direction and raised the gratitude of her young vanity to a very good purpose, for she found her decidedly more sensible than before of Mr. Elton's being a remarkably handsome man, with most agreeable manners; and as she had no hesitation in following the assurance of his admiration by agreeable hints, she was soon pretty confident of creating as much liking on Harriet's side, as there could be any occasion for. She was quite convinced of Mr. Elton's being in the fairest way of falling in love, if not in love already. She had no scruple with regard to him. He talked of Harriet, and praised her so warmly, that she could not suppose anything wanting which a little time would not add. His perception of the striking improvement of Harriet's manner, since her introduction at Hartfield, was not one of the least agreeable proofs of his growing attachment.

Here we have one long tissue of abstract terms making moral attributions. And this is what we tend to have not

---

[1] Quoted from *The Real Life of Sebastian Knight*, with the permission of New Directions. Copyright, 1941, by New Directions.

only in Jane Austen, but in the narrative line of most novels before Flaubert. Of course the novel did not suddenly then abandon such moral terms; nor did the novelist suddenly begin to compose his narrative line of nothing but physical detail. But novels after Flaubert tend to consist much more of the sort of physical description we find in this chapter opening of D. H. Lawrence:

> Meanwhile Ursula had wandered on from Willey Water along the course of the bright little stream. The afternoon was full of larks' singing. On the bright hill-sides was a subdued smoulder of gorse. A few forget-me-nots flowered by the water. There was a rousedness and a glancing everywhere.
>
> She strayed absorbedly on, over the brooks. She wanted to go to the mill-pond above. The big mill-house was deserted, save for a labourer and his wife who lived in the kitchen. So she passed through the empty farm-yard and through the wilderness of a garden, and mounted the bank by the sluice. When she got to the top, to see the old, velvety surface of the pond before her, she noticed a man on the bank, tinkering with a punt. It was Birkin sawing and hammering away.

Such details give the impression of carrying the story forward, instead of merely filling out the physical background, because they do advance the narrative by virtue of figuring the feelings of the character, Charles Bovary or Ursula.

Flaubert's analogies, become standard technique, have turned the routine texture of fiction from psychological abstraction to a physical documentation which is dense with significant specificity. The cumulative physical impressions of *A La Recherche du Temps Perdu*, the analogical leitmotivs of *Tonio Kröger* and *Death in Venice*, the literally infinite analogies of *Finnegans Wake*, share a common heritage with hosts of minor and even ephemeral novels.

Thus made to underlie the appearances of things is the reality of the secret life their analogies embody; they mutely surround characters who loiter beside "sad" rivers or "joyous" seas, under "confusing" rains or "draining" suns. "The real life of his books," Nabokov says of his own work (*Conclusive Evidence*), "flow[s] in his figures of speech . . . windows giving upon a contiguous world . . . a rolling corollary, the shadow of a train of thought."

In his earliest practice, as Pound says, Joyce's technical achievement is getting Flaubert into English;[2] and in *Ulysses* he has "taken up the art of writing where Flaubert left it." "The art of writing," refers to Joyce's comparably exhaustive pains at shaping sentences and choosing words; but Joyce's doctrine of "epiphanies," the atoms of observed significance that go to make up his novels, are also Flaubertian analogies pure and simple. The inner life and the outer world, stream of consciousness and epiphany, stand to one another as appearance to reality:

> Under the upswelling tide he saw the writhing weeds lift languidly and sway reluctant arms, hising up their petticoats, in whispering water swaying and upturning coy silver fronds. Day by day: night by night: lifted, flooded and let fall. Lord, they are weary: and, whispered to, they sigh. Saint Ambrose heard it, sigh of leaves and waves, waiting, awaiting the fullness of their times, *diebus ac noctibus injurias patiens ingemiscit.* To no end gathered: vainly then released, forth flowing, wending back: loom of the moon. Weary too in sight of lovers, lascivious men, a naked woman shining in her courts, she draws a toil of waters.
>
> Five fathoms out there. Full fathom five thy father lies.

The sea in Stephen's eye images his feelings, protean in this Proteus episode. The sea's rhythms are his; in unifying his impressions, they hark him back to the earlier morning when the presence of the old milk woman prompted Buck Mulligan to sing a snatch of a scurrilous song ("hising up her

[2] Joyce's definition of epic, lyric, and dramatic in *A Portrait of the Artist as a Young Man* simply erects Flaubert's point of view into a more general prescription for all literature.

petticoats"). The sea reminds him of his mother, of the monotony he wakens to after the slow anguish of class, of his theological background's Latinate undertones, of his vaguely persistent concupiscence. What St. Ambrose expressed and what Stephen feels are made one in the described concreteness, the epiphany, of the tide.

Stephen, of course, wears unwittingly the mantle of Telemachus; the *Odyssey*, too, has a reason why he should be on the seashore now: in beginning to think of his mother he is beginning to seek a spiritual father, one drowned in the metaphorical sea of Dublin. "Full fathom five thy father lies." The observed authenticity of his concrete impressions, which the precise descriptions and careful rhythms create, lends reality to the arbitrary *Odyssey* analogy; the sea is more convincingly epic if it stands first for the feelings of the character observing it.

Stream of consciousness: stream of epiphanies. The analogical texture of *Ulysses* stands midway between its allegory of the *Odyssey* and its documentative catalog of the intuited sights and smells of Dublin; it is the nerve center of *Ulysses'* complexity.

The simpler scope of much modern French fiction has left the moralizing tradition that runs from Madame de la Fayette through Stendhal for a well-made procession of analogies à la Flaubert:

> Le tramway, feu de bengale mouvant, éclairait une seconde les ifs et les charmilles nues d'une propriété, puis l'enfant écoutait décroître le vacarme des roues et du trolley, sur la route pleine de flaques, qui sentait le bois pourri, les feuilles. Il suivait alors le petit chemin qui longe le jardin des Courrèges, poussait le portail entrebâillé des communs; la lampe de la salle à manger éclairait ce massif contre la maison où, au printemps, on plantait les fuchsias qui aiment l'ombre.

> (The streetcar, a moving Bengal fire, lit up for a second the yews and bare hornbeams of a household; then the child heard the noise of trolley wheels die down, along the pud-

dle-filled route which smelled of rotten wood and leaves. Then he followed the little walk running along the Courrèges' garden, pushed the half-open door of the privy; the dining room lamp lit up this thicket against the house where, in the spring, were planted fuchsias, which love the shade.)

The trolley rattling through a "désert de l'amour" is an analogy to Maria Cross. On this very trolley she will encounter Raymond, *l'enfant* of this passage. She too is a kind of "feu de bengale mouvant," a firework with suggestions of luxurious, almost oriental, mystery. She too lights up first Courrèges *père*, symbolized in the "stable property," with its yews (symbolic trees) and *charmilles* significantly *nues*, before *l'enfant* hears the noise of her wheels. The road through the *désert* which the city incarnates is significantly full of puddles, smelling (as does the love) of rotten wood and leaves. The propertied people who plant fuchsias, flowers colored the purple of passion, flowers "qui aiment l'ombre," reveal emotions like those flowers when the characters perform the symbolic (and literal) act of planting.

Mauriac's characters seek God through their feelings for one another; Colette's strive for equilibrium in the psychological hothouse of concupiscence. These writers resemble each other not only in subject matter, sexual love, but in their Flaubertian composition: this passage from *Duo* recalls the texture of *Le Désert de l'Amour* because, for different ends, both are using the same tradition:

> Elle versait d'une main fine, toute en os et en tendons, le cidre foncé dont la mousse même se teintait de jaune, et son oeil, petit et brillant, cherchait celui de son maître avec une sorte de coquetterie sans âge, si pénétrante que Michel frémit. "Cacher quelque chose à Maria, comment y arriverons-nous?" Il se sentait si faible, si mal défendu, qu'il accueillit avec un soulèvement heureux le retour d'Alice, qui revenait vive, inquiète, poudrée d'une main distraite, le nez trop blanc, la bouche trop rouge. Mais ses yeux, toujours

plus confiants à l'approche du soir qui les bleuissait, s'ou-
vraient, vigilantes et pâles, sous la frange noire.

(With a slender hand, all bone and sinew, she poured
the cloudy cider whose very foam was tinged with yellow,
and her eye, small and gleaming, sought her master's with
a sort of ageless coquetry, so piercing that Michel trembled.
"How will we ever hide anything from Marie?" He felt so
weak and defenseless that he started happily at Alice's return; she was coming back excited, disquieted, powdered
with an inattentive hand, nose too white, mouth too red.
But her eyes, more and more confiding at the onset of the
evening which deepened their blue, opened up watchful and
pale under their black fringe.)

Maria, the pouring maid, stands as a silent pictorial
sounding board for the distance between Michel and his
once unfaithful wife. The translucent cider resembles the
desire between husband and wife, which Michel's rigor will
not allow to be fulfilled, though he longs for it as much as
Alice does; its mustiness and sadness are in the yellow tinge
of the cider. Maria's eye penetrates Michel's discomfiture
with such vividness that he trembles; and thus he has a rare
happy start at the return of Alice, whose own feelings,
"vive, inquiète," are given away in the very excess of attempting to mask them by makeup. Alice's eyes will change
in the amorous time of evening to a blue which, as it were,
transforms the "yellow" desire to the possibility of physical
reconciliation. Now, though, her eyes are anxious, "vigilantes et pâles" for fear of the rejection Michel will make
in a climactic scene.

The less composed novels of Malraux use Flaubertian
analogies to sound a gamut of final political moralities which
would seem to require the moral statements of a James or
a Conrad. Flaubert's aegis allows Bernanos to filter Dostoevskian apocalypse through impressions; de Montherlant
assumes it to express a titanic sensuous disgust. Even the
documentative statements of Céline owe some of their

verve to a conscious composedness of analogical significances. In *Mort à Credit* the fake Chinese Buddha enticed
out of Ferdinand's hands, causing and symbolizing the
agony of his misunderstood childish impotence, is a symbol
as well as an item of the decadent subreligious bric-a-brac
eclecticism of the modern spirit: in the money mad jeweller
who is selling it, his obscene wife who purloins it by horrible
seduction, and the frivolous neurotic collector for whom
it has been made.

The Great Gatsby has the formal finish we attribute
to the French novel; and in the texture, as well as the title,
of his most important novel, Fitzgerald adapted the Flaubertian method: scene embodies feeling in *Tender is the
Night*. Here Dick Diver is riding a funicular:

> The conductor shut a door; he telephoned his confrère
> among the undulati, and with a jerk the car was pulled up-
> ward, heading for a pinpoint on an emerald hill above. After
> it cleared the low roofs, the skies of Vaud, Valais, Swiss
> Savoy, and Geneva spread round the passengers, in cyclo-
> rama. On the center of the lake, cooled by the piercing
> current of the Rhone, lay the true centre of the Western
> world. Upon it floated swans like boats and boats like swans,
> both lost in the nothingness of the heartless beauty. It was
> a bright day, with sun glittering on the grass beach below
> and the white courts of the Kursaal. The figures on the
> courts threw no shadows.

Dick Diver's physical ascent here parallels his social climb
to Nicole, whom he encounters in this funicular and decides shortly to marry. The plot has pulled him too "with
a jerk . . . upward," toward an unseen psychological flaw
in her beauty, "a pinpoint on an emerald hill above." As
he climbs to survey her beauty, the flaw that previously
loomed to prevent his involvement with her will become
a pinpoint; a pinpoint that will later tragically puncture
his life. At the highest point he will be overlooking the
countryside of his life, as here of Switzerland, "in cyclo-
rama"; in his psychological loss of fineness, as well as in

Lake Geneva, through the significance Fitzgerald wished for his novel, lies "the true centre of the Western world." Dick himself is a swan like a boat, a boat like a swan, "lost in the nothingness" of Nicole's "heartless beauty." In the world he makes for himself it is impossible to tell whether he fails through excess of fineness or lack of toughness, through praiseworthy generosity or culpable imprudence: the point of the novel lies in our inability, like his, to discover whether he is boat or swan: because the figures, in the gentle pitilessness of Fitzgerald's tragic vision, metaphorically throw no shadows.

Fitzgerald's people inhabit a world with all the soft profundity of their feelings; Hemingway's are trapped in a world whose hard intensity their feelings recognize. Hemingway's scaling down of vocabulary to the sensory and the vague qualifier gives him a more limited palette of the *mot juste*. The sharply perceived items of his situations —of café life, bullfight, fishing party, beach—express and embody the feelings of the characters in *The Sun Also Rises*. The beginning of *A Farewell to Arms* describes a scene portentous with the emotions which the novel will make substantial:

> In the late summer of that year we lived in a house in a village that looked across the river and the plain to the mountains. In the bed of the river there were pebbles and boulders, dry and white in the sun, and the water was clear and swiftly moving and blue in the channels. Troops went by the house and down the road and the dust they raised powdered the leaves of the trees. The trunks of the trees too were dusty and the leaves fell early that year and we saw the troops marching along the road and the dust rising and leaves, stirred by the breeze, falling and the soldiers marching and afterward the road bare and white except for the leaves.

Death, what the troops mean and cause, passes and leaves its "dust" on Henry's feelings. At the end of the novel he will walk away from the hospital into the night, his strong

sentiments "clear and swiftly moving and blue in the chan-
nels," his mind, like the road here, "bare and white except
for the leaves."

In the method of Flaubert and his followers, each physical
detail, so to speak, figures a feeling. There is another analogical method which seems to derive from Turgenev and
Chekov and to be so general in modern Russian fiction as
to be found in such otherwise different writers as Pasternak
and Babel. For these writers the single detail may or may
not be metaphoric; more important is the elusive pattern
formed by all the details together, a pattern that it is impossible to call simply order or simply chaos—though one
might call Flaubert's pattern simply order—as it is impossible to call it simply appearance or simply reality.

For Katherine Anne Porter the dumb objects purveyed
in the narrative are eloquent of more than they symbolize.
A life sense, concrete as the tree, abstract as the political
ideas in the background, reveals its aching existence through
and beyond "the flowering judas." The tree, as the title
indicates, is not only a metaphor for the admixture of sexual
vigor and ruthlessness which confronts like a betrayal
Laura's spiritual puritanism with her own potential fe-
cundity; it is also a piercing insight into the structure of
feelings so elusive that only such superbly constructed narratives can express them. Likewise the cracked looking glass
in the story of that name does more than suggest Joyce's remark that Irish art is the cracked looking glass of a servant.
(The characters of the story are Irish, conscious of an Irish
isolation.) The looking glass, where "the wavy place made
her eyes broad and blurred as the palm of her hands and
she couldn't tell her nose from her mouth in the cracked
seam, . . ." mirrors Rosaleen askew because her world is
askew. And it also shares with her other possessions as an

item of apperception of that world. "Pale Horse, Pale Rider," an explicitly metaphorical title, shows death, the death of "Adam," grazing for life with its paleness the emotional existence of the narrator who loved him.

Carson McCullers tallies such objects in her fictions as the weight and visible sadness through which her "hearts," "lonely hunters," yearn. The husband in *A Domestic Dilemma* realizes through looking at his drunken wife surrounded by her garments, drenched as it were in sadness, that his love can compass her failing, that their very muteness unites them: "Little by little, mysteriously, there came in him a change. . . . Her high-heeled shoes with the carelessly dropped stockings made to him a mute appeal. Her underclothes were flung in disorder on the chair. Martin picked up the girdle and the soft, silk brassière and stood for a moment with them in his hands." The process, begun by the feelings clustered on her possessions, continues through contemplation of her sleeping presence, till "his hand sought the adjacent flesh and sorrow paralleled desire in the immense complexity of love."

Henry Green builds his sensible objects into an appearance of riddle which the characters guess through the correspondingly enigmatic sensibilities of their dialog. In *Loving*, the eggs stored in waterglass mirror the delicacy of their love. Mere servants are the characters, but not all mere servants could understand such feelings, as the heroine's best friend shows by marrying the gross keeper of the peacocks. In *Back*, metaphor becomes name; Rose, the name of the vanishing beloved, sheds roses on the book, finally on the naked body of her counterpart in the climactic passage which describes her abed through a series of rose images.

William Sansom constructs his well-made fictions around a central metaphorical object, often a landscape whose appearances are charged with a significance felt to be so real that he himself confesses his stories to be a hybrid genre, half travel literature, half fiction. The theme of these fictions is the necessity of the reality of deceptions to the appearances of truth; the illusory bodies are a necessary face of innocence; and the scene, as in the marvellously rendered trip down the Thames in *The Body*, interacts, as a collapsing backdrop of deceptively palpable density, with the paradox of duplicity and deep sincerity in the moral relations of the characters.

In Ford's *Parade's End* there is a kind of cold hardness in the objects (recalling the curious coldness of Conrad, his earlier collaborator). There is also a kind of refracted displacement between Tietjens and the brutal appearances of the world he too well understands, between the callous loveliness of Sylvia and the fragile incorporeality of Valentine Wannop (*Some Do Not*), between disaster and fake glory, between the appearances and the realities of love and war. ("Macmaster went down the tall steps to the car that gleamed in the summer sun. The roses shone over the supremely levelled turf. His heel met the stones with the hard tread of a conqueror. He could have shouted aloud!")

A novel's undercurrent sense of time may be rendered the more vivid through details so closely worked that they veritably shine with the significance of their transience. Eudora Welty, in *The Golden Apples*, makes things mirror what almost all novelists but Proust assign to plot, the qualitative change of characters. Each disparate consciousness in the Mississippi community is rendered by the analogical concreteness that surrounds it. All move from a felt childhood to a felt middle age so deep that the story creates, through many concrete details, a myth of life, perceived but unattainable, lost and paradisal as the golden apples of the title. In the capitulating chapter, "The Wanderers," the feelings of the most sensitive character, Virgie Rainey, have kept her at home while all the others have gone as far afield as San Francisco (one twin), as suicide (caused by the other). Virgie drives away from the funeral of her mother (the opening narrator) feeling through a significant rain all the mysterious mortal weight of her middle age; she comes into a town square dense with significance:

> She had often done this, if only to turn around and go right back after a rest of a few moments and a Coca-Cola standing up in Billy Hudson's drugstore. MacLain pleased her—the uncrowded water tank, catching the first and last light; the old iron bell in the churchyard looking as heavy as a fallen meteor. The courthouse pleased her—space itself, with the columns standing away from its four faces, and the pea-green blinds flat to the wall, and the stile rising in pepper grass over the iron fence to it—and a quail just now running across the yard; and the live oaks—trunks flaky black and white now, as if soot, not rain, had once fallen from heaven on them, and the wet eyes of cut-off limbs on them; and the whole rainlighted spread roof of green leaves that moved like children's lips in speech, high up.[3]

Her thousands of days ("She had often done this") charge the place, her many associations conscious or unconscious. From leaves like these, children once watched her enter with a sailor the vacant house of her music teacher; that old German woman was about to return and symbolically set it afire. Virgie's lived experience breeds a mortality in the physical objects of the town. Her feeling recalls to her a picture of Perseus grasping the head of Medusa on her music teacher's wall, and through the picture the meaning of the relationship, of all relationships. "With her hate, with her love, and with the small gnawing feelings that ate them, she offered Virgie her Beethoven. She offered, offered, offered—and when Virgie was young, in the strange wisdom of youth that is accepting of more than is given, she had accepted *the* Beethoven, as with the dragon's blood. That was the gift she had touched with her fingers that had drifted and left her." The memory makes her stand bare-headed in the rain. And as the book closes, the splendidly particularizing description of the rain is united with its myth: she "heard through falling rain, the running of the

[3] Quoted by permission of Harcourt, Brace & Co.

horse and bear, the stroke of the leopard, the dragon's crusty slither, and the glimmer and the trumpet of the swan."

In *Nightwood* the nostalgia of transient details becomes transmuted to an anguish in whose crepuscular heaving objects lose their literal, narrative base of reference to become pure metaphors, at once freer and less fictional than in other novels I have been discussing: "Sleep, the slain white bull," "the tree of night is the hardest tree to mount, the dourest tree to scale, the most difficult of branch, the most febrile to the touch, and sweats a resin and drips a pitch against the palm that computation has not gambled." It is no disparagement to the vision of this novel to say, with T. S. Eliot, that it exists at the margin of its genre and of another, poetry. Literal or not, the metaphors still extend the characters who handle them or name them. Doctor O'Connor's owlishly open-on-suffering eyes, and his penchant for the marvelously farfetched illustration are one with his character. He is what he imagines a prostitute to say: "I'm an angel on all fours, with a child's feet behind me, seeking my people that have never been made, going down face foremost, drinking the waters of night at the water hole of the damned, and I go into the waters, up to my heart, the terrible waters!" The splintered narrative, the striking exfoliation of unliteral detail, exist here in a hypertrophy reminiscent of *Ulysses;* and its characters, like those of *Ulysses,* tend to petrify into types, to twist, through the style, into grotesques more distorted than those of *Winesburg, Ohio.* One step farther and we have the novels of John Hawkes, where a litmus-quick sensibility parades characters so unformed as to be neither types nor grotesques.

This chapter's epigraph applies most pointedly to Nabokov's Russian forebears. In Gogol, Turgenev, Chekov, appearances figure as a reality that overreaches the analogical. Reality so inheres in the appearances of things that they cannot be metaphors. They are at once too evanescent and too outside the people to image feelings in any way but in the whole complex of the fiction.

The sensibility of Turgenev appears all the more compelling, all the more taut in its rendered details, for the beautifully conceived characters whom he defines by their response to the face of a world so represented. "Character, character expressed and exposed," James says of his work. "Turgenieff's sense of it was the greatest light that artistically guided him; the simplest account of him so to say that the mere play of it constitutes in every case his sufficient drama. No one has had a closer vision, or a hand at once more ironic and more tender, for the individual figure."

Turgenev's characters perceive, in their several ways, things which teem with a dim significance. "Ondoyant et divers," the objects stand as ciphers for a pathos not closed, as in the methodically single analogical references of *Madame Bovary*, but as open as that twilight horizon so mysteriously present in all his work from *A Sportsman's Sketches* on. Antennae among these shifting, open, suggestive details, characters like Litvinov in the significantly entitled *Smoke* respond to the tingling of their diversity. Things are felt as the substance of life; but even the great powers of a Rudin, a Bazarov, an Insarov, cannot master them. The stories express an ineradicable discrepancy between the simple, rather superficial ordering of Nikolai Kirsonov in *Fathers and Sons*, of Volintsiev, whose lives they charge with an easy melancholy, and the Dionysiac reeling among their felt disorder of the superior, enigma-subdued wakefulness of a Rudin or a Litvinov. The anguish of disorder, excruciating though sweet, can break out at any time. Litvinov, for example, after glimpsing a strangely familiar woman, has just received a letter from his father:

Litvinov was lost in thought over this document; it brought to him a breath of the remote and isolated steppe, the impenetrable gloom of a life moldered and fusty, and it seemed remarkable that he had read this letter in Baden of all places. Meanwhile midnight had long passed; he got into bed and blew out the candle. But he could not sleep; the faces he had seen, the speeches he had heard, kept turning and circling, strangely interweaving and jumbling in his burning head, which ached terribly from the tobacco smoke. Now he thought he heard Gubariov's bellow and saw his downcast eyes with their dull and obstinate gaze; now suddenly those same eyes flamed and danced, and he recognized Mme. Sukhanchikova, heard her crackling voice, and involuntarily repeated softly after her, "She slapped his face, she slapped his face"; now Potugin's awkward figure rose before him, and for the tenth, the twentieth, time he recalled every word he had said; now, like a jack-in-the-box, Voroshilov sprang up in his close-fitting coat, which enveloped him like a new uniform; and Pishchalkin sagely and gravely nodded his perfectly trimmed and undoubtedly well-intentioned head; and Bindasov shouted and cursed, and Bambayev exulted lachrymosely. . . .

But, above all, that perfume, that persistent, importunate, sweet, heavy perfume did not give him any rest, but pervaded the room more and more strongly in the darkness, and more and more insistently reminded him of something that he simply could not define. . . . It occurred to him that the scent of flowers in a bedroom at night is detrimental to the health, and he rose, groped his way to the bouquet, and carried it into the other room; but even then the exhausting perfume penetrated to him on his pillow, under the blanket, and he turned over fretfully from side to side. Now a fever was beginning to steal upon him; a priest, "a master against enchantments," ran twice across his head, in the form of a very lively hare with a beard and pigtail, and Voroshilov, sitting in the enormous plume of a general's helmet, as though in a bush, began to twitter like a nightingale in front of him . . . when suddenly he raised himself in the bed and, throwing up his hands, exclaimed: "Surely it isn't *she?* It can't be!"

Each of the impressions, in unleashing its significance, gives rise to a contiguous but conflicting one. The sense of dis-

THE SPECIALIZING SENSIBILITY

order is reinforced by the silences of inexpressible emotion which Turgenev has here represented by dots at three points of tension. At these points the thought, through the void of the mute emotion for which the dots stand, leaps to the further haunting chaos of another idea, culminating in the superbly imagined hallucinations where human beings become a bearded hare, a nightingale twittering in a plumed general's helmet.

Turgenev's offset plot structure and lapses of narrative —often long years are left vacant between successive episodes of his novellae—enhance the diversity of the felt surroundings with a chaotic time sequence. The characters, preconscious in their actions, cannot help but bungle until they release the life feeling in themselves. Life feeling all the time underlies the inscrutability, masking temporarily as meaninglessness, of the disorder in which they find themselves. The reawakening described above is not strong enough to frustrate, it only discomfits, a reconciled Litvinov. But it kills in *Fathers and Sons* a Bazarov who has failed to come to terms with his potentiality for sensibility.

The emotions of these characters are chaotically in tune to the changes of their world's appearances. They enter like a breath of air those social occasions—teas, visits, dances —so stable in Jane Austen, so mysteriously dissolving and unsummarized in Turgenev. The family histories of all the characters, a tangle of frustrations and eccentric triumphs, are shrunk in the memory to the compass of the single long paragraphs to which Turgenev habitually foreshortens their presentation.

The narrative line—the plot, its prehistory and its outcome—strengthens what the details of sensitivity incite. The crux is always the grand fatality of a love which cannot culminate in marriage, a love incarnating not physical desire, not Stendhal's life mystique or Jane Austen's cultivated sympathy, but this nodal point of life feeling. The love yearns toward an impossible order and destroys the possible

order of political mastery. In the cases where the woman
is free to marry, whether the man capitulates like Insarov,
refuses to marry like Rudin, or hesitates like Bazarov, it
comes to the same thing: he has radically altered his orienta-
tion to the too abstract, inhuman, political ideal, and the
diversity of the world scatters his forces and his life. Love
and revolution are the mutually incompatible polarities of
this world: life's chaos comes to a head in their conflict.
Rudin suffers displacement and obscurity because he cannot meet the demands of love; and the obscurity makes him
desperate enough, years later, to be killed in Paris during the
Revolution of 1848. The felt appearances of life are so bent
on evading order in Turgenev's world that even without
politics they triumph. Lavretsky, because his evil wife's
death is falsely rumored, entangles Liza in a love that will
frustrate them for life. Her religion will not allow her to
live with him; yet it is the sensibility of which her religion
is an expression that makes him love her. So they pine in
a sort of living death, their only comfort the anguish of his
visit, years later, to her distant convent: "In going from
one choir to the other, she passed close to him—passed with
the even, hurriedly-submissive gait of a nun—and did not
cast a glance at him; only the lashes of the eye which was
turned toward him trembled almost imperceptibly, and her
haggard face was bowed a little lower than usual—and the
fingers of her clasped hands, interlaced with her rosary,
were pressed more tightly to one another. What did they
both think—what did they both feel? Who knows? Who
shall say? There are moments in life, there are feelings . . . we can only indicate them—and pass by."

    In indicating them, Turgenev portrays religion as no
adequate consolation, the most idealistically organized politics as an illusory sieve of the Danaïdes. Life's illusion of
reality makes chaos of any order in the full vision of this
fictional world. Turgenev's sensibility expresses an empathy
with the illusion underlying the reality of the world, neither

moral nor tragic but purely fictional. Motive, submerged in a partial illusion of reality, emerges through the actions of the characters into the total reality of illusion. This is the meaning of the peerless artistry critics attribute to him.

In Chekov the details seem to cohere into an order which the protagonist tragically cannot master, though he may apprehend it. What the apprehension loses by impotence it gains in a tragic sensibility which perceives an almost religious order. More often than not a feeling of chaos is an illusion, a symptom of sin in *The Horse Stealers* or of approaching death in stories like *The Black Monk* and *A Dreary Story* (as Chekov explicitly says in a letter about it, denying an interpretation of the chaos as more than an illusion). The despairingly chaotic illusion of stories like *The Kiss* and *Ward No. 6* is counterbalanced by a sinewy, healthy reality of order, explicit in stories whose setting is the religious life, *Easter Eve* and *The Bishop*. The social mastery of an Aksinya in *In the Ravine* is not so much illusory, like that of such Turgenev characters as Insarov or Bazarov or Potugin, not merely brutal like Stakhov or Panshin, as it is radically evil. Aksinya is coldly rejecting an order in the pathos of the textural detail and in the lives of the other characters. What she fails to feel, what Lipa feels for her red wailing child (Aksinya has killed it by throwing boiling water on it), reaches toward an order implied by the poetic significance of the detail. (Lipa, who screamed at the scalding, has just come silently to take her dead baby home):

> The hospital, a new one recently built, with big windows, stood high upon a hill; it was glittering from the setting sun and looked as though it were on fire from inside. There was a little village below. Lipa went down along the road, and before reaching the village sat down by a pond. A woman brought a horse down to drink and the horse did not drink.
>
> "What more do you want?" said the woman to it softly, "What do you want?"

A boy in a red shirt, sitting at the water's edge, was washing his father's boots. And not another soul was in sight either in the village or on the hill.

"It's not drinking," said Lipa, looking at the horse.

Then the woman with the horse and the boy with the boots walked away, and there was no one left at all. The sun went to bed wrapped in cloth of gold and purple, and long clouds, red and lilac, stretched across the sky, guarded its slumbers. Somewhere far away a bittern cried, a hollow, melancholy sound like a cow shut up in a barn. The cry of that mysterious bird was heard every spring, but no one knew what it was like or where it lived. At the top of the hill by the hospital, in the bushes close to the pond, and in the fields the nightingales were trilling. The cuckoo kept reckoning someone's years and losing count and beginning again. In the pond the frogs called angrily to one another, straining themselves to bursting, and one could even make out the words: "That's what you are! That's what you are!" What a noise there was! It seemed as though all these creatures were singing and shouting so that no one might sleep on that spring night, so that all, even the angry frogs, might appreciate and enjoy every minute: life is given only once.

The vaguely felt significance of the sights and sounds Lipa walks through, of the anonymous woman with the horse who refuses to drink, culminates through the stated mystery of the bittern's melancholy in a feeling of comfort, of religious order, underlying the chaos. If life is singular, it is nevertheless life. "After the first death there is no other," as a poet has said in another refusal to mourn a child's death by fire. And at the end Lipa, reconciled to the dimly apprehended order, meeting the disconsolate father of her murderous sister-in-law and counterfeiting husband, speaks to him from a charity that draws tears to his eyes. Giving him food, she and her impoverished mother cross themselves in the last act of the story.

The missed life expressed by the plots of Chekov's plays, embodied in the diversities, often in the cross-purpose dialogs, of the characters, is tragi-comic in sentiment; in the stories, coupled with all the illusory substance of a world the narrator's sensibility gives significance to, the missed life ceases to be either tragic or comic, or tragi-comic, and becomes a mirror for a human limitation underlying the elusive real order of an apparently illusory chaos.

❦ VIII ❧

THE PORTENTOUS INTELLIGENT
STILLNESS

HENRY JAMES

Where the novelists who specialize each in an area of sensibility have followed Flaubert's use of physical detail, Henry James adopted, and advanced, Flaubert's tightness of structure. The sensibility is present in James as much as in Joyce or Turgenev, but instead of fixing on physical objects it is brought to bear on the very overtones of the whole novel itself. The detachment of the perspective, the rendered sense of the novel as a novel in the reflexivity of the given work, is identified by James with the sense the perceptive character has of that same novel's events. Thereby a "portentous intelligent stillness" is made to brood over the whole novel. The process of a secret life, present in all fiction, is generalized by James and built at the very center of plot and style in his novels; so that one could almost consider James's technique, as Lubbock did, a norm for the entire genre of fiction.

James carries point of view a step farther than Flaubert. Flaubert's detachment remains constant from *Madame Bovary* through *Bouvard et Pécuchet*. But James posits a self-conscious fictional system anew with each novel through the process defined abstractly in the *Prefaces* and *Notebooks*. By *The Ambassadors*, the idealized narrator,

134

as Lubbock diagrams the perspective of that novel, stands at no less than three removes from the bare events of the narrative. What is made to go on in Strether's mind *is* the theme.

Flaubert, too, is acutely conscious that his words are clumsy signs; they make bears dance when he would have them move the stars. James, in his attitude toward the unity of his own style, is a meta-Flaubert. As Hugh Vereker describes the (Jamesian) unity of his own work in *The Figure in the Carpet*, "It governs every line, it chooses every word, it dots every i, it places every comma." For James the consciousness of the theme ("it," the "figure") is one with the fictiveness of the fiction. The appearance holds reality, the meaning is fictive—as in any novel; but a James novel asserts this as one (the key) dimension of its theme. "It's the very string," Vereker summarizes, "that my pearls are strung on!" The exclamation point is a eureka. "It's" is ambiguous: "it is around the figure that I have organized my pearls," but also, "the figure is identical with the string." In the ambiguity of technique creating meaning (string helping figure) and technique being meaning (string one with figure), the reflexivity of James's fiction—ambiguous at the heart because it envisions life as equally ambiguous—unifies into autonomy. Surface is depth, depth is surface, as Strether describes Paris: ". . . some huge iridescent object, a jewel brilliant and hard, in which parts were not to be discriminated nor differences comfortably marked. It twinkled and trembled and melted together, and what seemed all surface one moment seemed all depth the next."

No wonder so many of James's fictions are about artists; one needs a reflecting consciousness when a novel shows, reflexively, not only its device as device, as in Flaubert, but its theme as theme. No wonder, too, that the relations of characters in James's plots become tighter and tighter, so tight that Blackmur has been led to oversimplify them and call them fables. In their abstract significance they are fables, as James is the heir of the romancer Hawthorne. Yet he is equally the heir of Balzac, whom Hawthorne, though he admired a Balzacian realism in Trollope, scarcely resembles. James's plots are not romances, or fables, but fictions that resemble romances in their tightness. In James, plot is not a cipher of meaning, as it is in romance. His tightness is the aesthetic coherence of a fiction which knows its theme as fictive. When this tightness slackens, the "subordinate parties" run the danger of being "pieced on," as James puts it; minor characters like Maria Gostrey may have a "false connection," be exclusively (and not reflexively) fictional, be, to use the term James borrowed from dramatic criticism, *ficelles* (strings without pearls). James, however, is too severe on himself; he realizes, as he says in the preface from which we have been quoting, that Maria Gostrey's relation does, after all, become legitimate in the end. Actually all his characters are *ficelles* by virtue of his consciousness of them as fictive appearances, and none are *ficelles* by virtue of their reality. This paradox is true of any fiction. Only in James is the paradox between the artifice and the reality of the characters in a plot made to reflect —veritably to coruscate with—the theme of the novel.

If James's fictions, then, are radically fictive, in what sense are we to believe them? Are they real and to what extent, James more than once asks himself in the *Prefaces*. To ask how far Peter Quint is a hallucination of the governess, how far the doppelgänger Spencer Brydon sees is real, brings us to the outer reaches of our problem's ambiguity. Of course Henry James the elder, and probably the younger as well, believed in ghosts. Yet we cannot believe *Maud-Evelyn* and *The Sense of the Past* so fully as we believe, once inside the fiction, the splendidly credible events described by Balzac, Tolstoi, and Dickens. There is less ambiguity, and more literal certitude, about the occult powers Doctor Minoret experiences in *Ursule Mirouet*, about the Devil's visitation to Ivan in *The Brothers Karamazov*, than about the occult in James: his ambiguity rises not from the nature of the experiences recounted but from the modality of the fiction in which they occur. The children in *The Turn of the Screw* die as surely as Morgan Moreen does in *The Pupil;* the supernatural evil in which they find themselves suggests the same source as the deep, trance-like selfishness of the Moreens. Yet the source reflects an unresolvable ambiguity (Hell or the governess's mind), which the title's ambiguity expresses both in its words (what kind of a turn?) and in its relation to plot (the turn of death? of the evil? the whole process?). "The apparitions of Peter Quint and Miss Jessel," James says, ". . . the elusive presence nightly stalked through the New York house by the poor gentleman in [*The Jolly Corner*] are matters as to which in themselves, really, the critical challenge (essentially nothing ever but the spirit of fine attention) may take a hundred forms—and a hundred felt or possible proved infirmities is too great a number. Our friend's respective minds about them, on the other hand, are a different matter—challengeable, and repeatedly, if you like, but never challengeable without some consequent further stiffening of the whole texture . . . the spirit engaged with the forces of violence interests me most when I can think of it as engaged most deeply, most finely and most subtly (precious term!)." James's stories, then, become occult because they are reflexive, not reflexive because they are occult.

To construct any hypothesis about one, or all, of James's fictions that allows literal certitude violates the subtlety or, as we have called it, the ambiguity of his meaning. We cannot read this ambiguity as the fictive implication of unliteral fancy (romance) or allegory; whether direct, as in *Gargantua* and *Don Quixote;* comically self-doubting, as in *Tristram Shandy* and *Dead Souls;* or seriously putative, hypothetical though unliteral, in *Euphues.* Nor is this dubiety in James a "willing suspension of disbelief"; Coleridge's term applies to a suspension in the mind of the reader, while James poses the suspension inside the fiction itself. Nor is it even the complex reversal between literal and allegorical which Singleton traces in *Inferno III* at the outset of an unliteral but real journey. James's dubiety represents so intimately the crucial reflexivity between his theme and his meaning that it cannot be formulated in terms other than those a full examination of that meaning can provide.

Once we have stopped trying to confine James's situations (and the perceptions of his characters) to the baldly literal—once we have fixed our attention on that shadow between apparent reflector and real reflected, of which James's occult stories are only a particularly intense embodiment—we can make it out in nearly all his works. In what dim density other than this do the candles on the altar of the dead shine; does Marcher's realization in *The Beast in the Jungle* take place where absence (the shadow of the dead's silence, the fictiveness of reality) is felt as a moral quality just as nothingness in Heidegger has substance? Thence Madame Merle in *The Portrait of a Lady* derives her precariously powerful badness, thence the Princess Casamassima—a false Christina, a false Light—her siren-like lure to destruction. In obedience to this ambiguous shadow do the foursome in *The Golden Bowl* evolve their fearsome ballet. Recognition of its corruption, in supernaturally fictive and not theological terms, persuades Guy Domville to enter what is probably the same monastic order that George Dane dreamed about in *The Great Good Place*. Deference to its inscrutable intricacy gives the magnificently suggestive indirection to James's own narrative style.

James's reflexivity expresses the silence that inheres in his novels, as the silent knowledge of his characters becomes one with each silent plot which has given it birth. "He dived once more into his story," he says of a character writing in one of his fictions, a fiction, "and was drawn down, as by a siren's hand, to where, in the dim underworld of fiction, the great glazed tank of art, strange silent subjects float." The very beast in *The Beast in the Jungle* is a fictive silence, an absence, a nothingness. James puts it significantly in *The Figure in the Carpet* (speaking of the search for the "figure"): "He would bring down the animal with his own rifle" and later, "It's the thing itself, . . . that has simply sprung out at him like a tigress out of the jungle. . . . [the pages] fell, in all their superb intricacy, into the one right combination. The figure in the carpet came out." Came out, that is, in a silence not communicated, as in James it never is, unless too late; the same silence is kept about evil in *The Portrait of a Lady, The Princess Casamassima, The Golden Bowl, The Ambassadors, What Maisie Knew:* the evil are silent to the good, the experienced to the innocent, even the evil and the experienced to each other. His characters live in the silence of a violation which is absent in *Washington Square*, present in *The Portrait of a Lady;* of a separation in *Madame de Mauves* and *The American;* of a renunciation in *The Ambassadors;* of the monitory presence of the absent dead in *The Wings of the Dove;* of the meaning of the silent dead in *Daisy Miller* and *The Altar of the Dead.*

Not only are the dead silent, but a Jamesian adept can sense this silence to achieve a silent rapprochement with another watcher before the altar by observing the silence of the unlit candle, which stands, as it must, for the mutual friend doubly silent as dead and as candleless. The silence can express the impossible contingency, what might have been, in Strether's silent longing to have experienced Europe young (though—paradoxically—he has to be old [1]

---

[1] James often played on the ambiguity of "old" and "young." He says, for example, that "The Wings of the Dove . . . represents to my memory a very old—if I shouldn't perhaps rather say a very young—motive."

to long for the knowledge; his honeymoon trip to Europe had kindled no such longing). The essence of Europe is silent to him, silent as America is noisy, though it is splendidly silent even in its very noise to the becrusted James coming home to write *The American Scene;* silent to James because, unlike Strether, he has lost his life to find it abroad and looks out at the American noise from the diving bell of thirty years devoted to contemplating the silent past of Europe. This all-embracing silence is powerful enough to allow the dead and, finally, in *The Sense of the Past,* the living to cross the insuperable barrier of death. And the silence, like the novels whose theme it identifies and surrounds, is reflexive. "What their silence was charged with therefore," James says in the aptly titled *The Story in It,* "was not only a sense of the weather, but a sense, so to speak, of its own nature."

The initiation into the past's mystery of silent evil is itself silent; the silence of the present—in Isabel Archer, in Ralph Pendrel—tends to displace the silence of the past but at the same time to get desperately involved with it. In the ghostly tales, silence is ghostly, is a ghost. It is what we do not hear the (silently evil) ghosts say in *The Turn of the Screw* to the children; we do not even know—and the unliteralizing dubiety is precisely the overtone of the silence —whether the silence is of the governess' mind or of the ghost's real but unheard words. Silence calls the tune for the dance steps of *The Golden Bowl:* what the leader of the dance at each turn does is refrain from speaking about the crucial matter, and this silence evokes the succeeding step. In James's abundance of fictiveness, in his intensity of vision, in his copiousness of words, the silence becomes a fullness, brimming with itself.

Mrs. Munden's dialog with the narrator in *The Beldonald Holbein,* might be taken by extension to summarize the action in any of his fictions:

"All the same I don't think, you know," my interlocutress said, "that Nina will have made her a scene or that, whatever we do, she'll ever make her one. That isn't the way it will happen, for she's exactly as conscientious as Mrs. Brash."

"Then what *is* the way?" I asked.

"It will just happen in silence."

"And what will 'it,' as you call it, be?"

"Isn't that what we want really to see?"

"Well," I replied after a turn or two about, "whether we want it or not it's exactly what we *shall* see; which is the reason the more for fancying, between the pair there—in the quiet exquisite house, and full of superiorities and suppressions as they both are—the extraordinary situation. . . but she tasted of the tree."

The taste of the tree was taken first in the Garden of Eden; it is silently reenacted here, first in the "quiet exquisite house," later in an unbroken silence across the ocean. The knowledge of good and evil, which the taste silently imparts, silently kills the knower in this story.

All is aesthetic appearance to James; and at the same time moral reality. He is an "aesthetic idealist," in Stuart Sherman's phrase, with, as Eliot puts it, "a mind so fine that no idea could violate it." Yet while the past is an aesthetic presence and embodies itself scenically in buildings and landscapes, in Strether's view of Paris, which is one with his moral judgment of Chad, it is equally a moral presence. We are no more able to disengage the moral in James from the aesthetic than we can disengage the real in his work from the fictive, the round characters from the *ficelles*, the facts (was Peter Quint a real revenant?) from the relations (governess-children as present, evil servants as past), or, to use his phrases about the least credible of his fictions, the "right relation" in its "verisimilitude" from the palpable untruth of a mortal's stepping physically back a hundred years, an untruth to Ralph Pendrel so visibly palpable that as we read we scarcely know what is happening or can isolate the moment. The aesthetic is fictive as the moral is real; each in James reflexively becomes the other, expands out (back) into the other.

Strether discovers Chad and Madame de Vionnet at the same time and because he was out appreciating a country scene like his memory of a Lambinet painting. Isabel Archer's feeling becomes free in the darkness only after her last renunciation of Lord Warburton; Ralph Touchett, chapters back, out of his own fine aesthetic (moral) sense, would not violate her fineness by revealing the facts his silence in the garden hides before she marries Osmond; he knows that at this point her moral, as her aesthetic, ear is too weak and she must silently live her way into that silent communion. She cannot know the aesthetic depth of Europe's darkness till she has committed herself morally to it through a love deep enough to entangle her for life to the aesthete Gilbert Osmond. She cannot yet see his moral side; so she does not know the full measure of his aestheticism, that his fineness of sensibility is morally evil while hers is good. In matching her good with an evil both moral and aesthetic, he is, tragically, a truer husband to her than Caspar Goodwood [2] might be, whose lack of aesthetic feeling makes his moral feeling obtuse. And Ralph Touchett is too far ahead of her, in life and in time: he is silent; he is to die.

No knowledge of the past can be complete till the moral is seen behind the aesthetic, and vice versa. Owen Gereth's lack of aesthetic appreciation for the spoils lends

---

[2] The name "Goodwood" strikes a range of irony, as does "Caspar," too, if we can allow Caspar to suggest the most famous Caspar of the nineteenth century, Caspar Hauser, the idiot who could see the stars by daylight.

his moral integrity an obtuseness, an ignorance; he has no ear for the unheard moral melody because the aesthetic is closed to him, which makes him a truer husband for Mona Brigstock than for Fleda, who tragically loves him; and her own perceptions take on their last refinement when she admits this through her renunciation. Strether's aesthetic feeling for Paris can only culminate when what had seemed a merely aesthetic refinement, Chad's relationship with Madame de Vionnet, is seen to conceal (the silence of) a moral evil, none the less evil for both parties equally because Chad bears the deeper guilt by intending all along to abandon her; and no less refined, no less aesthetic, for being evil.

Knowledge of evil is knowledge of the silent past. The past is present as the limiting term of mortal action; the temporal aspect of human limitation is the paradox that one hears the silence of the past only by becoming fully involved as victim (Milly Theale) or as agent (Kate Croy, Merton Densher). The knowledge, like the hours themselves on the motto Strether remembers from a Spanish clock, deals mortal blow after mortal blow and finally kills. *Omnes vulnerant, ultima necat.* The ultimate moment of realization demands of a victim the deepest loss (from Christopher Newman and Hyacinth Robinson to Milly Theale and Madame de Vionnet); of a partial victim, renunciation (Strether, Kate, Densher); of an agent, a hardness that carries its own damnation (M. de Mauves, Gilbert Osmond, Madame Merle).

And if the aesthetic is always moral in James, the moral is always the aesthetic; the church which provides the candles and an altar of the dead, which throws up a real, second stone wall for Christopher Newman to stare silently against (the first being the retreat of the Bellegarde's into pastness), is not envisaged as theologically true (or false) though it is moral (and aesthetic); it is merely the supreme

hive of pastness, an intensity of burning lights, a profundity
of sound in the weird chant which heightens Claire's own
chant and seals it off from the American.

James, like Hawthorne, Eliot says, "had that sense of
the past which is peculiarly American, but in Hawthorne
this sense exercised itself in a grip on the past itself; in
James it is a sense of the sense." James's fiction unites the
knowledge of the past with its silence: the silence of the
past is the silence of the fiction, and vice versa. What one
of James's illuminated characters silently knows at the end
of the novel—as a Jane Austen character knows sociable
loving-kindness or a Stendhal character, the ironic mystique
of *amour-passion*—is the past of that novel generalized. The
knowledge produced by the conclusion, as in all fiction, is
identical with the theme of the novel. A novel, after all, is
only the sum of its events, which have taken place in time
and at the end become past. But in James the silence of
this knowledge is reflexively brought to bear, throughout
and in the very texture of narrative and dialog as well
as by the plot they further, on this specific (moral) set of
past events.

Emma Woodhouse and Fanny Price and Anne Elliot
are free to apply their insight broadly to their future life,
bounded as it is by the given circumstances of Mansfield
Park and Donwell Abbey; they look forward, not back.
With Proust the knowing silence of the past is not an interdependence but a kind of resuming identity. With Stendhal,
the knowledge, rising as it must out of an accidental series
of specific events, identifies itself passionately, ironically,
masterfully within its limitations of previous commitment,
to an iridescent present; beauty and love are not interde-
pendent with moral good as in James: they simply rejoice
in moral good and largely repudiate (even occasionally commit) the moral evil from which James's characters must
abstain as they are becoming reconciled to it.

Through his knowledge of that specific past which the

events of the novel represent, through the very tightness of his relations to others, a James character looks back in human bondage to that past. "The figures in any picture, the agents in any drama, are interesting only in proportion as they feel their respective situations. . . . Their being finely aware *makes* [italics James's] absolutely the intensity of their adventure, gives the maximum of sense to what befalls them."

In James's novels the dramatized observer, or James himself as the postulated narrator, proceeds by analyzing what has already happened—a most unusual practice in narrative. This preoccupation with analysis of the past, paradoxically (for how can talk about the past get us ahead?) furthers the action. And the new stage is, in turn, only a version of the same tight set of relations which the perceptions of the characters demanded anew. James's style asserts the pastness of the silent past through being wholly occupied with discussing it (or sometimes keeping silent).

The late style in particular, as in this example from *The Golden Bowl,* illustrates the superb thematic relevance of James's texture:

> Yes, Charlotte had seen she was watching her from afar and had stopped now to put her further attention to the test. Her face was fixed on her, through the night; she was the creature who had escaped by force from her cage, yet there was in her whole motion assuredly, even as so dimly discerned, a kind of portentous intelligent stillness. She had escaped with an intention, but with an intention the more definite that it could so accord with quiet measures. The two women, at all events only hovered there, for these first minutes, face to face over their interval and exchanging no sign; the intensity of their mutual look might have pierced the night, and Maggie was at last to start with the scared sense of having thus yielded to doubt, to dread, to hesitation, for

a time that, with no other proof needed, would have completely given her away. How long had she stood staring?— a single minute or five? Long enough, in any case, to have felt herself absolutely take from her visitor something that the latter threw upon her, irresistibly, by this effect of silence, by this effect of waiting and watching, by this effect, unmistakably, of timing her indecision and her fear. If then, scared and hanging back, she had, as was so evident, sacrificed all past pretences, it would have been with the instant knowledge of an immense advantage gained that Charlotte finally saw her come on. Maggie came on with her heart in her hands; she came on with the definite prevision, throbbing like the tick of a watch, of a doom impossibly sharp and hard, but to which, after looking at it with her eyes wide open, she had none the less bowed her head. By the time she was at her companion's side, for that matter, by the time Charlotte had, without a motion, without a word, simply let her approach and stand there, her head was already on the block, so that the consciousness that everything had now gone blurred all perception of whether or no the axe had fallen. Oh, the "advantage," it was perfectly enough, in truth, with Mrs. Verver; for what was Maggie's own sense but that of having been thrown over on her back, with her neck from the first half-broken and her helpless face staring up? That position only could account for the positive grimace of weakness and pain produced there by Charlotte's dignity.

The light and shadow in this scene (previously described in the text), the formal card game, even the caged beast and beast-prey imagery are Flaubert's kind of analogy, and their correlations have been perceptivly outlined by Marius Bewley.[3] Yet in James the cage image, the lights and shadows, the formal room, produce only one of a meta-Flaubertian range of effects reflecting and discussing the action they narrate. While such metaphors throng the paragraphs of Flaubert—or Joyce—they stand off in James, like his characters, in nearly solitary isolation amid the verbal abstractions of the style.

[3] "Appearance and Reality in Henry James," *Scrutiny*, XVII, Summer 1950.

Abstractions which analyze the progressions they forward constitute James's chief element of style: terms of mental attitude ("sense," "doubt," "dread," "hesitation," "instant knowledge," "definite prevision," "consciousness," "perception"); of psychological action (all the previous ones, and "discerned," "intelligent stillness," "measures," "effect of silence," "timing her indecision," "past pretences," "produced dignity"); of temporal progression (many short adverbs and adjectives, the punctuation itself in its suspending presence, "a single minute or five?" "interval," "throbbing like the tick of a watch"); of qualification (again, all the stylistic elements constitute a large qualification, "absolutely," "completely," "positive grimace," "intensity," "irresistibly"). There is an interaction of virtual equivalence among these terms: mental attitude not only becomes but is psychological action, itself both constantly bewildered by and reacting to a hypertension and consciousness of the "throbbing" time through which they are happening; the acts constitute what they produce, the constant qualification. The qualifications themselves, all the terms together and all separately, are self-consciously analytic ("measures," yes, measures, that's what in fact these women are taking by their attitudes, their "portentous intelligent stillnesses"; "stillness" yes, that's what it comes to, etc.).

The analysis suspends, and even rifts the very rhythms: "yet there was in her whole motion assuredly, *even as so dimly discerned*, a kind of portentous intelligent stillness"; the italicized phrase, analyzing the result of reflection, breaks, like the crack in the golden bowl, between the act ("motion") and its interpretation ("stillness"). The phrase adumbrates its own silent knowledge (neither woman will speak of what is on her mind). And this silence, in being prescient with perception ("dimly discerned"), prefigures the discerner's (Maggie's) supersession of Charlotte's "stillness," here "portentously intelligent"—the portent then being of her (Charlotte's) own defeat. And the defeat remains, like all else, reflexive with its own past; the formal rigidity of the novel, as well as the metaphorical ascription, renders it a cage.

But a change is being analyzed as it takes place; the analysis makes it take place. "Portentous intelligent stillness" meets in the next sentence "quiet measures" which it has, as potentiality, as portentous, already changed itself to and set itself against. These measures in turn become, and create, the "intensity of their mutual look"—a look, of course, silent, or, in James's analytic phrase, an "effect of silence." Analysis transforms this in turn, through "timing," "indecision," and "fear," into an "immense advantage"—which, in the moment of meeting, confounds past and present, "blurred all perception of whether or no the axe had fallen." The axe, irrationally, as possible only in fiction, has both fallen and not fallen at once. In this blur of perception (which blurs because it cannot yet unravel the intricacies of the relationship) guilt—and innocence, knowledge and ignorance, move the pitted quartet forward.

In the end not only these characters, but all James's protagonists, in the silence of their knowledge of the past, in the tightness of an involvement with the past necessarily preliminary to the knowledge, must preserve the silence unbroken in order not to violate it, must wed themselves to the renunciation which Joseph Warren Beach and others have found to be James's central theme. Winterbourne, almost like Marcher, only realizes his affinity with Daisy Miller at her death; Longmore in *Madame de Mauves* finds his knowledge through a moral gulf beside which his actual separation from the guilty woman seems trivial (except insofar as the separating Atlantic Ocean is a metaphor of that moral gulf). Strether can no more marry Maria Gostrey than Merton Densher can marry Kate Croy: each, by the silent presence of the past, by the tightness of his involvement, is forced to renounce the other. Ralph Touchett must die at the very moment Isabel Archer's knowledge catches up with his; it is, in fact, just her final involvement which has killed him, as the showdown between the Moreens and Pemberton in *The Pupil* kills the preternaturally perceptive Morgan. Hyacinth Robinson's utter solitude, which he cannot accept, as much as the bitterness of his knowledge, makes him commit suicide. Not only is the revolutionary movement unworthy of his martyrdom, and the beauty of the Continental past unobtainable; but the Princess, who embodies the revolution in her ideology and the past's beauty through her personal wealth and splendor, is horribly unfaithful, unbearably self-centered and aestheticizing in all her relations. Hyacinth has neither the normal aristocratic background of the Prince nor the coarse vigor of Captain Sholter to reconcile him with this knowledge; Vetch, who might have saved him, is too remote in his relationship; and so, appropriately, he arrives a moment too late to share that silent knowledge. Maggie's sharing with the Prince implies at the end of *The Golden Bowl* a renunciation of the past—of the Prince's once innocent, then guilty relation to Charlotte, of Maggie's devotion to her father. The difference between their pasts restrains each from really sharing the other's knowledge; what they agree to, husband and wife, loving and reunited though they are, is a renunciation of inquiry, a diplomatic silence about the other's past.

In terms of technique, the renunciation, the solitude, serves, and can alone serve, to close the circle of the plot, to make it tightly sequent with the past of the verbal fiction. The structure of a James plot, as well as the style and characterization, confirm through the algebra or logic of its relations (as James calls them), the solitude, the necessity of renunciation. If, as Forster (*Aspects of the Novel*) points out, *The Ambassadors* has an "hour-glass" form; it is an hourglass with an overlapping bottom half; it grows in time into a solitude and silence beyond that which it had before being switched from top half at the beginning of the novel:

Strether does change places with Chad from beginning to end (Foster's criterion for hourglass form), with the difference that Strether knows more than Chad can know: what he knows is the finality of life: he is old; and what he gains, the insight into life, is inseparable from what he has already lost, the life that has uneventfully elapsed behind him. What makes him finer than Chad is precisely the sequence of events in *The Ambassadors;* Chad runs through the same sequence, but he is a different person; and he must be different by virtue of the tightness of a James fiction, which allows only one character for each term in an equation.

Gloucester can resemble Lear, Emma can resemble Mr. Knightley or Fanny Edmund; in the total fiction of a James novel there is no room for a double plot or even for a complete unanimity between two characters, and we need only the pairs from Jane Austen to reveal by contrast how defective the rare Jamesian unanimity, that between Maggie and the Prince say, really is.

If one may call the constant counterbalances, the diagram, of a plot, spatial, one may say that the solitude produced through the very functional differentiation of the characters in the spatial tightness of James's plot corresponds to the loss felt as involved in the plot's sequence of events in time. In the tragic limitations of human experience, the bottom of the hourglass must expand; it is forced to expand by the very events which pass through it. Gain is inseparable from loss as sharing is from renunciation. The plot, starting the fiction anew, constitutes a fresh beginning in time; so a character at the outset cannot have lived through the events which will bring illumination. Nor as a human being can he be capable of transcending the limits in which the tightness of his character individuates him. He cannot be both European and American, both youthfully innocent and cognizant of evil, both wealthy and exempt from the corrupt motives of others who befriend him at

least partially for his wealth, both poor and free of the stig-
matized impotence of poverty. Even if he is sensitive both
morally and aesthetically, both European and potentially
rich, both young and full of commanding insight, as is only
Nick Dormer in *The Tragic Muse,* then he must be impli-
cated through the tight plot of the novel with characters
who lack either moral or aesthetic sensitivity, who are
either evil or poor; even if they possess all redeeming traits
in potentia, the plot will not allow more than one person to
do so *in actu.* Any completeness is precarious, and one must
live beyond it. When a completeness is invulnerable, it has
an artificiality, for which Miriam Rooth stands, in which
her centrality consists: ". . . she was always acting; . . .
her existence was a series of parts assumed for the moment,
each changed for the next . . . [her] identity resided in
the continuity of her personations . . . she had no moral
privacy . . . but lived in a high wind of exhibition, of fig-
uration—such a woman was a kind of monster, in whom of
necessity there would be nothing to like, because there
would be nothing to take hold of." She is their tragic muse,
tragic in that her tragic acting, while tragically only artificial, will, in its very artificiality, serve as a muse for the
successful resolution of the dilemma her presence poses. The
characters, thanks to her, several times just miss the false
identification of amorous infidelity. Through her extra presence they create the new, and only possible, terms of fidelity. Here too, as in less extreme James novels, the plot, as a
fresh start in time, as a tightness in the equation of its spatial
form, traps a James protagonist in the necessity of limits.

Almost like the progression of a single James novel, the entire sequence of the novels he selected for the New York
edition begins under the domination of time, with a journey
into the future but toward the past (*Roderick Hudson, The*

American, The Portrait of a Lady). Then the (for James) rather relaxed spatial structure of *The Princess Casamassima* develops through the period of his dramatic training into the predominance of space, the counterbalancing of character antitheses from the bewilderingly checkered equations and pairings of *The Tragic Muse* through the increasingly simplified (and deepened) agons of *The Awkward Age, The Spoils of Poynton, The Sacred Fount, The Golden Bowl*. In the interval between the last two comes a mature reunion of space and time; first in the journey of Milly and the spatial counterbalance of Densher and Kate, which coalesce to realize the final counterbalance in the terminal journey (to Venice and death); then in an identity of journey and balance, already precariously achieved in *The American*, through the centrality of Strether in *The Ambassadors*, whose journey evolves the counterbalance as his consciousness is one in its development with that of the action. After this supremacy—and James spoke of *The Ambassadors* as "quite the best all round of my productions"— all that was left (except to execute *The Golden Bowl*, conceived before though executed after *The Ambassadors*) was to fictionalize his visible past in *The American Scene* or to turn the ultimate characters back for a reexploration of the past: *The Ivory Tower* opens on a past already bewilderingly dense in the land of the future, reversing the formula, and *The Sense of the Past* is so extreme in its absorption with the past as to deal verisimilitude an almost irrecoverable shock. The finality of the past comes out so top-heavy toward the end of the sequence that it can attain its splendid pyrrhic victories only in the relatively short temporal compass of the supreme later tales, the occult-skirting journeys of confrontation with the past in *The Great Good Place, The Altar of the Dead, A Round of Visits, The Beast in the Jungle, The Jolly Corner* (some, to be sure, dating back to the dramatic period, when his fiction intensified through his relative idleness). James, at least, must have felt this intensity as a kind of limit in order to have violated his superb artistic conscience to leave unfinished for years before his death the only two collected novels he began after *The Golden Bowl.*

From the beginning of the sequence, the protagonist is forced to enter the lists with too little equipment, with terms on his side of the equation less than those life (the plot) forces him to equalize with on the other side (the end of the novel). The plot's self-containment in time keeps the upper half of the hourglass narrower than the expanding bottom, making it impossible for the character to master the situation before he has lived through it.

Roderick Hudson's insufficient equation expands into the Alps (thereby metaphorical as well as literal), and the thin air (of the novel as of Switzerland) through which, impotent, he totters into the abyss: the ambiguity of his death, suicide or accident, mirrors the ambiguity of the James problem, just beginning to set itself, as it rises from the hazy ambiguity of Christina Light's desire. By the time she hardens into form, when James clarifies his theme first in unexpectedly political terms, she will cause a suicide as unambiguous as the despair of Christopher Newman. Roderick's Alpine air, through which he falls, becomes, for Newman, a convent wall through which he cannot pass, though he understands the density of the music behind it; the American's magnificent renunciation of revenge against his fate, his refusal to expose the Bellegardes, consoles him for the fact that his illumination will remain totally unshared, even by Mrs. Bread. Isabel Archer can share hers, but only with the dead; unhappily superior to the plunging Hudson and the walled-off Newman, she does penetrate Europe by unwittingly having bartered her initial inviolable freedom for inextricable pain. Journey, having travelled in three novels its road to Rome (as "Light" has become, through the cipher of the Roman tongue, "Casamassima" Grand House), resolves itself into the naked, oblique spatial interpenetrations, the unexpected encounters which further and constitute the plot of *The Princess Casamassima* from its first abrupt deathbed scene to the Princess' last impulsive call, too late in time as its motive is too shadowy and weak. Her betrayal resembles what it exceeds, Hyacinth's intolerable bond to the immediate past, his vow of self-sacrifice; it also transcends Isabel Archer's terms of renunciation, as this novel's vast social problem, James was to imply twenty years later in writing of the meaning of the First World War, transcends individual relations. Hyacinth's despair does not find itself outside him in Hudson's mountain air or Newman's wall; it has become a horrid internal darkness. An end has been reached; no further depths were possible for this vision, whose ultimate term it had taken James five years to achieve—the five years between *The Portrait of a Lady* (1881) and *The Princess Casamassima* (1886). Journey had already become space, through the spatial antitheses of an oblique plot, and the Americans had given way to Europeans.

After another four years, a rebeginning, a new definition and vision, showed once more all the shallowness and complexity of an early stage through a plot structure of spatial counterparts: *The Tragic Muse* shared the spatiality and nationality of the last of the previous sequence with the problem set by the first (the relation between an artistic vocation and choice in love).

Through seven years of short restatements and new explorations, of dramatic experiment, the next novel he was to choose as definitive reduces the spatial counterbalance to an alternation of rapprochements around a movement of ballast (the constant shifting of the spoils) in *The Spoils of Poynton;* the defective equation remains defective and simple, deepening at once in the same year to the isolated rapprochements of Maisie, a figure more innocent and deprived than Fleda; she must cap Fleda's renunciation by breaking with her own parents. Nanda Brookenham in *The Awk-*

ward Age goes beyond Maisie; as her knowledge is deeper, her series of rapprochements is more severely dramatized and more isolated (and isolating) for all concerned; the spatial design of this novel assigns each of the main actors a book for his center: all are bypassed from book to book but the sensitive future, Nanda, whose book culminates and resumes the others; only Vanderbank can understand her without having her; only Longdon can have her without fully understanding the knowledge she shares with Vanderbank; the dramatic tightness renders false choices impossible, having already separated everyone; there is nothing to renounce, except the future itself, by marrying one who embodies the past.

Reaching again a profundity and pessimism perhaps as intense, though not as devastating, as the social horror of *The Princess Casamassima,* the Jamesian representation of interdependence, in its tightness, begins to envisage the one body[4] formed by a couple in marriage as necessarily parasitic. Love, as Osborn Andreas formulates this motif in James, is "the deterrent to a full life." In *The Sacred Fount* what serves as ballast is no longer an external group of aesthetic objects, the spoils (though these will serve again ten years later in an uncollected novel, *The Outcry*), but the alternation of host and parasite in the love relationship; while this is internal to the actors, "the deeply involved and immersed and more or less bleeding participants," it is external to a partially involved observer, the narrator of *The Sacred Fount.* (The spoils, being external already, must matter equally to all concerned, even to the imperceptive Mona Brigstock.) Illumination can have a success like that of *The Tragic Muse* without being compelled to Fleda's renunciation, to say nothing of Hyacinth's suicide; so the

---

[4] It is noteworthy that the theological idea of concorporateness in its analogy and counterpart, the mystical body of the Church, is arrived at independently nearly at the same time by James's friend, C. S. Peirce; love means just this in *Chance, Love and Logic.*

depth of the illumination remains inconsequentially shallow.

It is deepened in the great novel of the succeeding year, as in *The Princess Casamassima,* by the introduction of a sacrifice figure, a dove for a Hyacinth. The dove, however, is displaced in its journey from the center of consciousness which Hyacinth had occupied in the novel's point of view. Milly's consciousness is rendered all the lovelier, all the deeper, by not revealing itself except as reflected in the counterpoise of the other characters. She dies in the Venice Hyacinth only visited. Lord Mark, less sensitive than the Lord Warburton of *The Portrait of a Lady,* is, for all his pretended morality, more brutal than Osmond, even than the Princess Casamassima herself; so his friend Aunt Maud is more brutal, in her very superior imperviousness, than the guilty Madame Merle. To identify herself with a world peopled by such transcendent brutalities, to put behind her a father as brutal, guiltier, and more ruthless, Kate Croy, fighting her defective equation of past poverty, desecrates the sanctity of her own contingent marriage, commits herself to a sin which, in James's deepening vision, will become the pivot of the following major novels, the last he will complete. After the sacrifice (Milly's of life, hers of virtue), her collusive brutality with Densher, scarcely less brutal for having been suggested by Aunt Maud through a horribly decorous silence, has killed Milly; but the dove, whose consciousness we have known only in its effects, whose illumination we have felt only as her own pain, becomes completely victorious in death, as Hyacinth could be only tentatively:

> "You must choose."
> Strange it was for him then that she stood in his own rooms doing it, while, with an intensity now beyond any that had ever made his breath come slow to him, he waited for her act. "There's but one thing that can save you from my choice."
> "From your choice of my surrender to you?"

"Yes,"—and she gave a nod at the long envelope on the table—"Your surrender of that."

"What is it then?"

"Your word of honour that you're not in love with her memory."

"Oh—her memory!"

"Ah,"—she made a high gesture—"don't speak of it as if you couldn't be. *I* could, in your place; and you're one for whom it will do. Her memory's your love. You *want* no other."

He heard her out in stillness, watching her face, but not moving. Then he only said: "I'll marry you, mind you, in an hour."

"As we were?"

"As we were."

But she turned to the door, and her headshake was now the end. "We shall never be again as we were!"

Milly's is a third presence, in the unopened envelope, overshadowing a repentance powerless because it cannot go back in time to revive the dead. The wings of the dove cover Densher and Kate in the fixed silence of death. The aesthetic fineness of their moral inviolability, the moral fineness of their beauty, supervenes, at once opening up perceptions and forbidding actions. They exorcise the evil which, paradoxically, Densher has already sufficiently expiated by feeling for Milly not a deceiving but a true love, perceived and dreaded by Kate, who stands equally under the wings. Through the sequence of question, declaration, and exclamation in the last three statements about the same past "as we were" (yes, as the past is reflexive; no, as we have lived through it), her hopelessness silences the hope in Densher's renunciation.

The Wings of the Dove is the first full-length collected novel in over twenty years, since *The Portrait of a Lady*, which makes an American a central figure, which goes far enough to allow the defectiveness of the major equation to include the complication of the international theme. Milly's passivity is united with the consciousness of *The Sacred*

Fount's narrator, and the international theme moves to the center of the larger, second sequence of collected novels in *The Ambassadors*. It elicits a further renunciation; Strether can discover a fineness in Madame de Vionnet's very adultery. Perception is the deeper for being hemmed in on all sides by the Americanism, the imminent old age, the fineness, the complicity, the relative poverty, the unrelatedness of Strether's final state.

There could remain, for this sequence, the advance of bringing the international consciousness into full relation with the evil of the past. The steps of *The Golden Bowl*'s ballet contain a rift, a fault, an open end at each stage which cries out to be closed; and the closing leads to a new sequence (I am revising Stephen Spender's analysis in *The Destructive Element*):

Charlotte is the friend of Maggie and beloved by the Prince: the opening between the Prince and Maggie is closed by their marriage.

This leaves a gap between Maggie's father (Adam) and Charlotte, closed in turn by their marriage.

The implications of the past demand that the closed circle be broken, like the momento golden bowl still on the scene; that the Prince become Charlotte's lover, bringing Maggie back closer to her father.

This closeness and tightness throws up new barriers of silence between Charlotte and Adam, the Prince and Maggie. The bowl breaks at the silence.[5]

Maggie forces Charlotte's hand silently, till the bowl is healed and the marriages remain inviolate. But the limits of the equation exact a distance between the pairs, and Maggie must renounce her closeness to her father to preserve her marriage. The bowl is healed only in the imagina-

---

[5] The steps might be diagrammed as follows (revising Spender):

$$
\begin{array}{cccc|c}
\text{C–M} & \text{P C} & \text{P–C} & \text{P M} & \text{M} & \text{C} \\
| \quad | & | \quad | & | \quad | & | \quad | & | & | \\
\text{P A} & \text{M–A} & \text{M–A} & \text{C–A} & \text{P} & \text{A}
\end{array}
$$

tion. The past is an immense, permanent crack between the couples, of which the Atlantic Ocean, which actually separates them, becomes the physical correlative, as it had previously determined the duality between Europe and America, the spatial side of the fault at the outset of the novel. (The golden bowl has a fault in the first place through the poverty of Charlotte and the Prince: they are too poor to buy any, let alone one of the splendor, say, possessed by the solid gold piece of plate 270 James's admirers gave him on his seventieth birthday.)

Two sequences of collected novels had brought the theme to its limits; but it could still be intensified, and that intensification occupies the last stories, the two unfinished novels, and no less the "allegories" as Auden calls them (with buildings as characters) of *The American Scene*, as well as the personal recapitulations of an autobiography nearly as dense as the fictions it concludes.

Leavis, Winters and Ford rightly admire James for his masterful and deep characterization; Trilling for his uncanny social vision. Both his characters and his social vision achieve their density from the Sophoclean world they reflect, one in which the profoundest copiousness of health may yet be involved in the evil of others (*Oedipus at Colonus*), in which the deepest meaning of the past is silently present (*Oedipus Rex*), in which one can bridge the paradoxes of human limitation by a renunciation paradoxically uniting (*Philoctetes*). It takes a nearly total artifice, a reflexive identification of appearance and reality, to make this vision fictional, as it took a comparably high artifice, a ritual identification of the formal and the real, for Sophocles to make it dramatic. "Complexities as rich as life itself," Tate says, speaking of Dante; "I had almost said richer than life, if by life we mean (as we must mean) what we ourselves are able daily to see, or even what certain writers have seen, with the exception of Shakespeare, and possibly of Sophocles and Henry James." James is a model of the fictional technique he was the first to discuss abstractly because of the depth and consequent generality of his theme, just as Sophocles' rare profundity, pure in a normality that "business could not make dull nor passion wild," made him Aristotle's model for the technique of drama. It is James who formulates what his works alone purely illustrate, "What is character but the determination of incident? What is incident but the illustration of character?" Yes, and what, for James, is the silence of fiction but the fictiveness of silence? What is the pastness of the present but the presence of the past? What is the moral of the fictive, but the fictiveness of the moral? What is the silence of knowledge, but the knowledge of silence?

The terms of these identities in idea—James speaks of his "immense array of terms,"—the specificity of the characters in their plotted evolutions gives James's central vision of good and evil a complexity which Osborn has perceptively formulated as a Jamesian moral code. But what Osborn leaves out, as James might say, is everything, the element of fiction which brings this code, and other abstractions critics have devised about James, into unity.

At the same time any two terms remain separate in their identity. There is a duality between reflector and reflected as well as a unity. The defectiveness of an equation implies two halves, between the light of whose terms falls the rift of the reflexive equals sign (the novel), a rift wide as the Atlantic Ocean, a shadow between the past and the present, the silence and its expression, the knowledge and what it must renounce in knowing. In theological terms— if James may be supposed to be a kind of fictional moral theologian (Osborn makes him this, if too crudely)—the shadow is original sin; in epistemological terms it is the invincible subjectivity, in space and in time, of the human observer. (This too is the epistemological aspect of original sin; Adam cannot have known this rift, and it perhaps explains the name James gave him that Adam Verver is spared the fullness of the knowledge.)

The shadow, to alter James's terms into those of the most Jamesian of poets,

> Between the idea
> And the reality
> Between the motion
> And the act. . . .
> Between the potency
> And the existence
> Between the essence
> And the descent . . .[6]

is unbreachable. But in knowing the breach one can become reconciled to it by renouncing the attempt; and in the renunciation one falls between the two halves of one's illumination, one almost becomes oneself the shadow, almost entering, like Ralph Pendrel, the actual past. This perception of the division can throw light (or shadow) backwards on the events of the plot which have already happened to invest them too with the meaning of the final equation which they created and with which they become identified.

This resuming process is the ultimate unity of the divided Jamesian silence, the rightness for James's characters of what Conrad calls "the sophism of their mistakes." The golden bowl is rehealed only in the imagination, by submission, like that James wished in his writing, to the conditions of life. "The more we remain in *them*," he said, "all round, the more pleasure we dispense. . . . All of which amounts doubtless but to saying that as the whole conduct of life consists of things done, which do other things in their turn, just so our behaviour and its fruits are essentially

[6] From *Collected Poems 1909-1935* by T. S. Eliot. Copyright, 1936, by Harcourt, Brace & Co., Inc., and reprinted with their permission.

one and continuous and persistent and unquenchable, so the act has its way of abiding and showing and testifying, and so, among our innumerable acts, are no arbitrary, no senseless separations . . . to 'put' things is very exactly and responsibly and interminably to do them. Our expression of them, and the terms on which we understand that, belong as nearly to our conduct and our life as every other feature of our freedom. . . . But on all the ground to which the pretension of performance by a series of exquisite laws may apply there reigns one sovereign truth—which decrees that, as art is nothing if not exemplary, care nothing if not active, finish nothing if not consistent, the proved error is the base apologetic deed, the helpless regret is the barren commentary, and 'connexions' are employable for finer purposes than mere gaping contrition."

This compounded silence runs through all his work from the earliest collected stories. In *The Madonna of the Future, Roderick Hudson, The American, The Europeans,* it is unconquerable; Winterbourne through death, Longmore through separation, first envision it. Its presence as pain for the unmarried heroine of *Washington Square* is transcended by the more deeply trapped but finer heroine of *The Portrait of a Lady.* A false desire to avert its imagined evil in the father causes a mother to let her child die (*The Author of Beltraffio*). Society becomes its burden, its agent, its illusion, in *The Bostonians* and *The Princess Casamassima.* In *The Aspern Papers* the past demands impossible involvement for knowledge of it, a knowledge none the less sensed through the refusal of knowledge. It exacts a choice in *The Tragic Muse* and *The Lesson of the Master.* Others' contradiction of it spells the death of Morgan Moreen, and the loss of a fiction envisioning it after the death of the lion. *The Altar of the Dead* makes up its loss in *The Aspern Papers* through its presence as the matchmaking past. By now *The Figure in the Carpet,* having been traced, can become its own subject. Its fineness of insight is enough to console

Fleda for her loss; the heroine of *The Coxon Fund* had been consoled less deeply for an equal loss. Knowledge of it illumines, then isolates Maisie, through the same process and by means of the same sin, that sends Guy Domville to La Grand Chartreuse. In such an atmosphere as Nanda Brookenham understands it does *The Great Good Place* become possible. Its evil of union and separation *The Sacred Fount* finds in the implications of physical union. Its inverse in Kate Croy's fuliginous past makes her commit an equal horror; and at the same stroke it enables her to understand how its fineness renders her troth impossible. It is, for Marcher, the beast in the isolating jungle of his willed, incognizant past. Strether embraces it as the refinement of what might have been, while Maggie enlists it to force her mother's husband and her father's wife to do it the homage of the only possible marital propriety. Its equation, reduced to the simplest terms, then works itself out in the brief intensities of the last stories and the unfinished novels, in explorations of the real lived past and the visible past of buildings, embodying it the more purely in their very separation from the imperfect characters who in the novels moved among them.

Only after he has detailed its terms and extended them in novel after novel, after he has given voice to the mutations of this silence, can James say of the sound of a real city, "fury of sound took the form of derision of the rest of your woe, and thus it *might*, I admit, have struck you as brazen that the horrible place should, in such confessed collapse, still be swaggering and shouting." The cumulative insight of James's fictions informs this real observer, the actual James, allowing him to see the "horrible place" as "brazen," to see the "confessed collapse."

In the reality of his life, in fact, as he commented about Balzac's, we find the intensity of life coming paradoxically from one whose whole life is in his fiction. The insight seems none the less fictional when it comes in travel litera-

ture, in prefaces, in autobiography, even in notebooks occasionally and in letters like the one he wrote Grace Norton
in 1883: "In other words consciousness is an illimitable
power, and though at times it may seem to be all consciousness of misery, yet in the way it propagates itself from wave
to wave, so that we never cease to feel, and though at moments we appear to, try to, pray to, there is something that
holds one in one's place, makes it a standpoint in the universe which it is probably good not to forsake. . . . Only
don't, I beseech you, *generalize* too much in these sympa-
thies and tendernesses—remember that every life is a special
problem which is not yours but another's, and content your-
self with the terrible algebra of your own. Don't melt too
much into the universe, but be as solid and dense and fixed as
you can." We recognize the "terrible algebra" for the equations of James's protagonists, "solid and dense and fixed" in
their specificity. The knowledge, in life or in the novels, is silently its own reward, whatever terror the algebra evolves.
"It signified little whether the crouching beast were destined to slay him or to be slain," Marcher knows; and later,
"Now that the illumination had begun, however, it blazed
to the zenith, and what he presently stood there gazing at
was the sounded void of his life."

James, like Marcher, gazed; the whole past, his own
and society's, seemed later to him a void, sounded by the
war, which James interpreted in a Jamesian way as the last
of a series, reflecting and qualifying the past: "The plunge
of civilization into this abyss of blood and darkness by the
wanton feat of those two infamous autocrats is a thing that
so gives away the whole long age during which we have
supposed the world to be, with whatever abatement, gradually bettering, that to have to take it all now for what the
treacherous years were all the while really making for and
meaning [italics James's] is too tragic for any words." Is,
in other words, a silence. It was into a like silence that he
ordered his pen in the notebooks, describing the tomb of a

beloved sister in words that are an extension of the meaning of his fictions:

> Everything was there, everything *came;* the recognition, stillness, the strangeness, the pity and the sanctity and the terror, the breath-catching passion and the divine relief of tears. William's inspired transcript, on the exquisite little Florentine urn of Alice's ashes, William's divine gift to us, and to *her,* of the Dantean lines—
>
> > Dopo lungo exilio e martiro
> > Viene a questa pace—
>
> took me so at the throat by its penetrating *rightness,* that it was as if one sank down on one's knees in a kind of anguish of gratitude before something for which one had waited with a long, deep *ache.* But why do I write of the all unutterable and the all abysmal? Why does my pen not drop from my hand on approaching the infinite pity and tragedy of all the past? It does, poor helpless pen, with what it meets of the ineffable, what it meets of the cold Medusa-face of life, of all the life *lived* on every side. *Basta, basta!*

Taking the "all" ("unutterable" and "abysmal") ambiguously as a noun (and an adjective), James goal is none other than that of his master Balzac, on whose lesson he was about to lecture from coast to coast. Balzac assayed the all through the device of wanting to write a history which would detail everything; James, the anti-Balzac, made the same effort by fictionalizing totally that all. And each triumphed, with an unsurpassed generality and intensity. The action of Vautrin, the death of de Rubempré, the isolation of Goriot, the almost congealed pity of Pons, gain their depth from the postulated range of Balzac's historicizing, particularizing total comedy, which seems shallow till one sees what force its intended contrasts engender. That depth is unutterable and abysmal, ineffable too, with an ache that recalls the silence of Strether, Marcher, Maggie, Spencer Brydon, Merton Densher. If James, taking up where Balzac left off, excludes the particularity of life in which his master abounds, he is no more trivial and rarefied than Balzac

is merely platitudinous and shallow; his scrupulous fictiveness produces a meaning which, as a converse of Balzac's
realism, shares some of the same dense quality. Appearance
has been read so densely as to seem to constitute reality. It
is only a testimony to that density, as to the similarity between the two, that its grandeur in both led Blackmur to
call James's plots fables, Baudelaire to call Balzac's characters mythical.

The sense that the two, appearance and reality, stand in
an indissoluble relation rises out of James's extraordinarily
subtle control. The novel can offer us such density, in James
or Balzac, because its very indeterminacy of selected detail,
directness of language, and wideness of focus, all permit it
to force a high pressure on the smallest events. In a play
the event put under pressure loses its smallness and looms
on the stage by the strength of its dramatic effect. In the
novel the event may remain small, only a hint or even a
silence, as James magnificently shows us, and yet in and
because of its very smallness it will hold a density that the
whole novel has created, a density like that found in the
process of life.

℣ IX ℣

IDEA IN FICTION

If novels are made from sequenced observations of social behavior, what holds empirically in them will be felt to hold inductively; a novel sets its own real standards of behavior against apparent standards. So much is fiction bound up with a moral idea that novelists have a tendency to campaign for specific social reforms, like Dickens and Tolstoi; to pose as moral prophets, like Gide and Faulkner; or even to write abstract moral treatises, as Stendhal did.

A moral idea in fiction is given in terms of appearance and reality. "I am comparing, not liberalism and conservatism, which are to me, not the main thing at all, but the sham and the truthfulness of the characters." To what Chekov says here almost any novelist would assent. Appearances in a novel function dramatically as the false moral ideas of stupid or evil characters.

The novelist, who observes social appearances, breaks through them to give us his version of moral reality. Even James had not, in Eliot's phrase, "a mind so fine no idea could violate it." He had an idea so fine that no loose concept alien to it could find its way into his work (as loose historical generalizations find their way into the splendid moral order of *War and Peace*). The figure in his carpet amounts to a code of moral ideas. To what else do the impassioned Jamesians give allegiance? And even when a conservative novelist like Jane Austen or Proust or James celebrates the conventions, they are not the blind conventions of a Mr. Woodhouse, a Basin de Guermantes, an Aunt Maud; they are conventions rendered more "real" through the insight of the novelist.

Even when the comic dramatist, Molière or Jonson, ridicules shams, he does so in terms of preconceived moral abstractions and character types: misers and misanthropes, or melancholics, and phlegmatics. Usually the tragic dramatist, Sophocles or Racine, will exalt and heighten the conventions of his society.

Dostoevsky's radicals are confuted not because they are leftist but because they hold their ideas in bad faith. The radicalisms of Raskolnikov or Stepan Verhovensky or Stavrogin are shams, not utopian programs but neurotic projections; their bad faith will not recognize the real, for Dostoevsky the religious, implications of their motives.

Idea in Dostoevsky, as in any successful novelist, is still bound up with form, with the style and plot and characterization of the novel. A severe formalism may obscure the role of a novelist's ideas as ideas; yet there is no novel which exemplifies the aestheticism of some formalist critics; a purely aestheticist novel, if Proust's or Nabokov's are that, turns aestheticism itself into an idea, almost into a code.

While the notion of separable content has mostly been eradicated from the criticism of poetry, it lingers on among those who discuss fiction, partly because fiction has not yet received so full a scrutiny as poetry. However, the very fact that moral ideas are of the essence in fiction should put us on our guard, more than it has, against forgetting the formal and artistic side of any novel.

For example, many a modern critic, finding a sympathetic chord in Ivan Karamazov's long fantasy, "The Grand Inquisitor," has imagined that here, with uncritical and un-

imaginative directness, Dostoevsky has given his ultimate
social vision. Yet if "The Grand Inquisitor" constitutes such
a peak, why *The Brothers Karamazov* itself? It is tempting
to the modern anti-ultramontanist to accept unqualifiedly
the anti-ultramontanism expressed by Ivan in his "poem,"
his "ridiculous thing," as he calls it. But to do so is to ignore
character and plot. The brilliant parable is spoken by the
same Ivan who earlier, at the monastery, expressed exactly
the opposite idea, a thoroughgoing ultramontanism. And
soon thereafter, concurring basely with his father to taunt
Alyosha, he expressed another idea equally opposed to both,
a thoroughgoing atheism. Logically ultramontanism and
atheism are incompatible, as are both with the anti-ultramontanism of "The Grand Inquisitor." Ivan, the intellectual, actually believes none of the three. His spirit torments
his reason to juggle all these ideas as a substitute for the
deeply selfless human responses the plot demands of him.
Like all the brothers he will later become transmuted into
atonement. In "The Grand Inquisitor," as always, Ivan's
flaunting intellection is still hovering in the half-light of in-
adequate spiritual relationships.

Alyosha's instinct has just sent him to the tavern,
where Smerdyakov has said Ivan awaits Dmitri. Ivan, erst-
while bitterly jealous of his younger brother, suddenly
reaches out to his mother's only other son, and the two
begin their prolonged tête-à-tête, which leads them through
reminiscences of their childhood and poetic apostrophes
of nature to discussion of the very women who cause
Ivan's jealousy. The name of Dmitri, though, curdles
Ivan. (But has he inconsistently not just sent for him?)
"Am I my brother's keeper?" this surrogate Cain-to-be
asks Alyosha. Ivan then brings up religious questions, as is
his habit at moments of tension. He at once mocks and
adores God; an ambivalence that attracts and repels Alyosha. Soon he has talked himself into a series of sadistic,
heart-rending parables about tortured children, anxiously

testing Alyosha's responses. At the climax of the parables he introduces "The Grand Inquisitor," a "poem" which resumes the ambivalence of his emotions toward human suffering and his consequent complex response to Alyosha.

In this fantasy, Christ, resurrecting a child at his Second Coming, is jailed by the Grand Inquisitor who has watched the scene apart in his monk's habit. Ivan's dream is a brilliantly elaborated and rationalized piece of denigration which denies its own diabolism in spite of itself, as Alyosha kindly says. It is as if the monk of one subplot (Father Zossima) were imprisoning Christ's surrogate, Alyosha, for "resurrecting," by miracle rather than by love, the children of the other subplot.[1] Alyosha in fact at the moment is "imprisoned" by bewilderment about the monastery.

That society needs to be slavish, subdued by miracle, mystery and authority—this view which the Grand Inquisitor presents is a profound one, and Dostoevsky held some version of it himself. Yet in the action of the novel society does attain the freedom of love; mystery and authority without freedom are seen as a parody of love in the figure of Father Ferapont, who, while no Grand Inquisitor, is isolated by love and from love. And Alyosha, the agent of love, is himself reborn into freedom by seeing that miracle is not necessary for regeneration when the body of Father Zossima undergoes natural corruption. Ivan, in pleading the slavishness of society to Alyosha, is trying (for self-justification) to depress the Christlike bearer of freedom and love. In its idea, and in its dramatic purpose, "The Grand Inquisitor" runs counter to the novel's meaning. It pleads despair, not hope: it implies that society cannot be regenerated at the very moment when Alyosha doubts, before

[1] The later description of Ilusha's flower-decked coffin makes it seem like the coffin of the child Christ resurrects in "The Grand Inquisitor."

carrying through his individual regeneration that expands out into the society.

Ivan's perverse dream would frustrate all the rebirths of the novel, including his own. Alyosha, understanding deep in his charity the struggle of his brother, chides him gently and abides. But Ivan, disclaiming his fantasy grinningly, is bound to contradict himself; declaring his love, giving Alyosha a kiss that in sequence will have been a kiss of Judas, he runs off "overcome by insufferable depression." Immediately he entrains for a distant city, abandoning his brother and humanity forthwith, allowing by his absence the crime which will make his eventual redemption far more difficult and far more painful for others. "I am a scoundrel," he whispered to himself on arriving at Moscow. His feeling is the last wave in a self-disgust of which "The Grand Inquisitor" was a particularly brilliant crest. By blind slavery to diabolical depression, his act of immediate flight has belied the very ideal of freedom which his poem held up.

Narratives whose sole end is the illustration of an abstract moral system are too direct in their conceptualism to represent a novel's fine and free social interplay. For Rousseau the novel is merely an alternate means of exposition, a parable for the ideas expounded in *Le Contrat Social* and elsewhere. The characters in *Emile*, in *La Nouvelle Héloise* act out his leading ideas too directly, too univalently, to generate in their plot any of the mythical overtones of romance. The mountains in *La Nouvelle Héloise* are not so much metaphor, still less observation essentially, as a direct source of moral grandeur to the characters.

A Rousseauesque romance is only part of D. H. Lawrence's prophetic purpose. The felt reality of a fictional observer he turns to glowing evidence against the shoddy appearances of modern living; fiction's reality affirms the reality of the body's sacramental goodness. His rainbow surpasses the mere illustrative function of Rousseau's idealized mountains, as the texture of his style will illustrate:

> For some weeks the youth came frequently and was received gladly by them all. He sat amongst them, his dark face glowing, an eagerness and a touch of derisiveness on his wide mouth, something grinning and twisted, his eyes always shining like a bird's, utterly without depth. There was no getting hold of the fellow, Brangwen irritably thought. He was like a grinning young tom-cat that came when he thought he would and without cognizance of the other person.

The illustrative significance of Will's presence here is not laid on arbitrarily, as in Rousseau. It rises out of the keenly observed qualities of his person and action. His dark face is observed as literally glowing before the dark glow comes to symbolize that of the dark gods of the blood. His observed eagerness is a desire, almost hypostatized by the plot, for Anna's whole person. His derisiveness becomes the bold scorn, almost allegorical, of the young man who is supplanting the old father in his daughter's affections. Yet Brangwen received him gladly, and Lawrence continues to stress his liking for the young man. The father is to relent after the wedding, and his ambivalent reaction is here concretized in the look and feel of his response to Will. The superb description of mouth and eyes has a literal rightness of observation Tolstoi would not have been ashamed to own. Out of this authentic observation comes Will's metaphorical significance. The animal metaphor, too, as so frequently in Lawrence, serves as both the observed reality and the symbol of the young man's appearance. Metaphorically he is a tomcat to the father. And to Lawrence his eyes have both the appearance and the significance of a bird's shining directness, "utterly without depth."

Lawrence is compounded of novelist and prophet, and

one cannot separate the fictive meaning of his novels from the prophetic message they bear. They strain the component of idea in fiction, its always present conceptual side, to a breaking point which sometimes falsifies a character or wrenches a plot, even allowing the special use of plot and character Mark Schorer claims for Lawrence.[2] Yet it is the urgency of his idea, the glow of his message, which furnishes Lawrence with a heuretic principle for his brilliant psychological observations, for his "burning bush" nature descriptions like that of the moon on the lake in *Women in Love*, where the moon shatters its light on the water into the shattering emotions of Birkin and Ursula.

Lawrence wrote more than novels. His leading idea is strong enough to let him extend his interpretive eye into the nature of Sicily, Sardinia, Mexico, American literature, the Etruscan past. And for him literature in general was only part of his calling. He was a symbolic sufferer as well as a creator. "One sheds one's sicknesses in books—repeats and presents again one's emotions, to be master of them." Yet he was sedulous about the art of his novels. "The real naked essence of our vision. . . . One has to be so terribly religious, to be an artist."

The ambivalence between novels as sickness-shedding and novels as "the real naked essence of vision" is reflected in the novels themselves. The symbolic animals, the horse in *St. Mawr*, the fox in "The Fox," seem illegitimately to transcend the meaning given them in the novels. They are observed. And they are metaphorical. But their metaphor is at once too symbolic and not symbolic enough. They have neither the one-for-one correspondence of Flaubert's analogies nor the breath-taking concreteness of detail in Turgenev and Chekov. They are meant to bear a weight of meaning, a message, which the form of the story cannot sufficiently contain. To put it differently, there is a gap between St.

[2] *"Women in Love* and Death," *The Hudson Review*, VI, Spring 1953.

Mawr the real horse and St. Mawr the symbol of glowing bodily assertion. Flaubert's fiacre has no gap: its rattling, its blackness, its blinds, symbolize, and *are*, the disequilibrium, the moral vacancy, the deliberate exclusions, of Emma.

Lawrence's plots too, in *Women in Love*, as Mark Schorer tells us, and elsewhere, are parables that follow the choreographic progressions of romance, but often without realizing the firm outlines of the best romance plots. The novelist's obsession with representing the underlying emotions of the characters melts the sequence of incident into a limpness of causality, a diffuseness of impression. This looseness of structure can become an advantage, in the short fiction; Lawrence's best stories gain a vividness from their occasional open form which recalls that of Chekov or his friend Katherine Mansfield. In a novel it blunts the edges of even such successes as *Sons and Lovers* and *Lady Chatterley's Lover*. While no major novelist exhibits so marked a diffuseness of plot, this quality is to be found in much of the ephemeral fiction contemporary with Lawrence. He at least was able to enhance his diffuseness as an expression of his burning idea.

On the one hand his plots are too limp to show his meaning crisply; on the other, they are so simple in their romance evolutions that without the constant observed support of subtle characterization and astonishingly observed detail they would fail. Characters dwindle under the obsession of a novelist who, ironically, wanted that obsession to give them full being. In *The Plumed Serpent* they are already flatter than in the best novels of his middle period. In *The Man Who Died*, the characters are such bald, such unobserved, types, that not even the brilliant poetic texture of the narrative can redeem them for fiction. The plot, in its repetitions, has no cumulative effect; its structural simplicity gains none of the insightful boldness of, say, *Billy Budd*. Characters are always types in a romance, but the types, must themselves be ciphers of insight, not formulas for a doctrine. *The Man Who Died* fails for the same reason that other pietistic fiction fails; it tries to substitute foregone conviction for insight. Here the dying Lawrence, his powers failing, trails out of art into life, unable to make each become the other. More of a hero he becomes, but at the same time less of a writer.

Against the social appearance of death, Lawrence, man and novelist, asserts the bodily holiness of the psychic reality, life. For him, Mark Schorer points out, as for all novelists from Cervantes on, the internal ego was to make itself the objective self by looking inward and recognizing its true nature. Lawrence saw this idea ambiguously as both program and vision. He wanted in reality, for himself and for others, his vision of a resacramentalized personal life. All novelists would like the reality of life to resemble the best part of their visions; all are moralists to the core. But Lawrence pushed the word of contemplation into the word of action. This ambiguity is at once the defect and the achievement of his novels. His weakness is his strength. His vision is bound up with the precariously direct seriousness of his idea—perhaps because, unlike most novelists, he felt society's appearances as an intrusion on personal reality rather than a necessary enunciation of it.

Another novelist of ideas embodies them somewhat differently in his novels. Malraux is that *rara avis*, the genuine political novelist. Like Lawrence he has not confined himself, in life or in literature, merely to fiction. And his ultimate work is a critique of art whose vision surpasses, strangely, the achievement of his novels.

In *La Condition Humaine*,[3] as the title comes to suggest when set against the novel, action at once illustrates and incarnates idea; motive and act, attitude and character,

[3] Entitled *Man's Fate* in the English version.

will and destiny, become one under the purgative extremity of a revolution. The self-disgusted Tchen is the very person destined, as the book opens, to commit political murder. Murder changes his world; he willed and is destined for that change. He will die, as will less horribly the milder Kyo. The poison which Kyo takes has been given him by the uncompromising Katow. Keeping none for himself delivers Katow, consistently, to the full vengeance of his captors. We know his idea through his fate, and vice versa. His idea brings, and is the consequence of, his fate. Kyo's father, Gisors, the opium-smoking ex-professor of sociology, is detached enough from the action not to suffer more than personal loss. In the last scene of the novel, though, Kyo's Shanghai-born German wife, May, fuses this very same personal loss with the revolutionary hope which is at once her idea, her character, her professional role as a physician, and her destiny.

A sharply analogous, almost eccentric, background lends substance to the diversified world these people make of their ideas, to their *condition humaine*. And the very plurality of motives, the distinctiveness of the separate destinies, makes for the firm hope of eventual political success; the revolutionaries are all the more devoted to the common cause for their individuality. The bureaucratic adept Ferral, by contrast, is isolated; he betrays his decadence in the sadistic eroticism of his relationship with the White Russian Valérie. The striking mad scene where he uncages exotic birds and sets a kangaroo loose in her darkened hotel bedroom is tantamount to a confession of the ineptitude he shows by fleeing. The contrastingly sober and healthy love of May for her husband Kyo rededicates itself to the cause; if this revolutionary episode has failed, another cannot but succeed, the novel is saying. All the strength of the healthy characters is converging in the direction of such a destiny.

The coherence of Malraux's idea is fictive enough to be independent of any specific communist platform. His fictional vision, while inseparable from its leading political idea, has a temper and incisiveness unattained by even such perspicuous communist parables as Aragon's *Voyageurs de L'Impériale.*

In *L'Espoir* the vision of a purpose underlying individual destinies is made too explicit. Random documentation in this novel supplants the diversified analogies of *La Condition Humaine.* In an earlier novel, *Les Conquérants,* Malraux casts his burden of social idea not so much in the plot —otherwise similar on a simpler scale to the situation of *La Condition Humaine*—as in the character Garine. In China, where Garine has come for just this vision of pure action, he finds politics as existential as Malraux would have them. But the vision of reality is still fictive. And Garine's notion, "beyond good and evil," is nonetheless a moral idea, the end of a soul-searching, opposed in the novel to the mindless power functionalism of Garine's antagonistic henchman, Borodine. Society paradoxically needs a man like Garine with an idea of its idealess process: "Il [Borodine] veut fabriquer des révolutionnaires comme Ford fabrique des autos! Ça finira mal, avant longtemps. Dans sa tête de Mongol chevelu, le bolchevik lutte contre le Juif: si le bolchevik l'emporte, tant pis pour l'internationale. . . ."

For Lawrence fictional vision is an instrument of moral prophecy. For Malraux, fiction is an unparalleled instrument for mirroring the elusive nature of the historical process. For Hemingway, as for Malraux, the extreme situation provides a proving ground to exact crucial allegiances from characters. The free time of a war-disillusioned leisure class in *The Sun Also Rises,* war in *A Farewell to Arms,* sport, that hybrid of war's danger and leisure's gratuitousness— all become a moral gauntlet, without which the code would remain hidden in life, unexpressed in fiction. Honor is at once elusive and unmistakable. No one is taken in by its sham in the mere bravado of a Robert Cohn. It can be gained by a Francis Macomber, lost in the snows of Kilimanjaro. Hemingway's scaled down vocabulary becomes, under the aegis of the code, no longer simply the observed metaphors of his master Flaubert. The words of this style are almost a pastoral system, they strip the world to a concrete stage for the idealized emotions he pictures as elemental.

In these writers, and others, idea plays a special dominant role. But no novelist can help seeming to claim the status of moral truth for the underlying social reality his observations purvey.

X

THE MORAL VISION

TOLSTOI

If fiction is essentially concerned with the commitment of its characters to moral ideas, its main stream is more to be traced in moral observation than in the tributary of figurative implication. As the instinct of Leavis has shown us, the great tradition of English—as of any—fiction is a moral tradition.

Each original novelist, by virtue of the uniqueness of the world he creates, has a distinct kind of moral observation. We find that Hemingway analyzes the moral gestures of courage, Trollope of sincerity, Jane Austen of altruistic social insight, Defoe of economic and sexual scruple, Stendhal of crassness or fineness.

Tolstoi's world, for all its breadth, is no less single in its moral outlook. It is a truism that the greater the novelist the more sweeping his vision. We tend to combine the persuasive universality of the moral abstraction with the wide scope of the major novelist and attribute to Tolstoi a representation of all life. This ascription, praiseworthy as a tribute to the commanding imagination of a superb writer, has the pernicious critical result of disarming in advance the attempt to define the theme of *War and Peace*. Even so responsible a critic as Forster (in *Aspects of the Novel*) seems almost captiously, and at the same time indolently, content merely to gape at the masterpiece, leaving unchallenged Lubbock's equally imperceptive assertion of thematic disunity in the novel.

The meaning of *War and Peace* is, however large, single and coherent. It creates its characters and builds its panoramic universe of moral meaning out of a sequence of observed and analyzed moral gestures:

> Prince Vassily always spoke languidly, like an actor repeating his part in an old play. Anna Pavlovna Scherer, in spite of her forty years, was on the contrary brimming over with excitement and impulsiveness. To be enthusiastic had become her pose in society, and at times even when she had, indeed, no inclination to be so, she was enthusiastic so as not to disappoint the expectations of those who knew her. The affected smile which played continually about Anna Pavlovna's face, out of keeping as it was with her faded looks, expressed a spoilt child's continual consciousness of a charming failing of which she had neither the wish nor the power to correct herself, which, indeed, she saw no need to correct.

The surface of social life in the *soirée* of this chapter is presented as a kind of play. Most prominent are the most acting, the most hypocritical (Greek, actors); there are moving at the same time shyly and clumsily in the background, of this scene as throughout Book One, those dedicated beings we will come to know as the agents of a real moral life. Not that they yet know to what they are dedicated. Prince Vassily and Anna Pavlovna know; but their knowledge is not a true superiority; as here rendered, it is only the superficial skill of the actor. Their limit is that they know all they are to do; so they have chosen it.

In the keen individuation of Tolstoi's moral analysis, these two hypocrites are distinguished from one another: Prince Vassily is languid, Anna Pavlovna "brimming over with excitement and impulsiveness." These traits in turn are subjected to analysis. Every nuance of behavior undergoes a moral scrutiny.

What is the domain of Tolstoi's analysis? It is so perfectly fused with the theme of the novel that a short definition is not possible, but, roughly, he is always analyzing a character's attitude toward his own destiny, his own tempo, his own potentialities. Gesture always has become or is becoming moral habit in Tolstoi. He analyzes the certitude of the become, the hesitance of the becoming. Habit is subjected to time, transmuted and retransmuted, in a number of ways whose diversity his moral analysis renders, whose underlying interdependence the plot coordinates. The plot's grand scale of social process changes each phase's moral appearance into a new reality. To keep up with the times, wtih Time, to be morally real, a character must meet a challenge which faces everyone equally as it faces each at his own individual angle. What makes Anna Pavlovna Scherer and Prince Vassily superficial is their dedication to surface, implied in the meaning Tolstoi analyzes into their almost ritual gestures. Oriented toward mere appearance, they commit themselves toward their temporary social masks. This commitment affords them a certain adroitness, but it cuts them out of all the profounder resurrections of the years to come. Nine years and a thousand pages later the bumbling Pierre of the first scene of the novel will have become spiritually baptized and rebaptized into a moral giant. But Anna Pavlovna, withdrawn from the horribly contrasting background of devastated Moscow, will be giving the identical Petersburg *soirée*, politely and coldly ignoring the cataclysm that is to be the death through which the best will be reborn. And who is her honored guest but the same Prince Vassily, unchanged in his diabolical superficiality.

In *War and Peace*, the analyzed gestures of the characters find their stated meaning in what will become their final destiny. The appearance of detail is being compounded with the reality of the whole. The constant relevance of these analyzed components to the reflected whole lends, to

detail and overall canvas alike, a uniformity and propor-
tionateness which recalls the realism of Vermeer or Cara-
vaggio or better, Velasquez: what Blackmur has called the
"buoyancy and sanity of Tolstoi's novels."

The fifteen books and epilog of the novel are orchestrated into an almost contrapuntal order, war and
peace being not, as Lubbock thought, disorganized strands,
but the basic alternation, each defining the other, of the
plot's form and the characters' evolution. War is repeated,
and peace. A new stage of peace varies the war epoch immediately preceding it, and vice versa. Each book has a prevailing mood, a phase of the common life to which every
character responds in the very act of contributing to create
it. The mood of one person is, with the variation of destined
personality, the temporary mood of all, a mood to be re-
smelted from phase to phase till the final temper of the
whole novel's vision has been enunciated.

There is a dominance of superficies in the peaceful
Book One. Anna Pavlovna's ostentatious *soirée* sets the
tone for the preliminary interests of all the characters.
Pierre—first shy, then tactlessly professing Bonapartism,
finally deferring abashedly as he parts from Anna Pavlovna
—goes on to assert his mere surface in the very frankness
of his subsequent talk with Prince Andrey, in the sociable
inconsequence of his early morning tomfoolery. Prince
Andrey on the surface of his mind can express no more
probing reason for his military departure than that peacetime life is not to his taste. His unconscious reason is that
so far life is as superficial as his first marriage seems to
him here. Natasha is likewise enmeshed in surface. At her
name day she impulsively wakens to the world of the opposite sex in Boris Drubetskoi, the very puppet-like incarnation of surface, though her keen insight leads her to ask him,
symbolically, to kiss her doll before kissing her. Boris'
mother makes an abrupt shift of allegiance from the superficial service rendered by Prince Vassily to the superficial

hope that Pierre's naïveté can be prevailed on to assume the burdens of a merely external patronage. The death of Count Bezuhov entails not the soul searching of the novel's subsequent deaths but a mere squabble over an inheritance, a manipulation of surfaces about money. Marya's devoutness, as yet a mere form, presses on her departing brother an ikon to which he is indifferent. She has been corresponding with the stultified, pretentious Julie Karagina, not yet sufficiently awakened to cast off this mere husk of a friendship. Dolokhov's bravado is confined to mere surface acting in this book. Marya Dmitrievna's "terrible dragon" frankness is merely another social form, here analyzed in terms of its effect on polite society; its real effectiveness will come into its own only when it saves Natasha in the deeper Book Eight.

Yet Tolstoi is all the while individuating these people, analyzing attitudes of a specific bent and tempo which will recombine for deeper and deeper meaning. Even in the superficiality of Book One, sudden insight into destiny can pierce through the decorum of such shallow characters as the crudely, shamelessly driving Anna Mihalovna, and the bewildered Countess Rostov, friends from girlhood who "wept because they were friends, and because they were soft-hearted, and that they, who had been friends in youth, should have to think of anything so base as money, and that their youth was over. . . . But the tears of both were sweet to them."

In these tears, and throughout Book One, there is a meaning portentously present. People are brought mysteriously into each other's orbits; as Prince Vassily carries on the conversation which will culminate in Anatole's unsuccessful overture for Marya, the stupid Julie Karagina writes portentously of Nikolai Rostov, a man unknown to her correspondent, who will at last, through the transformations of war, become Marya's fitting husband. The circumstances of the Duc d'Enghien's death discussed in the very first

chapter's *soirée*—what do they foreshadow but La Belle
Hélène's death in Book Twelve as the outcome of a parallel
adulterous triangle? Pierre will then be liberated to marry
the girl he will love from Book Eight on, though here, in
Book One, he scarcely dreams, sitting across from her at a
dinner party, that the thin thirteen year old is to become
of such absorbing interest. Yet he must have some intima-
tion of this future, or why at her look has he "felt an impulse to laugh himself without knowing why"? Why does
her look keep straying from Boris to him; why does she feel
so amused in his presence and go up to ask him for a dance
(at her mother's prompting, to be sure) "laughing and
blushing"?

The peaceful surface of Book One can give us only
such hints as these. The foreboding grows and the breach
between people widens in Book Two, where war displays
its surface. In Book One we approached society from the
outside in, at a *soirée*. Here we approach panoramically,
from above, the campaign of 1805, which will turn out to
have been war's mere surface in the later light of 1812.
Parade, strategy, honor: surfaces and abstractions crowd
the stage; the wretchedness of the ill-shod soldiers is only
an uncomfortable logistic detail, and a death at the Enns
bridge will occasion a joke more brutal but of the same kind
that Bilibin regales his comrades with at staff headquarters.
Here superficial discipline, finding in Dolokhov a lack of
punctilio, demotes him to the ranks, when in the total upheaval of Book Fourteen he will be elevated to guerrilla
command.

Peacetime superficiality is replaced in Book Two by
the wartime superficiality of mere military reputation:
Bagration, Zherkov, the jocular but impassive Nesvitski
sweeping his field glasses across the walled nunnery, the
nameless regimental commander whose "quivering strut
seemed to say that, apart from his military interest, he had
plenty of warmth in his heart for the attractions of social

life and the fair sex." Kutuzov turns away sadly from this
show to avoid having his deep disillusionment, here incongruous, bewilder his subordinates. Nikolai, dreamily content or dreamily fearful, eats up surface, proud of his
initiation into what his shallow mind takes for the reality
of military life (the Telyanin incident), of battle (Schoen
Grabern). We know no more here of Denisov but his function, that he is an honorable captain. And Andrey is here
superficially disillusioned by war, just as he had been by
marriage and social life in Book One. A slight wound sends
him to the manipulators of this surface, the headquarters
staff at Bruenn, where Bilibin's interpretations of diplomacy
and strategy will invest these battles with all the meaning
they can yet have. Significances are more portentous here;
such is the nature of war. But no one can guess why. Tushin
parts from Andrey at Schoen Grabern "with tears, which
for some unknown reason started suddenly into his eyes."
Seeing the unjust and uncomprehending disgrace of the
hero Tushin "Prince Andrey felt bitter and melancholy.
It was all so strange, so unlike what he had been hoping
for." Nikolai's sorrowful dreaminess confuses the meaninglessness of the many wounded with disjunct recollections of
peace, bringing the book to a close.

The surface of war in Book Two looks back to Book
One; its note of frustration is the first of a chord which
looks ahead to the frustrated life of Book Three. Nikolai's
family misses him all the more for his wound. Natasha refrains from writing Boris, to whom her brother is telling
falsehoods about heroism. Pierre frustrates himself for
seven years by yoking himself to the voluptuous, heartless
Hélène.

Here mere surface, as a frustrating influence, asserts
its fullest power. The sheer spell of Hélène's body shakes
Pierre. Nikolai huzzahs the Czar and evaporates into dreams
more confused than those of Book Two ("Natache . . . sa-
bretache."). Boris' God, surface, empowers him with an

understanding of that unwritten code of confident tact which makes a lieutenant superior to a general. Andrey abandons all his illusions as he lies wounded under the sky at Austerlitz, his hero Napoleon dwindled to insignificance. He will await no longer his own Toulon; his depression more than his physical condition has classified him as a hopeless case. But Austerlitz, in all its dominance, is a mere surface beside the Moscow of Book Twelve; it is meaninglessness that Andrey feels under this sky. His frustration with surface is his own special descant to the mood of this book.

Book One: peace; Book Two: war; Book Three: war and peace. These three books state the thesis, antithesis, and synthesis which the rest of the novel works out. The frustration of war in Book Three breaks up after the truce of Austerlitz; in Book Four it invades peace with all the backwashing sterility of war ill concluded. There come from the battlefront a searing fusion of wastes, a series of false notes.

"All Moscow was repeating the words of Prince Dolgorukov: 'Chop down trees enough and you're bound to cut your finger.'" Berg is falsely supposed a hero, Andrey falsely thought dead, till he returns in time to witness the puzzling waste of his wife's death. Hélène takes the abrupt, brutal Dolokhov as a lover, and Pierre challenges him to a duel that drains both men. Denisov proposes to Natasha, who has burned her arm as a proof of love to Sonya. And when Sonya rejects Dolokhov's absurd proposal, his desperate, wasteful revenge is to entice Nikolai into the waste of heavy losses at cards.

The waste of Book Four plays itself out into the mechanism and flatness of Book Five. After Pierre's duel, "Everything within himself and around him struck him as confused, meaningless, and loathsome." "It was as though the chief screw in his brain upon which his whole life rested were loose. The screw moved no forwarder, no backwarder, but still it turned, catching on nothing, always in the same groove, and there was no making it cease turning." The mechanical image of stagnation receives a mechanical answer, the rational religion of Masonry. This book introduces the novel's flattest character, the Mason Bazdeev, who converts Pierre. The crotchety, obsessively mechanical old Prince Bolkonsky moves to the fore as director of conscription. Colorless Boris Drubetskoi dominates Anna Pavlovna's salon to become the lover of a "misunderstood" Hélène. Nikolai candidly recognizes the place of his military profession and returns to find the hospitalized Denisov strangely stagnating at his calamity. Denisov presses a petition on him; he abandons it in order to join a crowd cheering the emperor, and he gets drunk in the last scene of the book. Prince Andrey likewise stagnates, unmoved by Pierre's convert enthusiasm. Still the sight of the sky over the flat ferry raft where they have been talking reminds him of Austerlitz and awakens intimations of "new life in his inner world," the mood of Book Six beginning to gather force.

Against Book Five's stagnated winter rises the burgeoning spring of Book Six. As the flatness of Book Five brought dull Prince Bolkonsky to the political fore, the vitality of Book Six marks the sudden rise of the charismatic Speranski. Andrey, with the rest of society, is to be renewed like the apparently dead oak—"seared with old scars," on his ride out, throwing out a profusion of green shoots on his ride back. Natasha does not burn her arm for love here, as in Book Four; instead she dresses in a yellow gown to set off her black eyes and stays awake ecstatic at the moon through the open window, where Andrey hears her. All draw to her vitality; even Boris gives up Hélène to court her. Happily immersed in his Masonry, Pierre takes a joyfully melancholy consolation in urging Andrey to press his own suit, and the engagement is brought about in the general matchmaking spirit which also unites Vera and Berg. Out at Bogutchorovo Princess

Marya, weeping in an excess of love, "felt that she was a sinner, that she loved her father and her nephew more than God," losing herself in the joy of raising Nikolushka and entertaining "God's folk," the vital itinerant pilgrims.

Books Four and Five, waste and flatness, form a pair; so do Books Six and Seven: vitality and unearthly joy. In Book Seven Natasha is riding too high even for her earlier moon ecstasy. The incredible joy, the magically perfect success of a day's hunt, evokes from her a prolonged unearthly shriek:

> At the same moment Natasha, without drawing breath, screamed joyously, ecstatically, and so piercingly that it set everyone's ear tingling. By that shriek she expressed what the others expressed by all talking at once, and it was so strange that she must herself have been ashamed of so wild a cry and everyone else would have been amazed at any other time.

Hunting, dancing, food, moonlight—all of an unearthly perfection. The general elation has roused Nikolai home from the army where he has previously felt willing to vegetate.

This joy is too intense to be more than a phase. "It would be too happy," Natasha feels, if her engagement to Prince Andrey concluded in marriage. The unreality of this momentary joy is exemplified in the falseness of Nikolai's engagement to Sonya. It had been set off by a mere play, the moonlight masquerade ride with burnt cork moustaches and transvestite costumes. "Madagascar, Madagascar," Natasha surrealistically mulls to herself after a transvestite buffoon has told her that her children will be "fleas, and dragonflies, and grasshoppers."

The unearthly joy, at its moment, brings clairvoyant powers that forecast the final reality. In the crystal ball of her looking glasses Sonya sees the real future mirrored:

> "No, I saw. . . . At first there was nothing; then I saw him lying down."

"Andrey lying down? Is he ill?" Natasha asked, fixing her eyes of terror on her friend.

"No, on the contrary,—on the contrary, his face was cheerful, and he turned to me"; and at the moment she was saying this, it seemed to herself that she really had seen what she described.

"Well, and then, Sonya? . . ."

"Then I could make out more; something blue and red. . . ."

Not only Prince Andrey's ultimate deathbed vision is foretold here, but also Natasha's marriage to Pierre. For when the joy of Book Six sent her in curl papers and pyjamas to her mother's bedroom, Natasha said surrealistically of Pierre: "Bezuhov now—he's blue, dark blue and red, and he's quadrangular. . . . He's jolly, dark blue and red; how am I to explain to you? . . ." But her fear and her poise on the crest of the moment make Natasha here pass by the real significance of "blue and red," and she goes on to query Sonya about Prince Andrey's future calamity.

Unearthly joy, having forecast the future at its zenith of vision, gives way to the next stage. Peace is spent, and Book Eight is dominated by the crass pain of coming war, searing and wasteful in the manner of Book Four. Everyone is involved more deeply than he had been in Book Four, and consequently loss is more durable. Natasha quarrels with her future sister-in-law. Old Prince Bolkonsky flouts his devoted daughter and fanatically flirts with the heartless Mlle. Bourienne, who had drawn Anatole away from Marya in Book Three. Boris Drubetskoi contracts a loveless marriage with Julie Karagina. But the coldest horror comes when Natasha is nearly seduced by Anatole, at the perhaps jealous instigation of his sister Hélène. Natasha's attunement to the mood of this book brings her into spellbound fascination with this unholy pair. Prince Andrey breaks off their engagement, and the coming war will permanently widen the breach till the presence of death unites them.

Pierre, leaving Natasha in consternation at the end of the book, sees the comet of 1812.

Book Five's flatness follows the searing waste of Book Four; so after the crass pain of Book Eight comes the abstract mechanism of war in Book Nine. German strategy, formidably competent and colossally stupid, dominates the war planning of this book. Even Pierre supplies soldiers and contrives a Masonic abstraction to explain Napoleon as the 666 of the Apocalypse. The profoundly intuitive Andrey can only turn from the abstractions of this phase to find life again meaningless, while Natasha, on the heels of illness, embraces religion, for her an almost mechanical ritual (her true religious life going on through the high rightness of her acts earlier in Book Six, later when she is a wife and mother).

In Book Six, vitality followed a phase of mechanism; so Book Nine's abstract mechanism leads to creative destruction, the keynote of Book Ten. Pierre weeps with forgiveness for the badly wounded Dolokhov at Borodino. Andrey, wounded, sees the creatively swarming white bodies of soldiers as cannon fodder; he contemplates the creativity inherent in children who run for green plums through the threatened orchard. The death of her father is a creative release for Princess Marya. Into threatened Bogucharovo rides the gallantly rescuing Nikolai, led by the emotions this role arouses to become Princess Marya's only possible husband. The destruction of Borodino brings Anatole to creative atonement, Andrey to creative forgiveness. And the physical destruction of defeat, at the end of the book, is declared to have been a creative moral victory for the Russians.

In Book Eleven the destructiveness of Book Ten descends to an empty horror, as not Smolensk but now Moscow itself is under siege. Toward the end of this book the counterbalancing creation in Book Ten is transmuted to a growing joy. Horror holds sway as Princess Hélène takes

two lovers at once, as the innocent Vereschagin is torn to
pieces by the crowd, as Moscow is captured and bursts into
blaze. Pierre wanders dazed in the empty house of his dead
master Bazdeev, Andrey lies wounded on a cart. But
growth predominates: Andrey's cart is moved into the
procession of the evacuating Rostovs; Natasha comes to
him, and they forgive each other in a new, deepened devotion. At the end of the book Pierre saves a child from the
fire.

In Books Ten and Eleven destruction and creation
counterbalance each other. In Book Eleven they have already been separated as well as transmuted: the horror of
the beginning had to wait till the end for a growing gladness.
Book Twelve transmutes only the horror into a rigor under
which Hélène dies from physical exhaustion of her simul-
taneous lovers. Andrey dies. Natasha is speechless, Pierre a
prisoner, Nikolai perplexed, Marya misunderstood in the
train of the Rostovs.

Book Thirteen, however, transforms the gladness of
Book Eleven into a philosophical joy, as Napoleon's army
moves out of Moscow and Pierre learns the meaning of
Russian folk life from Platon Karataev's total reconciliation
to process.

In Book Fourteen, recalling the mood of Books Four
and Eight, a surreal cruelty emerges as the back thrust of
war. Dolokhov in his wierdly correct garb leads guerrillas
against the ragged retreating French. The saturnine Denisov, too, comes into his own as a guerrilla commander. And
Petya, induced to enlist in the general surface dedication
of Book Nine, is grotesquely seduced (Tolstoi develops the
notion through a horrible kiss Dolokhov gives him) toward
his death.

Book Fifteen establishes for good a calm reconciling
joy. Marya marries Nikolai, Pierre, a Natasha so transformed he does not at first recognize her.

In the epilog, process evens off. A retransmuting[1] is hinted in Nikolinka, hiding in the shadow as his elders reveal their fixity in the lax rambling of their manners and conversation. He combines the nobility of his real father with the strength of his adopted father and the sensitivity of his adopted mother. Existence can only remain substantially the same, appearance and reality one, for the middle life of our major characters.

I have deliberately exaggerated the unity of each book to bring out its dominant mood. There are in every book, in every episode, many strands which lead back or ahead. The more stultified characters—Anna Pavlovna, Prince Vassily, Berg, Boris—are out of tune entirely with the later developments of the novel and often act in contrast to the prevailing mood. Yet the over-all pattern of the plot is one of successive dominances orchestrated into unity.

Into this structured time, this process of phases, grow the individual rhythms of the various characters. Each phase subjects to itself the destinies of all. What separates Andrey from Natasha is as much 1812 as the baseness of Anatole; and the titanic force of national events, into which the individual destinies flow, parts Andrey from the Anatole he has desperately been seeking till the moment when, as destiny exacts, he will feel deeply enough to forgive him. Without the siege of Moscow he could never have plumbed the marvel of Natasha's love: but death follows reunion.

Through the phases, the individual destinies realize the tempo of their own development. Present is appearance, future is reality, till the time when there will be no real future. Neither society nor self get byond appearances until their reality can be embodied in time. Pierre's gradual maturation takes him through no fewer than nine stages: first,

[1] That Tolstoi might have carried this transfiguration into another large novel is suggested by his original plans for a vast epic about the Decembrist Revolt of 1825. Nikolinka would have been just of age to take part in that.

the flouted bastard, then the wealthy cuckold, then the stern, confused victor over Dolokhov, then the dedicated Mason; then the hopeless lover of Natasha, followed by the courageous dreamer at the siege of Moscow. Already he has worked up to such stamina that he can pull out of the dream and save his own life by looking Davoust square in the eye, but he has still to have a philosophical revelation of life from Platon Karataev, and thereafter a final calm happiness, distinct from that of his revelation. To Natasha, at last, he looks "exactly as though he had come . . . out of a moral bath."

The tempo of each character is peculiar to each. To Pierre's gradual, unaware changes, Andrey counterposes the abrupt, somewhat repetitive, self-torturing resurgences of his vast spiritual capacities. First one disillusionment with social life; then another under the sky of Austerlitz. Then the strange joy at the blossoming oak tree, the engagement. Then another bout of disgust, leading to the post-Borodino feeling where, at his death, all is subdued under the light of the Gospels, a light so faint, though intense, that Andrey cannot get the full word out.

Natasha is so sympathetic to phases that she develops only at the innermost heart of her spirit. In the superficies of the beginning she is frivolous, a would-be dancer. Hers is the psyche delicate enough to suffer each prevailing mood into symbolic expression: a burned arm in Book Four, moon-gazing in Book Six, a prolonged unearthly shriek in Book Seven, in Book Nine a rote religion. But her sacrifice to the spiritual demands of war is to submerge this real sensitivity into the appearance of a most ordinary woman— for her the halo of an even more extreme phase than any of the others, one so absolute that Pierre does not recognize her. "No one would have recognized her at the moment when he entered, because when he first glanced at her there was no trace of a smile in the eyes that in old days had always beamed with a suppressed smile of the joy of life.

They were intent, kindly eyes, full of mournful inquiry, and nothing more." Yet "Pierre's embarrassment was not reflected in a corresponding embarrassment in Natasha, but only in a look of pleasure that faintly lighted up her whole face." The light has gone out of her eyes for the radiance of a wholly inner light.

Nikolai combines the Rostov dreaminess with the Rostov practicality. He drifts with the tide, and the depth of its currents more than his own blind will conveys him at last to his true destiny, gentleman farming. Marya is enough like him to be his true wife; her religious passivity merely undergoes—though willingly—the ennobling phases. She seems to derive consolation from misunderstanding, first with her father, then with her husband. And at the end, "she felt a submissive, tender love for this man, who could never understand all that she understood; and she seemed, for that very reason, to love him the more, with a shade of passionate tenderness."

The real life of the novel transcends what it must grow out of, the harrowing appearances of war. What marks the stupidity of a public character like Napoleon is his failure to understand these deeper currents. Kutuzov's signal heroism is the sad realization of his own submission to process, of his underlings' opportunistic blindness to it. The national destiny is expressed by Tolstoi not only through the plot but through these historical characters on the top; on the bottom by the anonymous masses, or by characters who, like Platon Karataev or Lavrushka, are too low for responsive will. Top meets bottom only once, in Napoleon's brief conversation with Lavrushka; this is a mutual deception, though on the whole Lavrushka prevails.

The meaning of this novel, for all its vastness and variety, is so articulately single that it is hard to see how critics could see in it either thematic disjunction or vague grandeur. As Hugh Walpole says, "Its final effect is as concrete and symbolic as a sonnet by Keats; its theme is as simple and singlehearted as the theme of a story by Chekhov."

A world grounded in the moral life of national destiny had exhausted its implications for Tolstoi, or he would not have turned from his planned trilogy first for an abortive historical novel on Peter the Great, then for the changed emphases of *Anna Karenina*. This novel's moral reality lies in the appearances that indicate, as they conceal, sexual involvements which the narrative is constantly analyzing. The rhythm of everyone's gestures toward the whole of life is crucially embodied here in some mysteriously appropriate member of the opposite sex. Nikolai's death is foreshadowed in the almost catatonic cruelty of his attitude toward the rescued prostitute who shares his life. Stiva's callousness, his utter lack of the honesty on which he prides himself, is embodied in his successive, purely physical affairs. Sergey Ivanovitch's hollow intellectuality emerges strikingly in his nervous failure, tantamount to a refusal of life itself, to propose to the equally timid pietist Varenka.

Sex is the cause and effect of brightness or darkness, harmony or discord; and Levin's soul-searching is shown as depending on his real search for a harmonious fruitful marriage with Kitty. Sex is the point at which body meets spirit, a fitting point, then, for "the dialectic of incarnation" as Blackmur[2] calls the action of this novel (and Blackmur's analysis of it is so final as to forestall any duplicating attempt here): "The bodying forth in aesthetic form by contrasted human spirits of 'the terrible ambiguity of an immediate experience.' "

Deeply needing reality, Anna finds Karenin most intolerable because he is a sham, and he loses her at first by

[2] "*Anna Karenina:* The Dialectic of Incarnation," *Kenyon Review*, XII, Summer 1950.

insisting on keeping up appearances, his voice rising habitually to a histrionic shrillness as he cuts off contact with
a reality he finds hideous. Vronsky's presence is excruciating from the beginning, but real, for Kitty as for Anna.
Sham too is the piety of Madame Stahl and Varenka; under
the appearance of charity lies the reality of sexual estrangement—Madame Stahl's old marital trouble and invalidism,
Varenka's sterile impatience with the vulnerability of love.
The hesitant reality of the sick artist Petrov's love for Kitty
cuts through these shams, sending her home cured as she
refuses to maintain that connection on a false basis of pity.
False, because sexless, is the overindulgent mutual adulation
of the separated Lidia Ivanovna and the abandoned Karenin,
and she sears with all her own falsity the unbearable, if
sinful, reality of Anna's attachment.

The reality observed in the statements of the novel's
narrative is appropriately moral, and, as always in Tolstoi,
redolent of destiny; he delineates reactions to the whole
complex of what always amounts to a sexual situation,
whatever disguise it may wear:

> Left alone, Darya Alexandrovna said her prayers and
> went to bed. She had felt for Anna with all her heart while
> she was speaking to her, but now she could not force herself
> to think of her. The memories of home and of her children
> rose up in her imagination with a peculiar charm quite new
> to her, with a sort of new brilliance. That world of her own
> seemed to her now so sweet and precious that she would not
> on any account spend an extra day outside it, and she made
> up her mind that she would certainly go back next day.

The agony concealed under the strained elegance and pretended frankness of Anna's sexual situation has caused this
reaction in Dolly. Before her visit she had thought of taking
a lover; now, faced with the reality of a suitor, she rejects
what was the mere transient appearance of a desire and refuses Veslovsky as definitely as Kitty had, though less sum-
marily. Her home situation previously wore the aspect of

intolerable frustration. Now it seems "sweet and precious," a fruitful reality in contrast to the willed sterility (they have been discussing birth control) of Anna's. Anna leads Dolly to redefine her sense of her own (sexual) destiny. The heart of the home now "sweet and precious" is the husband whose sexual conduct previously exasperated her. Tolstoi here tells us she said her prayers, and the prayers are, we may imagine, a protection against the forces of sex that are rending Anna and Vronsky. Anna, so frank before, is lowering her eyelids "just when the deeper questions of life were touched upon."

So Dolly's confrontation of Anna. Anna, too, confronts Dolly, and the departure of her friend saddens her:

> She knew that now, from Dolly's departure, no one again would stir up within her soul the feelings that had been roused by their conversation. It hurt her to stir up these feelings, but yet she knew that that was the best part of her soul, and that that part of her soul would quickly be smothered by the life she was leading.

Anna's tragic flaw is a kind of impatience with the subjecting appearances of the moment, as well as an obscure desire for a life only precariously whole. She at once faces and averts her crises; so she at once wills and resists unbearable pretense; she shortly commits suicide out of despair at holding Vronsky to the situation he chafes in. Analogically, as Blackmur points out, Vronsky has earlier broken the back of his mare Froufrou by not shifting position fast enough to balance her course; and he does not shift fast enough for Anna, who runs to her suicide because he has delayed writing in reconciliation. There is an unconscious will to murder in his sexual involvement, as Tolstoi shows in the images of sadism by which he describes their first love scene. And Anna is a preconsciously willing victim.

Society has an inertia of health, and Anna is miraculously restored to the life of her home by her almost fatal puerperal fever at the birth of her illegitimate daughter. That upheaval would have cut the Gordian knot of cross purposes in the triangle; in accordance with her earlier dream, the two Alexeys, husband and lover, close in forgiveness. But as well as its health society has the germ of original sin. Anna's brother Stiva interrupts to assert the lover's claims; and Vronsky, recovering from his own suicide attempt, would have gone off to leave Anna and Karenin in peace had not Stiva harried Karenin into the fatal interview that determined the unexpected situation; at a stroke the reversal was undone, and there resulted a deeper and wholly inextricable version of the previous tangle. No Stiva, no more Vronsky; but Stiva is present, Anna's demon and brother. And since it was to extricate Stiva from his own adulterous guilt that Anna travelled to Moscow in the first place, she owes her meeting, as her fatal reconciliation, to the offices of her brother.

A single sin is not the same for two different people. Around the basic sexual situation crystallizes a circumstance unique for everyone. We measure the depth of Anna's degradation by the shallowness of her brother's. And we measure the spiritual majesty of Anna, petrified in sin, by Levin's response toward the very end:

> Besides wit, grace, and beauty, she had truth. She had no wish to hide from him all the bitterness of her position. As she said that she sighed, and her face suddenly taking a hard expression, looked as if it were turned to stone. With that expression on her face she was more beautiful than ever; but the expression was new; it was utterly unlike that expression, radiant with happiness and creating happiness, which had been caught by the painter in her portrait.

Levin is a spiritual barometer, like Anna. And he is contrasted to her in the lawful health of his relationship, typified as hers is individualized according to the pattern set down by the novel's first sentence: "Happy families are all alike; every unhappy family is unhappy in its own way."

His destiny rises out of her disaster; God creates good out of evil; if Vronsky at the beginning had not abandoned Kitty for Anna, Levin could never have married the woman who initially refused him for Vronsky. And at the end it is confronting Anna that brings home to him the rooted spiritual sense he has been striving to achieve. For her, though, the "light was quenched forever." For him: "my life now," he says at the novel's conclusion, "my whole life apart from anything that can happen to me, every minute of it is no more meaningless, as it was before, but it has the positive meaning of goodness, which I have the power to put into it."

So Levin at last comes into his destiny in the unity of all his acts, here perceived as religious. For everyone destiny is unified or perilously not; sex is the index of the unity, in living and in career. At the ascendancy of sham and cuckoldry Karenin's career arrests and begins declining. Levin's farming has meaning which it finds, and funds, in his relationship with Kitty. Vronsky's agricultural methods, as he advocates them in his council dialog with Levin, are harshly mechanized, lacking the intuitive sense of land and peasantry which signalizes Levin's health: Vronsky's career is his sexual displacement; he realizes at the outset that to take up Anna is to forego the opportunities exemplified in the career of his friend and advocate Serpuhovsky; and after her suicide he departs for the Servian campaign with all the riffraff of Russia, a man stalled in career as in sex. His rather plodding selfishness has become the downfall of his sound capacity.

Levin is all the time working toward spiritual perception; Vronsky, like Karenin, toward special failure. The unity of destiny, objectified in the sexual action, is present at every moment in the feelings of the characters. Anna and Vronsky know, when the peasant throws himself under the train in the portentous scene of their meeting, that she will thus commit suicide; that is why she is so profoundly disturbed, why Vronsky sends two hundred rubles to the nameless widow out of apparent generosity and real self-protection. Both dream at particular moments throughout of the strange unkempt peasant, bearded and nasty, who suddenly materializes into reality on the train platform where Anna does commit suicide. Spiritual insight at moments of tension, as in *War and Peace*, materializes into clairvoyance. But all know in their perceptions, and act with the loaded unity of their sexual destiny; this they are constantly creating and responding to.

There is no deep change from part to part of *Anna Karenina*. The unity of Tolstoi's insight in this novel is at once more polished, simpler, and less breathtakingly concrete than in *War and Peace*. Still it is grounded in the unity of a moral plot, of sequenced moral statements which analyze, point by point of the narrative, the moral destinies of the characters.

Reality in some strange way seems to have broken Tolstoi as he turns from moral insight to moral program in his insane last years. His penchant to substitute shallow abstraction for deep perception is prefigured by *War and Peace*'s disjunct disquisitions on a meaning already commandingly present in the analyses of the narrative itself. This tendency to disrupt fiction for tendentious theorizing is held in abeyance by the formal finish of *Anna Karenina*. But it breaks out shortly in Tolstoi's abandonment of art for the half-lights of nightmare abstraction. Sex, mastered in the vision of *Anna Karenina*, has become an obsession in those conversations Gorki records; in his writing it becomes either a platitude in *Resurrection* or an obsession with the extreme and narrow force of *The Kreutzer Sonata*, itself a gargoyle on the cathedral of *Anna Karenina*.

A novel must fully realize its center of moral insight in order to characterize its people fully and consistently, as Tolstoi does. His people are inward, and they grow in process, lucidly enunciated, into whole selves. But they exist in society, and their psychology, however inward, is defined through the consistent social insight which a moral idea implies, into a world widely coordinated in its relations and its temporal process.

The novel, perforce implying moral ideas, demands the social life for the existence of its characters. Even Robinson Crusoe is not so much an isolated individual as a society of one.

XI

PLOT AS DISCOVERY

CONRAD, DOSTOEVSKY, AND FAULKNER

The relations of the characters in a novel—that is, the plot—are determined by the characters' inner lives. And so the causal woof that makes a plot of a story tends in a novel to rest on rather tenuous connections. Climaxes are not necessarily built. Every character is not necessarily kept fully busy furthering the action. Seldom is the action of a novel rigorously structured. Slowly, in the fine process of their small actions, the characters must be shown to arrive at a state of being that is likely to involve more discovery for us than for them. The plot is the discovery: it discovers the subtle center of the secret lives of all the characters.

Its dependence, too, not so much on moral categories or ritual as on pointed social observation tends to give a fictional plot a much more individual shape than the plots of plays. *Hamlet*, the *Oresteia*, and *Ghosts* have at least comparable plots, but the original novelist tends to invent a plot which is as much of a personal signature as the kind of social observation on which it depends. Tolstoi's series of interlocking climaxes admirably build the alternations of war and peace, of sexual virtue and vice in *Anna Karenina*. For Stendhal's world of coruscating irony there is singular aptness in his iridescent buildups, his checkered flashes, a veritable *feu d'artifice* of innumerable tiny incidents. Jane Austen's characters move at minuet pace from social event to more advanced social event, any outlandish break in the pattern revealing crucial alignments; as everyone darts to cover the break, he reveals himself and recognizes the step demanded of him, toward which the whole action has been tending. The plots of *Madame Bovary* and *L'Education Sentimentale* set up a slow, fateful immersion for the central character. He drowns in the impressions that saturate deeper and deeper crises. Hemingway's characters move through a plot of pared simplicity and exacting monotony: they must do the same thing over and over again. Days accrete into vacuity, the tempering process of disillusioned courage.

The more completely a novelist assigns to plot the process of a secret life evolving between appearance and reality, the more tenuous his plots will appear. In Conrad, Dostoevsky, even Faulkner, the moral life becomes so elusive, and so final, that the meaning of the plot's causal pattern—in *Brothers Karamazov, Chance* and *Wild Palms* the pattern itself—nearly vanishes from view.

Conrad's plots offer what Forster (*Abinger Harvest*) calls a "central obscurity" in his work. The protagonist is maneuvered through a tightening nexus of incident that exacts a recognition of a void at the plot's heart. The motives— the "dreams" or "illusions" as Conrad is given to calling the life views of his characters—permute into a situation complex in its extent but simple in its tightness; they discharge a final void-revealing action. Out of the side of the dark mountain in *Nostromo* comes inconspicuously that pale value, the silver which is to dominate the destiny of the society facing the gulf. And the indispensable servant of everyone, the miraculously competent stranger, Nostromo, as events pivot his way, becomes so central that he comes to seem incorruptible. The void prevails, though: *corruptio optimi pessima*. The society's own indomitable perseverance toward health restores it without the silver; but Nostromo is lost, as the horrible vacancy of his smile shows to Doctor Monygham, whom the same events have restored from abysmal humiliation to a semblance of self-respect; only a semblance, however, for one who has gazed deep into the void. An islanded woman, the betrayed Linda, will carry within her forever the knowledge of the betrayal:

> She stood silent and still, collecting her strength to throw all her fidelity, her pain, bewilderment, and despair into one great cry.
> "Never! Gian' Battista!"
> Dr. Monygham, pulling round in the police galley, heard the name pass over his head. It was another of Nostromo's triumphs, the greatest, the most enviable, the most sinister of all. In that true cry of undying passion that seemed to ring aloud from Punta Mala to Azuera and away to the bright line of the horizon, overhung by a big white cloud shining like a mass of solid silver, the genius of the magnificent Capitaz de Cargadores dominated the dark gulf containing his conquests of treasure and love.

Nostromo's corruption has not been motivated by the plot: it has risen through the interstices of the plot which the moral cross purposes and mutual misunderstandings of the character already suggested. "Dark and, so to speak, inscrutable spaces being met with in life, there must be such places in any statement dealing with life." Thus the narrator of *Chance*. In this novel, as in Conrad's others, a character is forced to muster all his resources for a difficult situation. The causal nexus of this situation is not coincidence, nor is it so positive as a divine order. So Marlow at the end puts his belief only negatively: "For all my belief in Chance I am not exactly a pagan." Conrad locates his tone, and the causality of his plots, between a despair of chance and a hope of providence. Here lies the "gap" James attributes to him. Each character must face this gap uniquely. Disparities are envisaged not aesthetically, as in Turgenev, or with the furious resignation of a Céline, but skeptically. Conrad's skepticism is not negative; it denies no more than it affirms, facing the void.

The ruthlessness of purposes that do homage to the void sets up a chain reaction of murders in *The Secret Agent:* the void that colors almost lividly the pathos of Stevie, that darkens the ridicule of Verloc, that falsely arrests and perhaps even secludes in his horrible pale fatness the harmless Michaelis, that deepens the hard baseness of Comrade Ossipon, closes in silence over the murdered head of Winnie Verloc: as the plot resolves, the absolute apostle of void ("anarchy"), the Professor, wanders forth with his touchy bomb, "unsuspected and deadly, like a pest in the street full of men." It penetrates to the remote jungle bastion Lord Jim has won against the void in himself, to cause his death. Void has won cold allegiance from Schomberg in *Victory*. Void has disillusioned Heyst, challenged Jones, seduced Ricardo, terrified Wang, seared Lena. It keeps one step ahead of everyone, so that the narrative must constantly "hark back to make up" in presenting the plot to account for the advance it has silently been taking. Heyst's suicide is his only possible victory against the void of his father's philosophy—and of the plot. Agent of the void in *Under Western Eyes* is the hebephrenic Nikita, finally disclosed as himself a traitor, who bursts the eardrums of the entangled, at last of Razumov himself who cannot bear the cold embrace of the void after he has betrayed Haldin, realizing that under the appearance of revolution lies the reality of the void.

Conrad's plots have a kind of displacement which their central object, a "nothing" (the last word of *Victory*), induces. Yet against nothing, total void, the human spirit

can remain indomitable in victory. Chance may bring it
about that the shamed and wronged daughter of the de-
graded de Barral be allowed to marry—and remarry.
Immersion in knowledge of the void permits the first tempering of life in *Youth* and *The Shadow Line*. While the
abominable void of cannibal rites is the last reality of im-
perial conquest in "the heart of darkness," the narrator
brings back a tactful void-flaunting lie to Kurtz's intended.
Jim's integrity outlasts his death.

   "At any rate," Leavis says (*The Great Tradition*),
"for all the rich variety of the interest and the tightness
of the pattern, the reverberation of *Nostromo* has something hollow about it; with the colour and life there is a
suggestion of a certain emptiness." Exactly! This "something hollow," this "emptiness" is not a defect in Conrad's
work, but the core of his theme, man braving in his mortality the heart of darkness. Toward this insight is directed
Conrad's scrupulous construction, evidenced in the closed
plot, the tightness of the pattern, and in his frequent hall-of-
mirrors points of view. What Penn Warren (Modern
Library *Nostromo*) calls his "irony," his (quoting Conrad
himself) "scepticism . . . the tonic of life" reflects in the
radical ambiguity of one or more detached narrators who
color events in the very telling.

   In his shaping of words, too, Conrad's Flaubertian style
expresses his meaning. Many have found in his texture of
detail, as in his structure, a curious, and equally revelatory,
coldness. There is something leaden, dull, imprecise, in
Conrad's painstaking diction; something at the same
time too suggestively abstract. This coldness, too, reflects
the void it is his whole fictional vision to render. The odd
juncture of abstraction with description in Conrad's statements has a hard clarity about it. The phrases, often two
of them cobbled in rugged imprecision to describe a single
fact (violating Flaubert's cardinal principle of not repeating
adjectives or phrases, except for some preciser purpose)

mirror, as with the cold hardness of polished stone, the void.[1]

Conrad's statements are alternately, at times combinedly, moral and analogical. The cosmic feeling of his characters, the void around which his plots crystallize, makes his moral statements at once sweepingly abstract and somehow empty-looking. To put it differently, the moral analyses are so seemingly gratuitous in their cosmic assertions at times that Conrad has been accused of banality: Leavis supports his ascription of hollowness to Conrad by this quotation from *Nostromo:*

> It had come into her mind that for life to be large and full it must contain the care of the past and of the future in every passing moment of the present.

Yet the disparity here between Mrs. Gould's cosmic feeling and her situation equals the disparity between the void and the events pitted against it; the total plot envisages a similar disparity.

Conrad's images, especially those of the sea, are analogs of the void: all the fleeting colors and shapes of the water described in his early work merely coruscate coldly on the surface of a central heart of darkness. Consider the conclusion of that story:

> Marlow ceased, and sat apart, indistinct and silent, in the pose of a meditating Buddha. Nobody moved for a time. "We have lost the first of the ebb," said the Director, suddenly. I raised my head. The offing was barred by a black

[1] Was he not writing in a foreign language, some would ask, committed to a cold surface through the deliberateness of his idiom? Of course: but this is only to push the question one step back: why did Conrad's unconscious artistic purpose choose to write in a foreign language except to set up for himself a limitation which would become a vitally expressive advantage? Perhaps, too, he chose the heavy, ponderous, intractable English, rather than his more fluent, rational, literary, French, as a robuster medium—the stolidity of English would better bear up under Conrad's void than the spidery discriminations of French.

bank of clouds, and the tranquil waterway leading to the uttermost ends of the earth flowed sombre under an overcast sky—seemed to lead into the heart of an immense darkness.

Here the significance is explicitly read into the visual sky. The timing—the stillness of Marlow and the others, interrupted abruptly by the Director—points to a kind of disparity of motion: the motion is at first stalled, then accelerated, by the presence of void in the meaning of the story just told. And the landscape which narrator and audience face is charged with a bank of clouds whose blackness is as infinite as that of Kurtz: the "tranquil waterway" is deceptively calm, just as Marlow's indistinctness and silence indicate the void he is contemplating, "in the pose of a meditating Buddha": *The Heart of Darkness* faces a void as deep as that described in "The Fire Sermon." Loneliness, sitting apart, is literally and metaphorically the price for full insight of void, for Marlow as for Heyst and others.[2]

If Conrad's moral preoccupation suggests Tolstoi, his concern with radical evil suggests that other great Russian novelist to whom he has so often been compared; particularly in *Under Western Eyes* is Conrad Dostoevskian. But this novel, or any of Conrad's, confronts the Dostoevskian problem in a formalistic way, as the title and the narrator's situation implies: it is Dostoevsky seen, as it were, through the eyes of Tolstoi.

The characters in Dostoevsky's own novels are transcendentally dynamic; the plot is constantly having them change before our very eyes. These constantly changing characters are constantly remaking their relations. Mysterious dispositions to good or evil direct the past's concatena-

[2] The discussion on Conrad has been reprinted, with some amplification, from *Nineteenth Century Fiction*, vol. XII, no. 4, published by the University of California Press.

tions: characters transcend and transfigure the plot. As Ortega (*Notes on the Novel*) says:

> To a perfunctory observation, he seems to define each of his personages. When he introduces a figure he nearly always begins by briefly giving a biography of that person and thus makes us believe that we know well enough with what kind of man we are dealing. But no sooner do his people begin to act—i.e., to talk and to do things—than we feel thrown off the track. They refuse to behave according to those alleged definitions. The first conceptual image we were given of them is followed by another in which we see their immediate life, independent of the author's definition; and the two do not tally. At this point, the reader, afraid to lose sight of the personages at the cross-roads of these contradictory data, sets forth in their pursuit by trying to reconcile the discrepant facts to make a unified picture.

This technical mastery at illustrating in action the changes of characters—at plotting—becomes a unique vehicle for mirroring the deep reality under the shifting ambivalent appearances of human motive. In the lineaments of their changing individuality, in their self-transcending oscillation between freedom and original sin, Dostoevsky's characters embody a plot of almost theological mystery. They measure up to the prophetic wonderment of Dmitri Karamazov:

> It's terrible what mysteries there are! Too many riddles weigh men down on earth. We must solve them as we can, and try to keep a dry skin in the water. Beauty! I can't endure the thought that a man of lofty mind and heart begins with the ideal of the Madonna and ends with the ideal of Sodom. What's still more awful is that a man with the ideal of Sodom in his soul does not renounce the ideal of the Madonna, and his heart may be on fire with that ideal, genuinely on fire, just as in his days of youth and innocence. Yes, man is broad, too broad, indeed. I'd have him narrower. The devil only knows what to make of it! What to the mind is shameful is beauty and nothing else to the heart. Is there beauty in Sodom? Believe me, that for the immense mass of mankind beauty is found in Sodom. Did you know that secret? The awful thing is that beauty is mysterious

as well as terrible. God and the devil are fighting there and the battle-field is the heart of man.

The "broad" nature of man, the "awful" coexistence of Madonna and Sodom in the same breast, make any act a wilderness of motive; one can never predict what act will out. So talk, endless talk, laceration, and soul searching, preoccupy these plots; broadness slows to a long narrative *sujet*, the relatively simple basic fable. Over nine hundred pages to set the stage and exhaust the implications of an old man's murder by an illegitimate son! These plots so inventively exhibit the growth of intangible inner states that we may well very deliberately ask what each plot hinges on.

Crime and Punishment, to begin with the first major novel, combines the simple fable of murder and confession with the complex *sujet* of a social situation that is contracting to a determined abyss at the same time it is expanding to a free, enlightened altruism. The plot is a series of circles, expanding—one might almost say throbbing—out wider and wider from the central situation. In the first two chapters of Part One Raskolnikov is already agonizedly working up to an abortive attempt at his planned murder, shrinking from Luzhin and Svidrigailov, forgetting his truncated existence; his guilty vertigo, sending him into a bar for drink, polarizes into generosity for the ruined Marmeladov.

Part One ending with the murder, Part Two mysteriously stirs the guilt into an all-embracing murk, till at its conclusion Marmeladov's ribs are crushed by a trampling horse; the weak Raskolnikov faints at the news. Part Three shows order vainly attempting charitable restitution, meaninglessly in the face of the chaotic, unexpiated guilt. These charitable appearances, which atonement might make a reality, are overshadowed by the arrival of horror, Svidrigailov. Raskolnikov has already, so to speak, anticipated Svidrigailov's arrival by employing what turns out to be Svidrigailov's trick, eavesdropping. Falseness grows in Part Four, culminating in the spurious confession of the house painter. In Part Five the masked unctuousness of Luzhin reveals Svidrigailov-like evil as he diabolically gives Sonia a counterfeit ten roubles and plants another hundred roubles in her pocket. While Luzhin is unmasked at the ensuing mad party, Katerina Ivanovna, under the mysterious mood of the evil which is embracing everyone, goes mad at her party, and dies coughing. At the pitch of horror in Part Six, Raskolnikov actually seeks out Svidrigailov: "He was particularly worried about Svidrigailov, he might be said to be permanently thinking of Svidrigailov. From the time of Svidrigailov's too menacing and unmistakable words in Sonia's room at the moment of Katerina Ivanovna's death, the normal working of his mind seemed to break down. But although this new fact caused him extreme uneasiness, Raskolnikov was in no hurry for an explanation of it." He knows "extreme uneasiness," because he knows he has invoked the diabolical climate by his murder, so that he is the spiritual murderer of Marmeladov and Katerina Ivanovna: thus he seeks out the devil Svidrigailov. "What he had to hope from that man he did not know. But that man had some hidden power over him."

Sonia, though, has been reading "The Raising of Lazarus" from St. John's Gospel. It matters not that Svidrigailov eavesdrops on this soiled good angel: Raskolnikov's atonement will foil him, and the knowledge sends Svidrigailov, without his quite knowing why, into utter despair. Even though Dounia too has been hovering mysteriously, and against her will, into his orbit, Svidrigailov shoots himself. Raskolnikov learns of his suicide in the police station immediately before confessing in the last words of Part Six. The rest is regenerative epilog in Siberia, "the subject of a new story."

There are three interacting spheres of causal influence in the plot of *Crime and Punishment:* first Raskolnikov's intent (to murder the old woman, to aid Marmeladov); second, his living situation (the pawn ticket, the family pov-

erty, the expulsion from the university, the friendship with
Razumihin); and third, a sphere of almost supernatural coincidence, that which brings the drunk Marmeladov twice
across his path, which makes him overhear in the Hay
Market that Lizaveta is to be absent the next evening, which
brings Lizaveta back the next day, which has it that Lizaveta will have done mending for Sonia.

Raskolnikov's intent is all-embracing: this is the central
mystery of the plot: the fact of murder stirs up to frustration and ill-timing the living situation, as it determines the
supernatural coincidences. We feel that the devil is being
allowed to tempt him in the Hay Market: had he not been
restlessly wandering about the city and mulling over his
intent to murder the old woman, he would never have happened to overhear Lizaveta.

Ironically Raskolnikov's living situation would sustain
him in what would have been sufficient time had his evil
intent not transmogrified it: Razumihin offers him the
windfall of some translation work. But he has already committed the murder, and he feels so subjugated to self-
destruction that he is powerless to make the effort at
restoring his finances. Because of the hidden murder the
unexpected presence of mother and sister is an added tor-
ture. His living situation too, brings him around to the
police station, not to confess the horrid effect of his murderous intent, but, first to pay his debt to his landlady, next
to claim his pawned pledge. (The landlady situation, and
Raskolnikov's expulsion from the university, suggest an
initial commitment to evil which finds its extreme form in
the murder: he broke off his engagement to the landlady's
daughter; he wrote an article justifiying murder for extraordinary men.) Living situation and supernatural coincidence, as well as leading him to atonement, are providing
aids to eventual restitution, in the growing sympathy of
Sonia who will accompany him to Siberia, in the marriage

of Razumihin and Dounia, thrown together in the living situation by the effects of his intent.

Raskolnikov's ambivalence between evil and charity thickens the atmosphere, making the whole sequence of action and detail in the events of the novel as overwrought as those hallucinations and dreams which characterize him throughout. Raskolnikov's suspended alternatives are characterized on the one hand in Svidrigailov's vision of hell: "We always imagine eternity as something beyond our conception, something vast, vast! But why must it be vast? Instead of all that, what if it's only one little room, like a bathhouse in the country, black and grimy and spiders in every corner, and that's all eternity is? I sometimes fancy it like that." On the other hand he is sustained by the suffering generosity of Sonia, who has victimized her chastity to feed a family to whom she has no blood relationship. "A sort of insatiable compassion, if one may so express it, was reflected in every feature of her face."

In their mysterious dependence on Raskolnikov, the other characters transcend the selfhoods they have brought to the enchanted metropolis: they oscillate on the concealed axis of the aboriginal crime. Most obscure in *Crime and Punishment* is the supernatural coincidence which sends these metamorphosed characters straying into one another's orbits: the "crime" of the title brings that "punishment" on all until the protagonist can volunteer for purgation. Porfiry's life is deep enough to make him want Raskolnikov to confess without being arrested, and even the minor police officers are too busy pursuing their own destinies to thwart the processes of atonement by premature arrest.

The next step for Dostoevsky's plotting is to center on someone who is foolhardy enough, like Don Quixote, to suffer, like Christ, vicariously for mankind: *The Idiot.* Darkness in the idiot causes the flash of light preceding a fit; Myshkin, like Christ, will perpetually atone, having failed to inspire more than intermittently a sincerity in others. Madonna and Sodom are united here not in the murderer Raskolnikov but in the victim Nastasya Filippovna. She is at once Sonia and Raskolnikov. Yet she has chosen to be the victim; having elected the Myshkin in herself, Myshkin himself, she revokes in favor of Rogozhin, who then murders her. At the same time she is caught like Sonia in the immemorial web of compassionate injustice: her ridden self-torturing psyche is the work of Totsky, who has taken Svidrigailov-like advantage of her. Crossing a severity of chastity with a prostitute's ostentation she doesn't know what to make of herself—even Rogozhin, even being murdered, is a kind of relief.

Myshkin substitutes light at the center of this plot for the murderer's darkness of *Crime and Punishment*. The light is fitful, and so dazzling that we only half see what it illuminates: it is eclipsed by the darkness of the end.

In Book One all respond lightly to his generosity. Aglaia can merely toy with him, and Nastasya Filippovna lightheartedly proposes marriage. Confession of one's worst deed is a game. But Ganya faints as the book concludes to see Rogozhin's money left burning in her fireplace: the game's tests emerge as real.

In Book Two the characters crucify this reality by reasserting their status against the light. It is summer, the time of villas and parties. Myshkin is mocked by Aglaia as a Don Quixote, a poor knight. Ippolit slanders Myshkin at the prompting of radical friends. Rogozhin, after exchanging crosses, assaults him murderously, sending him into that extreme joy which flashes the epileptic back completely into his privacy (Greek, *idiotes*, private). Aglaia, then, on the ascendancy of her pride, can repulse him. He moves to the Lebedyevs', to the home of one who interprets the Apocalypse's star that is Wormwood as the network of European railways.

Having crucified, then resurrected, Myshkin playfully

as Don Quixote in Book Two, the characters are prepared
to own the light. The Epanchins, who dominate Book
Three, embrace him. It is his Palm Sunday. Aglaia meets
him on the green seat to become engaged, opens a correspondence with Nastasya Filippovna. A false duel is averted
by generosity. Ippolit makes a public confession: the dream
of a diabolical reptilian insect had failed to kill him; he fails
to kill himself because the gun does not go off. Nastasya
Filippovna is so irritated by the falsity of universal joy that
she whips an officer who has insulted her. The fly that will
buzz blackly over her dead body in Book Four stands in
this book as the symbol of Myshkin's momentary joy:

> All at once the bird darted out of the tree, and at the
> same instant he recalled the "fly in the warm sunshine," of
> which Ippolit had written, that "it knew its place and took
> part in the general chorus, but he alone was an outcast." The
> phrase had struck him at the time; and he recalled it now.
> One long-forgotten memory stirred within him and sud-
> denly rose up clear before him. . . the brilliant sky below,
> the lake, and all around an horizon, bright and boundless
> which seemed to have no ending. . . . He remembered now
> how he had stretched out his hands to that bright, infinite
> blue, and had shed tears. What tortured him was that he was
> utterly outside all this. What was this festival? what was this
> grand, everlasting pageant to which there was no end, to
> which he had always, from his earliest childhood, been drawn
> and in which he could never take part?

Anguish, Gethsemane, is present in this Transfiguration;
but exaltation calms into a sleep here from which Aglaia
wakes him, laughing aloud.

Yet it is all unreal: the meaning is not yet: Aglaia no
more intends to marry Myshkin than her father has previously wanted Nastasya really to become his mistress.
"These letters too were like a dream." "But how was it
that you could at the same time reconcile your reason to
the obvious absurdities and impossibilities with which your
dream was overflowing?" "But even before he had unfolded

them, Myshkin felt that the very fact of the existence of the possibility of them was like a nightmare."

The nightmare, the hideous reality of everyone's secret will, dominates Book Four. Ivolgin's madness extends to include Napoleon. Having broken a precious vase at a social gathering, Myshkin in extreme generosity lets his fiancée Aglaia run away while he tends the feverish Nastasya —and all respectable doors are closed to him. Wedding is nightmare; Nastasya is spirited off by Rogozhin in her wedding dress; to be murdered, as she foretold and darkly wished, by the knife he had purchased and flashed to Myshkin. Myshkin falls into a crucifying fit at the sight of her body. Rogozhin is sent away for fifteen years in Siberia; and the novel does not tell us he will be regenerated there. Myshkin, far gone, recognizes no one, not even Aglaia and her mother.

Except for such minor characters as Vera, Radomsky, and Kolya, all these self-transcendences have been downward. They are shying away from the light of the plot in Myshkin. Afflicted with St. Paul's thorn in the flesh, he himself possesses only the humanity of Christ without the divinity, so that his mysterious lack of sin is an unconscious attribute but not a power. All face not the Second Coming in him, but their own best similitude, and they contort in ways that transcend their previous abasements and momentary allegiances. Private enough to evoke the secrecy of letter after letter, his coming is also public enough to stir up the feverish proximities of the impromptu parties that throng this novel.

All oscillate between the Sodom of their own worst nature and the light of their best which he shows them. Aglaia tries to scorn him at first by calling him trite; reaches out to him; tries to transform him to a mere social appearance in urging him to defend his honor at a duel; sinks into the delightful abeyance of engagement; and, at last kills the Myshkin in herself by turning from a regenerated Radom-

sky to marry a scandalous son of the Roman church Myshkin deplored. Her sisters, the aping, ear-passive musician
Alexandra, the sprightly, eye-dominated painter Adelaida,
are too superficial to know the Christ when they see him.
All these are ordinary people as Dostoevsky defines them
at the beginning of Book Four. "When anything extraordinary happened, Madame Epanchin used to open her eyes
very wide, and, throwing back her whole person, she would
stare vaguely before her without uttering a word." She is
opening her eyes, so to speak, to prevent the light from
sharpening her inner eyes. And her husband "preferred to
appear to be carrying out the ideas of others rather than
the promptings of his own intellect, to pose as a man 'dis-
interestedly devoted' and—to fall in with the spirit of the
age—a warm-hearted Russian." The alternation in General Epanchin between status-worship and inner delicacy
reaches a spiritual height in that youngest daughter, to
whom the whole family instinctively feel they must sacrifice everything. But Aglaia, spasmodically, betrays that
fineness. Her family has given her empire—so she wants
empire over Myshkin, where only subjection will induce
her own rebirth. She constantly puts up a mask of rejecting
him forever, from the very first snub, through the threat
that she will break off if he talks seriously at a social gathering. And she does break for good when she leaves him
tending the Nastasya her scorn has prostrated.

Ganya, to whom she turns on rejecting Myshkin, is
her more ordinary male counterpart, hence the secretary
of her father: "Passion and hatred were strangely mingled
in his soul." As he alternates between defense of Myshkin
and indifference to him, it is his willed destiny to be no more
than agitated at the presence of the prince; he is clever,
Dostoevsky later says, but really one of the ordinary people. Rogozhin keeps a picture of Christ on the walls of his
home, one to which the characters revert in their devotional
dreams. But he flouts the surrogate Christ with whom he

wants to exchange crosses. So strong is his good side that he keeps it shrouded in the murk of his dark will. That dark will exceeds the hyena mask of a Ferdyshckenko, who is guiltless of the theft his manner has made even Myshkin suspect in him. Burdovsky and Keller are stiff, harmless in their surface chaos. Ippolit is redeemed, like his friend Kolya, who keeps a kind of safe distance from the prince, perhaps because he feels he is not yet keen enough to stand the light. But between the family he came to save and the idiot who does not recognize them in the last scene, total eclipse. Of the two great-souled women, one has thrown herself away as a murder victim, the other has married an excruciating stranger in a false country.

The light has failed, and all is character. The next step is for obsession of character to dominate plot from the outset, for a doomed society to be mirrored in deepening abasement: society is a herd of swine in *The Possessed,* jumping off the cliff into the sea.

Stavrogin is a Myshkin who has abominated himself into a Rogozhin. His unearthly beauty has something of the vampire about it; his Prince Harry wild oats lead to no real kingdom. The other anarchists desire to erect him as a man-god—as a political avatar of Myshkin, so to speak; this sends him to the monastery: he can confess but not repent of having seduced an oppressed girl and driven her to suicide. Stavrogin, having killed God, as the girl thinks she herself has done, cannot do more than make convulsive gestures toward that extraordinary spiritual leadership all feel to be his right. He shatters the cross of Tihon at the moment of friendship. Having married not his destined Liza but a cripple, he reaches out to the passive sister of another pathetic victim, Shatov, to join him and flee to the Switzerland that haunts this novel, as it does *The Idiot,* like some impossible vision of paradise. But when his mother comes to him,—the narrator's constant undercurrent of irony swells for major capitulation:—"The citizen of the canton

of Uri was hanging there behind the door. On the table
lay a piece of paper with the words in pencil: 'No one is
to blame, I did it myself.' " Nor is this diabolical possession
insanity, the last sentence of the novel insists: "At the in-
quest our doctors absolutely and emphatically rejected all
idea of insanity."

"No one is to blame," Stavrogin charitably confesses.
Yet his diabolism is partly a violent rejection of the false
liberalism, as is his sexual obsession of the sham chastity, in
his fuddled tutor, Stepan Trofimovitch. His mother, too,
that imperious foolishness, induces the reaction: it was she
who hired the tutor.

The depth charges of the devil blast wide open the
superficial society whose dependent Stepan Trofimovitch
is. Out of indolence he fails to write his political study. Out
of a cowardice for which Varvara Petrovna can never forgive him, he has rejected sex after the hinted impotence of
his first marriage and the brevity of his second; what he
leans on in women is their foolish rejection of their whole
selves. He can work for them or tutor them, but not marry
them—and his employer is only herself possessedly setting
about the devil's work in getting up an engagement between
him and his pupil Dasha.

He is not wholly indolent and cowardly, however.
The shallow obsession of French, an elegant defense mechanism, he turns to self-knowledge at the beginning: "Je suis
un simple dépendent, et rien de plus! Mais r-r-rien de plus!"
The confession denies what the stutter affirms; in saying he
is no more than a dependent, he is on the way to becoming
more. At the holocaust which envelops in one chaos the
high society and the low, he sets forth as a pilgrim, meets
a gospel woman (the same Lyamshin had mocked) who
understands his French. She reads to him, at his own request, that passage about the legion devils leaving a man for
the swine who jump into the sea, and while all the possessed
swine are rushing to destruction in this novel, Stepan

Trofimovitch is the freed man of the parable. His pilgrimage is toward a death of rebirth. As the darkness of the collapsing society closes about him, he affirms the light. The completeness of the opposing dissolution in others gives his solitary, unexpected metamorphosis the grandeur one occasionally finds when a nobleman turns pilgrim in the Indian epics. Even his sexual timidity emerges, at last, as the secret chastity, stigma of holiness, which Myshkin and Alyosha radiate.

His superficial counterpart, the vain writer Karmazinov, has been upset at the fête where the preoccupations of the possessed only draw their ears away from his narcissistic twaddle. Young Verhovensky, the Mephistopheles of the novel, rejects his father and Karmazinov too with a sly impudence. His blackness is total and all but causeless. He fawns on Stavrogin, apotheosizing him to betray him. With his pawn, the simple Erkel, he is the instigator and the sole undeviating executor of Shatov's horrible murder. He goads Kirillov into suicide, completing the work all the possessions have begun. Stavrogin is the Herculean center of character in this novel, Verhovensky its self-transcending total darkness of plot.

Verhovensky can bear Shatov's transcendence into light even less than the insult; he mocks the timid Virginsky who pleads, in the fellowship of cuckoldry, for the new man who stands before them. Virginsky's own truant wife is that minute performing her creative role as midwife to Madame Shatov. Because of the murder, the new mother exposes herself and the baby to the cold, and both die.

Yet at the climax of Part One Stavrogin has been humble enough, in the unflinching courage Dostoevsky insists on, to take a blow from Shatov full in the face.

Liza faints at this blow, as she is clubbed to death at the deeper blow of the climax.

Liza, palest of Dostoevsky's heroines, is extraordinary enough to respond to Stavrogin, possessed enough to abandon herself to him at the climactic scene. But he is not possessed enough for her: "Nikolay Vesyevolodovitch, since I've been with you I've discovered that you are very generous to me, and it's just that I can't endure from you." She oversimplifies reciprocal subjection into possession, as she had oversimplified history—and Shatov—in engaging Shatov to help her collect a year's newspapers to establish a pattern for events; so she had oversimplified courtship in allowing the devotion of Mavriky. At the climax she runs out into a "mist of fine, drizzling rain [that] enveloped the whole country, swallowing up every ray of light, every gleam of color, and transforming everything into one smoky, leaden, indistinguishable mass." There she is overjoyed to encounter her old tutor, in whom she sees the anti-Stavrogin of his old social self and not the anti-Stavrogin of his new religious self.

The characters of the others are contortions of their leaders. Kirillov writes treatises on the suicide his idol Stavrogin, and he himself, will commit. Lebyadkin is a more ordinary Stavrogin, brother-in-law and Falstaff to him, a sadist toward his crippled sister, a frustrated poet who sends versified eulogies to Stavrogin's Liza and somehow precedes Karmazinov on that obsessed literary program, finally getting his own throat cut by that plebeian Stavrogin, the convict Fedka.[3] Liputin, the usurer-nihilist, is sent on a drunken debauch by the events' transcendence of his puny spirit. Lyamshin is the give-away, the mere mimic of possession, who "would imitate a pig, a thunderstorm, a confinement with the first cry of the baby" (not knowing this early in the novel that the pig is the swine of the St. Luke epigraph, the thunderstorm the rain of the climax, the confinement and birth that of Shatov's wife); he goes to pieces and tells everything at the end.

At the center of this novel's plot a social world of

[3] Stepan Trofimovitch has, in effect, ruined Fedka, too, having sold him into military service to pay a gambling debt.

shallow optimism and status quo, exemplified in the existence and politics of Stepan Trofimovitch, clashes with an underground world of radical pessimism, the terror Shigalov formulates in the meeting at Virginsky's. These worlds crepitate from the beginning: both are possessed. As the plot opens, Stavrogin, the germ of chaos, tweaks a general's nose at a polite gathering, bites a governor's ear, and lapses into three years of insanity. The conventional world wears the mask of social mastery (a mask, because who here is less masterful than Stepan Trofimovitch, than the incapable *bon vivant* self-styled novelist von Lembke?); in the insistence of the anarchists, the radical world wears the mask of an underground to help the people—including ex-serfs like Shatov, who, however, denies that the people are anarchic.

As the tensions of possession mount in this closed situation, this "birdcage" (what Skvoreshniki means in Russian), the climax mounts, splendidly timed for self-transcendences. The social world reaches the chaos of the fête, the abduction of Liza, the momentary insanity of von Lembke; the underground world has the lurking outsider Fedka set fire to Shpigulin's factory, killing Lebyadkin and his crippled sister. Finally this spell holds the whole society in its grip like that "fine, drizzling rain" that made everything an "indistinguishable mass." Liza, fleeing from the upper spell, from Stavrogin, is clubbed on her way out of dark obsession by the lower spell in the confusion around Shpigulin's factory. And Verhovensky takes advantage of the confusion to get Shatov killed. No one but Stepan Trofimovitch, whom Liza has just passed on the road, can journey into the light away from this dark magic circle of evil.

The mysteriously infinite radiation of theological act is omnipresent. In this novel theology takes the form of politics; to prove that wrong politics is diabolism was Dostoevsky's immediate impetus for writing it. Actually in Dostoevsky's view, as Romano Guardini says and Shatov is coming to realize, the people is not a shapeless mass but precisely God—in (Shatov does not tell us this, however) their mystic communion and interpenetration as the body of Christ, the invisible church. To this truth the diabolically possessed do various violences, actual and ideological. "Dispossess a man of mind and sensibility," Blackmur says of this novel, "and he is likely to become possessed; that is to say, he is likely to be invaded by those forces which, by encompassing his own destruction, would strike a blow at the immortal part of society; which is, however it is phrased, the characteristic temptation of the possessed: the temptation of suicide to become murder, of politics to become anarchy, of man to become god. All three are phases of the one temptation." [4] The central climax of fête and fire constitutes a social transcendence: the plot has not fully prepared us for it; but the singleness, the society of this novel, in being political is as closely knit in its causality as ever in a novel by Dostoevsky.

A murder is the simple nucleus of worlds of meaning in *The Brothers Karamazov*. In *The Possessed* a monastery had been only another crazier version of possession; to social visits it offered only the white nonsense of block after block of sugar bestowed by the darkly capricious elder on some thunderstruck suppliant. When Tihon does make sense, Stavrogin breaks away from him. In *The Brothers Karamazov*, Zossima is equally cryptic, but with apocalyptic prophecy, defining the natures of suppliants in a phrase, predicting the hovering parricide, kneeling down—everyone feels symbolically—to Dmitri Karamazov.

Rembrandt and Goya, alone or nearly alone among painters, imbue their paintings with a light so supernatural that the observer can point at no supposed or actual window or sun as its source. Dostoevsky's plots have a Rembrandtian perspective. In *The Brothers Karamazov*, after a summarizing introduction whose shifting perspectives sug-

[4] "In the Birdcage," *The Hudson Review*, I, Spring 1948.

gest such hidden origins of light and shadow, the undefined source of light is revealed in the monastery. Alyosha has already preceded his family there from having contemplated the meaning of his mother's suffering. Everyone steps into that light and finds himself described, if at times mysteriously, by his reaction and by Zossima's summations. From the outset reality is theological, and the dominant chord is struck before the causality proper, the nexus of parricide, commences.

The self-transcendences in this novel are grounded in reactions and counterreactions not to a single person but to all. Katerina Ivanovna vacillates towards Grushenka because of her attraction for Dmitri, who in turn seeks out Alyosha to counter his own dark side. Ivan, attracted likewise by Katerina Ivanovna, oscillates between Smerdyakov and his full brother Alyosha. Katerina Ivanovna is torn between her abasing bond of guilt to Dmitri and her healthier fondness for Ivan. Smerdyakov and Ivan alike assert that they are not their brother's keeper; consequently Dmitri has too free reign to canvass the unresponsive egoisms of Samsonov and Lyagavy and Madame Hohlakov, finally to stall the plot into mystery about the murder. Clinging to the anguishing certitude of a self-destructive hostility toward some person, or even toward some evil, is a laceration of pity or contempt. "Lamentations comfort only by lacerating the heart still more. Such grief does not desire consolation. It feeds on the sense of its hopelessness. Lamentations spring only from the constant craving to re-open the wound." The demands of the murder, of mystic and real brotherhood, force these people against themselves to transcend their lacerations.

Guilt is the death through which they are reborn, their faith even as a grain of mustard seed sufficient to make them fruitful, to turn the lie of their superficial dark will into the truth (these the terms of the penultimate chapter). The courtroom is a new agony, a parody and rigorous version of the initial monastery, its harsh air evoking not only the false elaborations of the prosecution but the extreme, and revealing, responses of Grushenka's impulsive support of Dmitri, of Ivan's illness, Smerdyakov's private confession and suicide, Katerina Ivanovna's damning "sudden catastrophe" when she reveals the misleading letter that caps Dmitri's condemnation.

All this has exfoliated from the murder—and more. In mysterious sympathy to the theological timing of the action, Father Zossima, whose early career parallels the "murderer" Dmitri's, dies shortly before Fyodor Karamazov is murdered. Alyosha is reborn through the death of this spiritual father. The stench of corruption from Father Zossima is a willed stumbling block to Rakitin, who leads the dazed Alyosha out of the monastery and to Grushenka. But Grushenka takes him as an emissary of the light, leaps off his knees to tell him the parable of the onion which did not save the selfish woman from the burning lake. And shortly thereafter, dozing at the funeral of Father Zossima, Alyosha dreams himself into a deeper, more natural joy, the death of total involvement in the natural order, through the image of the funeral sermon: "Cana in Galilee" transforms the water of earthly existence into the wine of theological bliss.[5]

Alyosha realizes that Father Zossima's virtue is not supernatural sanctity but a triumph of the will and of grace, so firmly of the natural order that his body must have a stench of corruption. This empowers him to transcend the selfhood of his shallower adolescent piety, to become a full brother to Ivan and Dmitri, to get beyond the falsity of Madame Hohlakov's sentimental piety and the self-lacerating, equally sentimental reaction of her crippled daughter Lise.

[5] The marriage in the parable also suggests the sexual love which is to emerge in the novel as the concomitant and partial agent of redemption.

Not only do the adults benefit by the spiritual regeneration. The children of one subplot are linked to the sin of old Karamazov: Ilusha's father is in the employ of Fyodor and forbidden by Grushenka to seek revenge on Dmitri; he has been sent from the father to Dmitri with an IOU; Dmitri has pulled his beard, causing Ilusha to seek revenge by stoning Alyosha, who forthwith attempts to restore the family. Smerdyakov's devilish malice has incited Ilusha to give Kolya Krassotkin's dog a needle hidden in a piece of bread. The cumulative sins of the Karamazovs have brought Ilusha to such despair that he stabs his friend Kolya, sickens, and will shortly die.

But Alyosha is a Karamazov who will atone vicariously for these sins. His regeneration of the children breaks into the plot's rhythm; it is narrated between Dmitri's arrest and Dmitri's trial as Father Zossima's death is intercalated between the ominous evening of Smerdyakov's fit and the actual murder. The children are the future who will mysteriously suffer at the sin or rejoice at the regeneration of their elders. These real children are mystically to be identified with those of the heart-rending parables told by Ivan in his prelude to "The Grand Inquisitor," with those suffering children whose parents have earlier come to consult Father Zossima, with the starved child at the center of the burned town in Dmitri's prison dream. After dreaming of that Babe (the archetypal capital letter of the appellation linking these children with the Christ child of whose nature they partake), Dmitri walks out prepared to atone for the hateful wish which would vicariously starve the world of the future. " 'I've had a good dream, gentlemen,' he said in a strange voice, with a new light, as of joy, in his face."

These children, through the analogical and consequent death of Ilusha, become coadjutors of that joy, that new light. We learn of Dmitri's final determination not to accept Ivan's offer of escape to America, of Ivan's redeeming illness in Alyosha's final speech to the children, at once a funeral oration over Ilusha and a psalm of joy. And joy predominates in their final iteration, "Hurrah for Karamazov!"

Redemption is vicarious, and the connection between the subplots and the main plot is all the more vitally transcendental for its causal mystery. The personal link—between the subplots (deaths of Father Zossima and Ilusha) and the main plot (murder of Karamazov)—is Alyosha. He has initially elected vicarious atonement by going to the monastery against the wishes of his father, thereby meeting Father Zossima; and by leaving the monastery at the injunction of Father Zossima, thereby meeting the children.

Alyosha's shyness is deferential humility toward what he has not the prophetic power to know, or do more than act charitably toward. Dmitri's passions are fulgurations designed to obfuscate his full nature as a free soul, as his compulsive squanderings of money are designed to bring him back in hated subjection to his father, to bring him to the point where he will have to perform the act which will relieve him of his liberty: his father killed, he will, he darkly hopes, be forever unfree. The intellections of Ivan, mutually contradictory and internally vacillating, are smoke screens against the light; they are evocations of that father of lies, the devil, who finally overtakes him to converse with him, under the appearance of an aging gentleman, at the same moment his brother Smerdyakov is committing suicide.

But the transcendent spiritual ground of the novel's plot will not allow these wishes to have their own way. Alyosha is in the background vicariously atoning. Dmitri does not murder. Ivan does become his brother's keeper when something in him rebels at spiritual sickness to send him into physical sickness. Likewise are regenerated the children, the minor figures and the women, Grushenka and Katerina Ivanovna, who meet the challenge and transcend that prurience of the spirit, the Sodom which held them all alike spellbound in the beginning—all except Alyosha, and even he shows his Karamazov nature when he impulsively kisses Lise and visits Grushenka.

"Our habitual psychological concepts," Romano Guardini says (*Dostoievsky*), "intellect, intuition, imagination, will, action, creation, sentiment, and passion must be employed [for Dostoevsky] in a much more elastic and general sense, because here these faculties do not exist in the pure state; in each of them are presented all the others as well." Or, as Dmitri Karamazov puts it, "Man is broad, too broad, indeed." Dostoevsky has mirrored in his plots the transcendences of that broadness—in the interacting worlds of living situation, guilty intent, supernatural coincidence in *Crime and Punishment*, in *The Idiot's* community of dark reactions to the light of Prince Myshkin, in the mysterious rush of a society's total response to Stavrogin's perverted leadership, in the radiating force of atonement, personal and vicarious, which serves as a manna of light for the mystic starving Babe, a bond among the little groups of *The Brothers Karamazov*. By virtue of these transcendent plots, as Guardini again says, "There is no figure of a certain stature, no event of a certain importance, which is not, immediately or mediately, full of religious significance." Appearances in time change toward the hidden light of a steadfast theological reality.

The mysterious and expansive freedom of Dostoevsky's plots provides a measure for his characters' freedom, equally mysterious and expansive. So freed, they can range from abysm to exaltation, can fling dirty roubles at a singer and drive off into the tremendous night, can hang themselves or dream of the Babe in a charred village or stand in the witness box and stun everyone, themselves most of all, by the impulse of a confession. Every act, too, can emerge

suddenly after the character has vegetated or held out or
expostulated for hundreds of pages. Carrying such open
action is the voice of the narrator, akin, though rather
more raptly objective, to the long early-morning-hours'
voice of Conrad's Marlow. The fictive idea endows the
narrator's voice with the fiat to switch subject abruptly,
foist up a symbol, reveal new background, retale heart-
rending anecdotes, send someone offstage for good, let one
in on a secret conversation, all without the impulsion to
coherence which any presentation on a stage must carry,
even the "panoramic" stage of Shakespeare.

In Dostoevsky's theological vision, we get, Allen Tate
says (*On the Limits of Poetry*), a tremendous sense of actuality. At its high moments, in the immaterial light of the
action's chiaroscuro, this actuality will materialize into some
infinitely symbolic detail, the fly that buzzes over the corpse
of Nastasya Filippovna; the buzz, Tate says, "rises like a
hurricane in that silent room, until, for me, the room is
filled with audible silence."

Middleton Murry (*Dostoevsky*) praises, too, the
symbolism of the soap Stavrogin uses to smear his suicide
rope. These objects stand out all the stronger for their rar-
ity in context, as materializations of the total meaning. They
are symbols of the dense reality which the plot of the novel
has created. They are few and far between because the moment of theological plenitude is rarely embodied.

An outermost limit of actuality is seen where that fly
buzzes and that soap-smeared rope hangs; where the European network of railways is "the star that is called Wormwood that fell upon the fountains of waters"; where, inside
the house whose walls he obsessively remembers were pale
blue, Stavrogin before his sin stares at a red spider on the
geranium plant; where at a dance the young wallflower
Yulia Mihailovna wears a turquoise fly on her forehead;
where Smerdyakov sits on a green bench at twilight playing a guitar; where, stealing up on his solitary, head-band-
aged father, Dmitri Karamazov "murmured, not knowing

why, 'How red the white beam berries are' " and "raised himself on tiptoe" to see his father's bedroom divided in two parts by a red Chinese screen behind which he falsely imagines Grushenka to be standing; where the corpse of Nastasya Filippovna lies, one marble-like foot protruding, a white sheet pulled over her covering of "good American leather," between the four uncorked jars of Zhdanov's fluid, under the buzz of the fly.

Plot enables these characters to struggle into or out of such self-transcending illumination. Dostoevsky's inventiveness of incident, his plotting agility, compares favorably with Shakespeare's; it surpasses in depth what it cannot match in inclusiveness of internal reference, the plotting of that greatest of French novelists whom he began his literary career by translating. Balzac's achievement, too, lies in the plot, that total pattern which links novel to novel like so many incidents. Plot both controls and discovers the firmness and interrelations of observed insight in *La Comédie Humaine;* plot creates and informs the analogies which expand Balzac's world. It is plot that brings Rastignac to the arms of Delphine de Nucingen, née Goriot, and then makes him a half-willing colluder with Nucingen himself; it is plot that conducts du Tillet from employment under a doomed Birotteau into the power to refuse, with a sleight of signature in a letter to Nucingen, to aid his old employer; plot draws Daniel d'Arthez through contact with Michel Chrétien's *cénacle* and the great literary career he has been consolidating, into the arms of the Princesse de Cadignan whom Chrétien silently worshipped and related plots have already blackened. Plot concatenates these splendid insights into a world whose outer limits in time (apart from the Middle Ages and Renaissance of the *Etudes Philosophiques*) can include that strange abortive Breton by-blow of revolution, *Les Chouans;* and in a hidden back alley behind Notre Dame, decades later, the metamorphosed her-

oine of *Les Chouans*, Mlle. de la Chanterie, dispenses remarkable charity, aided by the analogically plotted involvement of a great banking house; this charity can itself step
forward into plot after plot to alter history for good as
silently (it is *L'Envers de l'Histoire Contemporaine*) as
Ferragus or Vautrin could for evil.

Balzac's imagination is such that his revelations only
begin with the sociological catalogs which are the skeleton
of his technique. He gives us a configured universe of emotions, and one where we cannot only find all the usual
emotions—not simply a catalog of emotions—but where the
interconnections reveal entirely new emotions, shot through
with the related emotions which give them their substance.
The whatness of de Rubempré's final emotion, a feeling of
reality, a loss of illusion, of Goriot's or de Marsay's; Chabert's or Pons'; Eugénie Grandet's or Joseph Bridau's or
Horace Bianchon's, extends laterally, as it were, but not
vertically, like Dostoevsky's. The characters know not their
own depths but some few strands more of the web of the
two thousand others. So Balzac in a sense spoke wiser than
he knew when he called himself a "sociologue." If Balzac
and Dostoevsky are our greatest novelists, they do not repeat one another. Beyond Balzac's lateral reach is the anguish of a Myshkin or a Stavrogin, the redemption of a
Sonia, the exaltation of an Alyosha. Beyond the reach of
his plot is that mysterious theological coinherence which
links Krassotkins and Snegiryovs with Karamazovs, that
governs the intuitive preferences of a Nastasya Filippovna,
that brings Raskolnikov into Sonia's orbit, that sends Stepan
Trofimovitch out onto the open road of pilgrimage and
death. Nor, to be sure, in Dostoevsky's world can we find
anything like the Balzacian analogies; he is not extensive
enough to include one of them. . . . Balzac was the only
novelist he could continue, as he did all his life, to look up
to.

Different in his use of plot from both Balzac and Dostoevsky is an American novelist who has often been compared to both. Yawknapatawpha County is dense not because of the differences between characters, or because of the complexity of a single character, as in Balzac, but because of the likeness: McCaslin and Sartoris, Snopes and Compson, Beauchamp and Sutpen, share modes of a common destiny, a simple plot, whereas Goriot and Vautrin, de Rubempré and Madame Graslin, Pons and Mlle. d'Espard, Nathan and Gobseck, all serve to complicate their world. Henri de Marsay, the spirited, worldly wise ministerial friend of Rastignac, is strikingly different from that bold comrade who figures in the hairbreadth escapades of *La Duchesse de Langeais,* as both are from their original, the obscure bastard son of an English lord in *La Fille aux Yeux d'Or.* But the Quentin Compson of *Absalom, Absalom* is only an extension, an explanation, of his identical self in *The Sound and the Fury*: the later novel leads us further into that hovering past to explore why he commits suicide in the earlier. Not analogical but historical is the common world of Faulkner's novels.

What binds Faulkner's characters is not the sort of theological coinherence found in Dostoevsky's plots. The anguish of Faulkner's best people is divine enough, the stultification of his corrupt characters gross enough, to be theological, to seem Dostoevskian in their purport as in their distortion. But actually they are bound in a plot of history.

In Faulkner's vision, the plot must expand. The two protagonists in *Wild Palms* wander not just to figure their souls, like Huck Finn and Ahab, but to enter a circle of plot that becomes possible only when they are out of their habitual circle. The plot in *Sanctuary, Light in August,* and *The Hamlet* arises only because Temple Drake, Lena, and Snopes are on the move. Let Henry Bon stay home in the West Indies and you have no *Absalom, Absalom.* Quentin must move from Mississippi to Harvard, from Harvard to a strange countryside, to destroy himself, as his sister and his namesake niece must seek a wider sphere for their slower self-destructions.

Beyond the mythic inevitability lies the widened plot, widened not into a tight causal knot but into a knot whose causal strands we cannot precisely define. Sartre (*Situations I*) has singled out this causal peculiarity of Faulkner's plots for us in his excellent Heideggerian analysis of *The Sound and the Fury*:

> You may seek in vain this knot in *The Sound and the Fury*. Is it the castration of Benjy? Caddy's miserable amorous adventure? The suicide of Quentin? Jason's hatred for his niece? Each episode, as you look at it, opens up and reveals other episodes behind it. Nothing happens; the story does not unfold: you discover it under every word, like an obscene encumbering presence, more or less condensed according to the circumstances.

No one comes to prominence; there is no agon without a protagonist. All are caught in the call to full freedom (rather than having their freedom surrendered to an all-embracing necessity, as Sartre and Gide, I believe, misread Faulkner's tone). And fullness involves process, the burden of a bond to the past you plumb, the fate of a horizon you confront beyond Jefferson in university or war or the search for a husband.

The land is the past; yet the land is a bond, and so the land is suspect, as a corrupter, once it is owned; only the wilderness is pure, as Ursula Brumm has shown.[6] You move beyond the land and to the land; in *Go Down, Moses* the earth fuses Palestine and Egypt, as parentage is lost, but ever present, in the complexity of past desires that have created the children, fated yet free, with desires of their own.

Faulkner's people seem unfree in their very assertions

[6] "Wilderness and Civilization: a Note on William Faulkner," *Partisan Review*, XXII, Summer 1955.

of love; they are bound toward the past. Dostoevsky's characters move toward God through love for the mystery in
each other; Faulkner's brood toward the past and are honorable or dishonorable to one another according to how
the past dominates them. Sex in Dostoevsky is a bodily
means of theological abasement or divine discovery, a way
of pressing the plot; in Faulkner it is a particularly treacherous mode of avoiding the plot, of disowning or corrupt-
ing the past—the past of the family (Caddy and young
Quentin), the meaning of one's own past as the ground-
work of a possible destiny (the teacher Labove in *The
Hamlet*, the interne who chooses sex as a self-destructive
break from his purpose in *The Wild Palms*), or the willed
but forgotten tragic flaw in the process of history (Sutpen's
negro wife, and the subsequent tragedy brought on his
house when the quadroon son of that marriage appears
from the West Indies to court his own chaste Judith;
Judith's chastity, again, is not so much a theological virtue
as an almost hysterical attitude toward her father's unknown but intuited past). The past's plot is complex
enough to drive a Darl mad, who has been trying to subdue
the past by a ritual that would make it a "mausoleum of all
hope and desire" (what Quentin's father said he was giving
his son with a watch), by symbolizing in his devotion to a
living horse what his brother Cash did more simply in making a coffin, "sawing the long hot sad yellow days up into
planks and nailing them to something."

Jason's lack of love toward Caddy and Benjy and
young Quentin and Dilsey has a freedom and a theological
implication the Easter analogy of the novel's structure and its
silent morality in Dilsey invite us to see. First of all, though,
before he lacks love, Jason lacks piety toward the past. His
mechanistic attitude toward the time of day or the genera-
tions of his family is the root of his almost catatonic hatefulness. His own hate is tragically unequivocal enough to
occupy the plot's causal center while being deflected from

the center of its deeper meaning in his brothers and sisters.

Faulkner's vision of pastness resembles that of the great American novelist to whom his style bears closest affinity. In Faulkner, as in James, the loftily pitched involutions, the suspension of time sentence by sentence into orotund universes of abstraction, point toward and describe the womb of the present as big with the meaning of the past. In James it is a moral past either contained within the plot of the individual novel or objectified in an external scene (Europe) or a formulable code (aristocratic manners). In Faulkner the concreteness is not only in the scene but in what the blood remembers or refuses to remember; it informs the intuition and gestures of the characters, relating them not so much backward and forward at the same time (as in James) as to a kind of past-dynamic present. The anguish in Faulkner is always now, and the full humanity of Dilsey accepts its presentness in all humility. The present of the plot harks back to reenactment of the past; but the reenactment is archetypical, *The Sound and the Fury*'s Good Friday-Easter Sunday progression. The resuming point of view is Dilsey's. Joe Christmas' analogy to Christ amounts also to a plot of reenactment, one which gives a theological overtone to the Southern past.

Faulkner's characters do have a full human freedom. Benjy begins the story in *The Sound and the Fury* not only because his consciousness is vividly timeless. He is also a completely passive character, one whose sole existence is to receive love; in his family's gestures toward Benjy, even as children, we see the whole will of each member; we see that underneath the hysterical concern of Quentin there is a willed, sick dissociation and abstraction from the real demands of love, that the weasel hatefulness of Jason rejects. In Benjy's simple anguish we see that however great a sinner Caddy may be, she brims over with love; that debauchery in her is a sickness and not a vice; that she is a victim of the past more than her hapless daughter is to be; or at least in a way that, set against the alcoholism and metaphysical despair of her father, allows her more human stature than her poor daughter Quentin is to have in rebellion against the mechanical sterility of Jason.

It is from a possible but unrealized plot of love, Dilsey's and Benjy's, that Jason drives away in the sick chaos of the conclusion. He is the counterpart of the Quentin whose going to Harvard he resents. Their father's sin of indolence (past paralysis) splits both sons off from an imaginable complete plot into the suicide of one, the mechanism of the other: one stops, the other watches, the clock. "Women are never virgins," the father says, weaving the excessive abstraction of metaphysical nonsense to further obsess the son already over-obsessed with these matters. "Purity is a negative state and therefore contrary to nature. It's nature hurting you not Caddy and I said That's just words and he said So is virginity and I said You don't know. You can't know and he said Yes. On the instant when we come to realize that tragedy is second-hand."

"Tragedy is second-hand" if one wills it to be, and father is inducing his son so to make it. The secondhandedness means that everyone in this family—the sentient Quentin, the loving Caddy, the spiteful Jason—will split off into that disjunction which the disparate sections of the plot underscore and express. These characters no longer have enough will for firsthand tragedy. Their will makes their tragedy secondhand, causing the distortion and anguish of plot, the impotent sense, with which the novel opens, that everything has already happened. Impotence or pride hands the present over to the past, a process the novel's violent disjunctions enforce. The father's intuition, along with that of the son here narrating, has become a parody of intuition, as his intellect has become a parody of intellect: a theorizing parthenogenesis of itself as it speculates insanely on virginity.

Another dominant secondhand tragedy lies behind

this one, and Quentin narrates it as well to his Canadian roommate. Sutpen and Jason Compson are both crying, "Absalom, Absalom." Quentin, Henry Sutpen, Charles Bon are ill-starred into a kind of identity, the last two by their tragic condition: their father has willed a history with a tragic flaw in its past-dominated plot. The Civil War overtakes and postpones the catastrophe that comes with a weight as final and hopeless as the huge tombstone Sutpen has been dragging with his baggage train through four years of war. The heir, Quentin, is willing his ill-starredness by fixing his attention on this past and on what he reads as the hopelessness of his situation.

The fluidity of the style, like the width of the plot, opens the tone of the novel beyond tragedy, and in the flashes of insight, humor and anguish are welded together; the deepest sense opens into a smile at terror; the old patient Dilsey and the young terrified Dilsey are the same, both capable of the gladness Gavin Stevens always breaks into out of his vision of things, a vision not comic or tragic but something partaking of both which Faulkner has made the novel bear. Process demands humorousness in understanding; lack of humor is fatal in an agonist like Joe Christmas and equally in an egoist like Anse Bundren; both are too present-oriented to understand the past and therefore master its multiplicity of harrowing process by a smile, any more than, for all his suffering, Hightower can master a past he transfixes into myth.

The retrospective one-voiced narration inflates the Civil War into a resuming unity of pastness, as the multiple perspectives of *The Sound and the Fury* and *As I Lay Dying* break the present into so many bright, past-haunted fragments. *The Wild Palms* goes even farther to mirror the dissociation of a whole civilization from a personal or a common past in juxtaposing two elaborately analogical narratives that scarcely touch causally: a doctor wilfully abandons his profession for sex and traps himself by the logic of events into a denial of fertility, into an abortion which leads to his imprisonment; the logic of events sets a prisoner free on a flood where he rescues a pregnant woman, then returns willingly to his prison: both protagonists end up, significantly, in the same prison.

In *Light in August*, archetypal situation has moved to the foreground, because of a spiritual bankruptcy from a past that Hightower alone can see, and then only in fitful hallucinations. Pregnancy and murder, theology and orphanage, bring the protagonists into precarious and disastrous involvement with one another, for a reenactment of a Christian drama without Christ.

The repetition of the past in the present suggests archetypes. And Faulkner's tendency, exceeding its proper limits in *The Fable,* is to construct his plots out of allegorical situations, to give his observed characters a significance of mythical dimension. To adapt a remark of Richard Chase's (*The Kenyon Reader*) "Faulkner works inward from the extremities, from the mechanics and ecstasy of life. And this relentless, bardic American bias often makes us wish he would reverse the procedure, that his consciousness would work through human manners into the human character and then outward towards the extremities it can contain or fail to contain." But Faulkner's meaning has it that he cannot "reverse the procedure." The pattern of the Civil War in the presentness of 1910, of virginity in its loss, of the significance in *Light in August*'s straight and curved lines (which Chase has himself demonstrated)—all demand that the characters find their way, or lose it, not through manners, but in the archetypal patterns the past has already ordained. Here Sutpen and his son face each other (the italics signify that the confrontation is being spoken by Quentin Compson, and also what is obsessing his sick imagination):

> *Henry says nothing. It is coming now. He says nothing, he merely stares at his father—the two of them in leaf-faded*

*gray, a single candle, a crude tent walling them away from
a darkness where alert pickets face one another and where
weary men sleep without shelter, waiting for dawn and the
firing, the weary backward walking to commence again;
yet in a second tent candle gray and all are gone and it is
the holly-decked Christmas library at Sutpen's Hundred four
years ago and the table not a camp table suitable for the
spreading of maps but the heavy carved rosewood one at
home with the group photograph of his mother and sister
and himself sitting upon it, his father behind the table and
behind his father the window above the garden where Judith
and Bon strolled in that slow rhythm where the heart
matches the footsteps and the eyes need only look at one
another.*

Here pace and setting, verbal rhythm and detail, all rise
powerfully from an observed base, to become those analogies which make Faulkner the stylistic peer of Flaubert,
Hemingway and Joyce. "Leaf-faded" his both literal intensity and metaphorical extent, recalling that image of
Homer's which compares the mortality of soldiers to that
of leaves. The metaphorical implications of candle and
maps and pickets make the country and the family define
each other, binds Civil War and Sutpens in a relationship
where cause and effect are so intertwined as to be lost; and
there is that further analogy to the Christian reenactment
in the library holly. The soldiers, like the Sutpens, are going to march backward. ("Retrograde" and its near syno-
nyms are favorites of the past-obsessed Faulkner.) The
whole is operating at a pitch of intuition, as of verbal mastery, which can achieve the magnificent "slow rhythm" of
the last sentence.

The past not only orders—or disorders—the plot; it
gives the sentient character an intuition into plot equal to
Faulkner's own. Not only Gavin Stevens, who uses his
creator's keen nose to ferret out crime, but nearly all
Faulkner's characters have the perceptiveness which in its
awareness of human nuances and the poetry of the objects
through which they move is constantly defining the plot's

indefinable. Faulkner's reputation among his fellow novelists may very well be due more than anything else to the high pitch with which he allows his characters constantly to give airy nothing a local habitation and a name: "Caddy smelled like trees"; "She seemed to be momentarily mesmerised by a completely inert soft surprise, big immobile, almost eye to eye with him in height, the body which seemed always to be on the outside of its garments"; "It was a forensic face, the face of invincible conviction in the power of words as a principle worth dying for if necessary"; "As I descended the light dwindled slowly, yet at the same time without altering its quality, as if I and not light were changing, decreasing, though even when the road ran into trees you could have read a newspaper"; "She has no mother because fatherblood hates with love and pride, but motherblood with hate loves and cohabits"— these successive insights not only keep the narrative at a vanishing point of perception: they create what they rise out of, the theological implications of the plot's pastness. As Sartre says, every event in Faulkner lies behind every other in a single novel: and their manner of relation is as intangible as the mysterious impingements of supernatural coincidence or vicarious feelings which connect the incidents in Dostoevsky's novels. The implications of his plots make Faulkner, as R. W. Flint observes,[7] verge on poetry. It takes poetry to describe such evanescent feelings. At the heart of Faulkner's best novels is the intangible past whose mystery all the insights define; or seem to define; the plot has been doing the defining actually, with a unity, and a transcendence, that in a way is an extension of Dostoevsky's. Dostoevsky is more comprehensive, finally more profound, than Faulkner: his transcendences go farther as his final effect cuts deeper. And Balzac's *Comédie Humaine* is more penetrating as well as incomparably more various

[7] "Faulkner as Elegist," *The Hudson Review*, VII, Summer 1954.

than Faulkner's, though Balzac is tone deaf in sensibility
while Faulkner's ear is attuned to the unheard music of the
fictive spheres as keenly as any living.

Every valid novelist, much more than every valid dramatist,
must discover anew for himself the ordering principles of
plot. The drama is a performance of reenactment. It can
fall back on an inherited or invented plot of archetypical
design, can fall back on versions of Aristotle and Ibsen. The
novelist must in a sense make as well as express his world:
his causes must be as fresh and observed as his single observations. For Dostoevsky and Faulkner and Conrad no less
than for Tolstoi and Trollope, the meaning, which the plot
discovers, gives their whole tenor to the observations which
would otherwise be not fictive but merely moral, not the
worlds of Tolstoi or Dostoevsky but the separate moral
maxims of La Rochefoucauld and Vauvenargues and Chamfort. The novelists who concatenate maxims out of concrete
situations are greater than these moralists. The greater the
reality which the novelist discovers, the larger and more
open his plots are likely to be.

❧ XII ❧

ROMANCE AS ALLEGORY

MELVILLE AND KAFKA

The plots of Dostoevsky and Cervantes are both fictive, both plots of process. Yet Cervantes' plot has some of the rigidity of design which we associate with allegory. His plot is a romance, one whose structure is something approaching a meaningful schema into which the detail is fitted like gems in a jeweler's box. Dostoevsky's plot, on the other hand, is more than schematized: there are mysteries in it; the detail is not set into the plot's fixed pattern, but, as it were, is transmuted by the plot: not gems in a jeweler's box but only lights and shadows intermingling.

Novel and romance, are defined by Northrop Frye[1] as elements in fiction. In our terms, they are two different strategies for representing appearance and reality. In a novel, each observation reproduces the contours of behavior as a reality which is also an appearance; each points to the further reality of the over-all plot. In romance the archetypical plot of the book is shown to be the underlying reality, the secret process, of life's mere appearances.

[1] *Anatomy of Criticism.* We may call Frye's third type, the Menippean satire or encyclopedia, a special version of combining romance with documentation: a comic tone will make the prototypes of romance into the types of caricature, shimmering with itemizations of social distortion. Frye's fourth type, autobiographical confession, might be defined as a partial or total arbitrary limitation for the novelist on the range of his observation.

242

In Aristotelian terms, the characters (*ethos*) in the plot (*mythos*) of a romance express and evolve the plot by their simple relations to each other, so that the plot is a cipher of the idea or theme (*dianoia*). In a novel the characters are complex, and their observed traits constitute a form. (One would not think a man with the trait of shyness would have the trait of violent social ideas. What a surprise when he turns out to have the trait of a potential murderer when he meets me in the dark hall of his home!) A character's action in each appearance, in Ortega's point about Dostoevsky, adds to the form, rather than simply reiterating it, as in a romance. In a novel the complex forms of individual characters combine in a way to express the theme (*dianoia*) so that the theme, if abstracted, would be another, inner, true plot, displaced slightly from the bare plot (*mythos*), which, in a romance could serve unchanged as a cipher of the theme.

These abstract types of plot are never wholly separated in an actual fiction. Cervantes' romance has a novel side to it, and nearly every novel has somehing of romance in its plot. The symbolic "night journey" Guérard finds in Conrad has the archetypal character of romance. Any novel is a quest, sometimes even a Quest: Fabrice not only ventures out of his country to be reborn at Waterloo; he receives there a thigh wound that recalls the one in the Chapel Perilous.[2]

Yet Conrad's symbolism results partly from the tightness of his plots, and partly from his post-Flaubertian tendency to use analogical detail. Cervantes, Melville, Kafka, and others, use romance more exclusively as cipher of meaning.

A romance tends to be allegorical. And however complex the figures are in allegory, they remain single, rather stiff and abstract. *Faux Semblant,* Slough of Despond have

[2] The researches of Frederick Locke into the Grail legend in Alain-Fournier and others have set me to looking for such motifs.

a single meaning, but a complex one: there are many implications to hypocrisy, to acedia. The White Whale can be read as nothingness or the supernatural or the divine nature of the sea or a blank concentration of all space into a single object or death or wonder or the infinite or the devil or various combinations of these. There is detail in Melville to support all these, and an infinite number of other interpretations. The White Whale is symbolic, not, Melville said —ironically, some think—"a hideous and intolerable allegory."

Still, the symbolism of the White Whale is allegory-like, different from the symbolism of Kurtz's cannibalistic religion in the heart of darkness. The romance of *Moby Dick* makes the White Whale seem allegorical: it seems to stand for something single, however infinitely complex; there is nothing single, first or last, in the darkness of Kurtz. The White Whale is a cipher, for however much. It is at once fact and cipher. Cipher precedes, or at least coexists with fact. The heart of darkness is first fact, then symbolic meaning, never cipher.

Balzac used romance as a means of investing his sociological system with mythical overtones. Melville, like all his best American contemporaries, found in romance a meaningful schema for an American experience which seemed excessively abstract, or excessively thin, as James indicates in his famous description of the impoverishment of American institutions.

In the romance of *Moby Dick*, the "elaborate synecdoche," as Auden calls it (*The Enchaféd Flood*), by which whaling stands for mankind is so total, so (complexly) single in its reference, that the plot needs no causal pattern other than the pure process of voyaging. Allegory is cause, rather than vice versa. Sequence is fortuitous in the vast Pacific, as on the vast Mississippi of *Huckleberry Finn*. Not only Manhattan and New Bedford and Nantucket and the *Pequod* are allegorized, but the process from Manhattan to

New Bedford to Nantucket to the *Pequod*. Not only Quee-
queg's face and his past allegorize out from their descriptions, but the fortuitous sequence of his acts. Not only are
the nine ships the *Pequod* meets allegorically significant, not
only the fact that there are nine, but the sequence, itself
causally fortuitous, in which she meets them.

Hawthorne's romances by contrast have a simple and
rather rigorous pattern of causality. Their titles often ad-
vertise allegory. Likewise allegorical is the mystery in Poe's
tales, whether unexplained in *The Fall of the House of
Usher* and *The Descent into the Maelstrom,* or ferreted out
in *The Gold Bug* and *The Murders of the Rue Morgue.*
When the mystery is ferreted out, fiction is the loser: the
detective tales lack imaginative depth for all their mythical
overtones and the legendary power of literary influence at-
tested to by their vast progeny. The maelstrom will stand
comparison with Moby Dick, but beside *The Scarlet Letter*
such popular mystery tales as *The Gold Bug* seem as inconsequential as Balzac's *Contes Drolatiques,* which that
great writer, conscious of his work's quality as the provincial Poe could not wholly be, called graffiti on the edifice
of *La Comédie Humaine. The Gold Bug* and its kin are
suggestive graffiti on the great romances of the American
renaissance.[3]

Hawthorne incorporates into his novels little of the
concrete observation that, by overcompensation as it were,
proliferates in his *Notebooks.* The documentation about
streets and cities and inns and people and ships, and above
all whales and whaling, which Melville works into his narrative, not only functions persuasively to substantiate the
credibility of the action. (This is the function of detail in
Gulliver's Travels, that romance which becomes fictional
only in its final hallucinatory vision of England.) The detail
in *Moby Dick* serves, further, to show the supernatural's

[3] Since I wrote this Richard Chase has come out with a full
study of the romance element in the American novel.

rootedness in the physical world. We never physically encounter the Brobdingnagians or the Slough of Despond; we do, or can, encounter land and sea and whales, even such white whales as Mocha Dick. And for Melville, the literal embodies the allegorical. Here is the way he describes light on a whaling ship:

> See with what entire freedom the whaleman takes his handful of lamps—often but old bottles, and vials, though—to the copper cooler at the try-works, and replenishes them there, as mugs of ale at a vat. He burns, too, the purest of oil, in its unmanufactured, and, therefore, unvitiated state; a fluid unknown to solar, lunar, or astral contrivances ashore. It is sweet as early grass butter in April. He goes and hunts for his oil, so as to be sure of its freshness and genuineness, even as the traveller on the prairie hunts up his own supper of game.

Here the whaleman uses a brighter light because his adventure is more spiritual, and whatever enters the comparison—mugs of ale, early grass, butter in April, game on the prairie—partakes of something of that spirit, as do the old bottles and vials, the copper cooler and the try-works and the ship at large. The *Pequod* is a Walden where spiritual wakefulness is rooted in observed physical detail.

The mystery is immanent and incarnate. Ahab's and Ishmael's attitude toward the mystery—as well as Pip's, Fedallah's, Starbuck's, everyone's—is qualified in the humorous tone of the whole, which admits the purpose of the whaling voyage to be a vast incongruity. *Moby Dick*'s humor is found in its narrator Ishmael's over-all attitude toward paradox; the humor permits a split resolution of incongruities in fictive process, the mystery of what Melville in his next novel will call "the ambiguities." The excitation of fantasy is induced by the presence of the supernatural: the half-sportive, half-sardonic smile is not Stubbs's "Laugh's the wisest, easiest answer to all that's queer" but a tentative and wondering acquiescence in the numinous.

Melville himself had an exquisitely precise sense of the work his style was doing: "blubber is blubber you know; tho you may get oil out of it, the poetry runs as hard as sap from a frozen maple tree;—& to cook the thing up, one must needs throw in a little fancy, which, from the nature of the thing, must be ungainly as the gambols of the whales themselves. Yet I mean to give the truth of the thing, spite of this." *Moby Dick*'s humor, like the similar fancy of Dickens, makes its romance fictive: humor mediates between appearance and reality.

Romance tends to be theological allegory. Melville echoes a kind of Calvinist transcendentalism as Dante echoes St. Thomas, though the fictiveness of his romance differentiates him more fundamentally from transcendentalism than Dante from Catholic doctrine. Likewise different from the theology of Kierkegaard, for which Kafka has often been read, are Kafka's romances.

In Kafka the meaning of the romance's ciphers dwindles into absurdity. Our several interpretations of the White Whale are partial but valid; what we say about the castle is not only partial but provisional. Its allegorical meaning is that it has no meaning, or that its meaning is to be found only in provisional action. It requires for completion the schema it seems to be giving but is not. The process takes its meaning from the schematization of itself; but as soon as the process ends, the meaning is lost with the ambiguity of the process. The schema has a likeness not to a single complex referent, but only to itself. This radical ambiguity, as Blanchot (*La Part du Feu*) says in his excellent essays on Kafka, falsifies any attempt to schematize the meaning of

his allegory; even so probing a schematization as Paul
Goodman's or Max Bense's makes of Kafka "a sort of
superior Max Brod." This allegory finds its ambiguity in
the unbridgeable gap between an illusion of abstract meaning and a reality of concrete; rather, the concrete so underlies the abstract, that the one cannot exist without the other.
In this sense Kafka's work is a parable for the art of fiction,
and so Blanchot has read him.

As Kafka himself says of parables (*Gleichnis*, likeness):

> All these parables really set out to say merely that the in-
> comprehensible is incomprehensible, and we know that al-
> ready. But the cares we have to struggle with everyday:
> that is a different matter.
> Concerning this a man once said: Why such reluctance?
> If you only followed the parables you yourself would be-
> come parables and with that rid of all your daily cares.
> Another said: I bet that is also a parable.
> The first said: You have won.
> The second said: But unfortunately only in parable.
> The first said: No, in reality; in parable you have lost.

In parable, in the *Gleichnis* of allegory to its meaning, the
act evades its own schematization ("in parable you have
lost"); the evasion is the meaning of the schematization.
Allegory is a truncated significance: process creates an appearance of design, and this appearance is as much as we
have of a final reality.

In process an act lacks meaning; its meaning can only
be given by more process, which in turn lacks meaning to
be given by more process. The meaning is not only paradoxical, but paradoxically inconclusive. So Kafka's novels
are unconcluded, all but *The Trial*, which ends in an unexplained death, a death the victim gives a wrong, because
impulsive, meaning to in an effort to perpetuate any meaning, even a false one: " 'Like a dog!' he said: it was as if he
meant the shame of it to outlive him." This statement is the

culmination of all his acts, which persist in seeking shortcuts to meaning, a tendency which may very well be his guilt.[4]

The priest in the cathedral has tried to get across to Joseph K how provisional the process in *Der Prozess* must be. The very sequentiality of time and the unknowability of all relevant detail make any interpretations of process provisional; all one can do is go on perfecting a burrow, a great wall of China, be a hunger artist against the absurdity of such unexplained but explicit guilt as Joseph K's, such sudden metamorphoses as are figured in the physical change of a Gregor Samsa.

These characters resemble the Abraham whom Kafka borrowed for his parables from that book of Kierkegaard's he studied most closely, *Fear and Trembling*. As Kierkegaard expounds it, Abraham's commitment is radically unknowable, and its unknowability is unknowable. Abraham's heroism lies in accepting the paradox that what you know is what you do not know. In Kafka's romance the provisionality of the meaning makes these characters unpredictable, like Dostoevsky's, and oriented toward the supernatural. But, as types in a romance, they lack the roundness of Dostoevsky's characters, and the concealment of their symbolism makes them caricatures of types, bare, present, and inscrutable.

They are the characters of Dostoevsky designated by letters or first names, stripped to the bone of an ur-humanity, faceless in all but their loneliness; and all their verbalizations are merely a superfetation of process upon itself.

The castle is at once near and far as Kafka describes it: at once meaningful and the "disappointment" of meaning,

[4] Kafka is unequivocal in calling Joseph K guilty, by contrast with the innocent Karl of *Amerika*, who is not guilty in a Kierkegaardian sense but only seduced.

at once visible and invisible, at once bureaucratic and theological. It is not, as some interpreters would have it, that the theological and the bureaucratic are levels of meaning; this would make Kafka a superior Max Brod, a facile allegorist. Theology and bureaucracy are not discrete levels but paradoxes of each other; they only become obscured in process. This tangle cannot be the full will of God; but it is all we know; K, like Kierkegaard's Abraham, has radically no grounds for hope. But hope is his only virtue; Tertullian's *credo quia absurdum*. Makeshift is temporary; but the need for makeshift is permanent. All that remains is change. And the meaning of change abides, though it cannot exist till change has ceased.

In its free associativeness Kafka's world is dreamlike but desperately real. Appearance is dream, but dream is reality. Frieda allows us to intrapolate reality into the novel by mentioning the south of France. (As the hunter Gracchus, suspended between life and death, says he comes from the Schwarzwald.)

K arrives at his nameless village "late at night," as the book tells us, and the snow was deep. *Das Dorf lag in tiefem Schnee*. The snow means itself, and more than itself: dream and reality. There was also a "surrounding . . . fog and darkness" so that "not the weakest light" indicated (*deutete an:* ambiguously both pointed out and told the significance of) the castle. Standing on the wooden (provisional?) bridge (like that which Bendesman dropped from in "The Judgement"), all K could do was look up to the *scheinbare Leere*, the emptiness which was snow and not snow, whose appearance was its only reality in that all he could know was its appearance, its being *scheinbar*. And Kafka added the paragraph I have been quoting as a revised version of *The Castle*'s beginning. He wanted at the outset to *deuten* the riddle of his significance.

In the "brilliant winter morning" of the next day, the castle is no more scrutable for being visible. Process adds meaningful detail without supplying any more meaning than the riddle's identity with itself:

> Now he could see the Castle above him, clearly defined in the glittering air, its outline made still more definite by the thin layer of snow covering everything. There seemed to be much less snow up there on the hill than down in the village, where K found progress as laborious as on the main road the previous day. Here the heavy snowdrifts reached right up to the cottage windows and began again on the low roofs, but up on the hill everything soared light and free into the air, or at least so it appeared from below.
>
> On the whole this distant prospect of the Castle satisfied K's expectations. It was neither an old stronghold nor a new mansion, but a rambling pile consisting of innumerable small buildings closely packed together and of one or two stories; if K had not known that it was a castle he might have taken it for a little town. There was only one tower as far as he could see; whether it belonged to a dwelling-house or a church he could not determine. Swarms of crows were circling around it.
>
> With his eyes fixed on the Castle, K went on farther, thinking of nothing else at all. But on approaching it he was disappointed in the Castle. . . . And in his mind he compared the church tower at home with the tower above him. The church tower, firm in line, soaring unfalteringly to its tapering point, topped with red tiles and broad in the roof, an earthly building—what else can men build?—but with a loftier goal than the humble dwelling houses, and a clearer meaning than the muddle of everyday life. The tower above him here—the only one visible—the tower of a house, as was now evident, perhaps of the main building, was uniformly round, part of it graciously mantled with ivy . . . as if designed by the trembling or careless hand of a child, clearly outlined against the blue. It was as if a melancholy-mad [*trübselig*] tenant who ought to have been kept locked in the topmost chamber of his house had burst through the roof and lifted himself up to the gaze of the world.

K is satisfied/disappointed. The castle is like/unlike the church tower at home, like in that it stands for the divine, unlike in that it has, Kafka implies, been built by other than human hands. Or is not this too ambiguous? In another sense the castle is more human, less meaningfully divine, than the tower of the church at home. What, still, does it mean? Is it diabolical? No more than it exudes grace. Is it capricious or merely enigmatic? It is closed up, its root name implies—*das Schloss (schliessen)*. One's hope can only respond to its inscrutability with a troubled melancholy, *trübselig*, like that surreal tenant whom K figures as a metaphor of the castle's appearance.

Change, change, though the snow looks the same, and the castle is presumed the same. (Further, "There seemed to be much less snow up there on the hill than down in the village.") As K's altering involvements with the altering people proceed, he will shortly hear the castle in the form of a telephone sound which the mayor later tells him is at once a confusion and "the only real and reliable thing you'll hear, everything else is deceptive."

> The receiver gave out a buzz of a kind that K had never before heard on a telephone. It was like the hum of countless children's voices—but yet not a hum, the echo rather of voices singing at an infinite distance—blended by sheer impossibility into one high but resonant sound that vibrated on the ear as if it were trying to penetrate beyond mere hearing.

This detail, like the sharply ambiguous description of the castle, is pregnant with a meaning it does not intend to deliver.[5] Only to those below does the humming seem children's voices. Actually it is those in the castle telephoning each other. It is the choiring of the blessed, too intense for human ears. It is those who have been freed from fatality, from the distortions of past, present, and future (time is always uncertain in this novel, and duration con-

The Waste Land, than the mysterious voices of children in the leaves "Quick, now, here, now, always" in *Burnt Norton*.
d'enfants chantant dans la coupole," which Eliot incorporates into
　　[5] The meaning seems at once more schematized and more universal (in the Kierkegaardian sense) than Verlaine's "*Et O ces voix*

tinually surprises K). In the process of village life the castle must appear as fatality, as a final past. However, in eternity bliss is free, a simple intense humming. The past becomes the future, the elect become as little children. The future is only the hope of time: so those who live in time see eternity, which is hope, as futurity, the voices of little children.

K's hope is that he looks forward to full acceptance from the castle. He grows impatient, even mocking; but of this he never despairs. He is the Prometheus of Kafka's parable, with the difference that he knows what he cannot know, that his sufferings will end. Meanwhile he can partake of bliss in drinking, like Alice in Wonderland, Klamm's magic brandy; in loving Frieda; in running with Barnabas, encouraging Olga, befriending Gerstaecker; in hearing the blissful humming. This humming gives him immediate hope, and he telephones miraculously without telephoning, being caught but being allowed to succeed in a well-meant attempt to trick the castle into believing he is his own old assistant. He oscillates between a *Seligkeit* of mania like Karl's in *Amerika*, and a *Trübseligkeit* of melancholia, as in *The Trial* (the terms those of Paul Goodman's perspicacious analysis in *Kafka's Prayer*). In *The Castle*, to adapt Goodman's summary psychoanalytic formulations in a direction he does not, K is gradually trying to work the melancholia of Joseph K's condition into a more deeply oriented version of Karl's mania. The bliss of *The Castle* is a visionary future enriching the tone of the present melancholia, beyond the tone of the two earlier novels.

The surprises of involvement have brought K new assistants who claim they are old. Dostoevskian self-transcendences in this novel—K's, his assistants', everybody's—become dimensions of inscrutable fatality. Often the meaning is written into poetic detail like that of the castle's appearance or the blissful hummings. Amalia's white silk gown, the assistants "their skin . . . a dusky brown, the blackness of their little pointed beards striking by contrast";

Barnabas' dress: "he was clothed nearly all in white; not in silk, of course—he was in winter clothes like all the others —but the material he was wearing had the softness and dignity of silk"; the faces of the peasants, "who stood gaping at him with their open mouths, coarse lips, and literally tortured faces—their heads looked as if they had been beaten flat on top, and their features as if the pain of the beating had twisted them to the present shape—and yet they were not exactly gaping at him, for their eyes often flitted away and studied some indifferent object in the room before fixing on him again." Here the peasants' look is transmuted before K's very eyes—first gaping, then flitting. And the appearances of others change, allegorically, with their characters: the assistants come to look "older, wearier, more wrinkled, but fuller in the face," and Barnabas shortly strips his fine garment to reveal rags.

The plot combines the freedom and the significance of the romance of *Moby Dick* (the significance of *The Castle* being cryptic) with the human interdependence of a Dostoevsky novel. Joseph K in *Der Prozess* moves more or less impulsively from one building and one kind of person to another. Karl in *Amerika* lets the situations define him because he has nothing else to do; he takes what comes till he is swept up into the mysterious elation of the Nature Theatre of Oklahoma. In *The Castle* K moves as in a dream, with religiously symbolic action, from one group to another causally, finding in the "turmoil of conflicting plots" (Goodman's phrase) that what he did before was all the time determining what comes after. Desire leads him to Frieda and wins him Frieda. Chance encounter brings him Barnabas' message from the castle, brings him the assistants, who chase Frieda. Frieda's assistance gets him a makeshift job, but his gratitude and concern lead him away to Barnabas' family, where he hears, through the solid middle of the novel, a shorter version of another's struggle with fatality under the figure of a high castle official's obscenity. He discovers another side to change; he has helped Barnabas, more than Barnabas has helped him, by providing the occasion for Barnabas' first commission from the castle. And he returns from decreased admiration for Olga, from distant association with a strangely transfixed Amalia, to find that this contact has initiated another change. Jeremiah, grown strangely older and truculent, turns out to have been a friend of Frieda's youth; he has supplanted K in her jealous affections. Process has estranged him, and estrangement leads him to Pepi, then to the examination by Buergel and Erlanger, then to Gerstaecker.

More and more K finds himself the center and ground of everyone's relations with the castle, changing all the time as he and everyone is changing. And they are his ground of change:

> "Then what did they miss doing?" asked the landlady. She was lying outstretched on her back now, gazing up at the ceiling.
> "To ask Klamm," said K.
> "So we're back at your case again," said the landlady.
> "Or at yours," said K. "Our affairs run parallel."

There is no cause in this plot; parallel lines meet only in infinity; cause is hidden and must happen before it is fully known. But by virtue of the fact that cause exists, by whatever retrospect, it remains present: it is both dream and reality, like the people wandering in winter clothes through this castle village. And everything leads back to the castle, is the temporal aspect of the castle. "This turmoil," Goodman says, "is so managed and so kept in motion by the protagonist's character that it can never come to an end."

Salvation is only provisional; the process itself is inexorable and melancholic. But to go outside the process is the negation of salvation:

> . . . it seemed to K as if at last those people had broken off all relations with him, and as if now in reality he were freer than he had ever been, and at liberty to wait here in this

place, usually forbidden to him, as long as he desired, and had won a freedom such as hardly anybody else had ever succeeded in winning, and as if nobody could dare to touch him or drive him away, or even speak to him; but—this conviction was at least equally strong—as if at the same time there was nothing more senseless, nothing more hopeless, than this freedom, this waiting, this inviolability.

This is the end of a chapter. At the beginning of the next, ". . . he tore himself free and went back into the house—this time not along the wall, but straight through the snow—and in the hall met the landlord, who greeted him in silence and pointed toward the door of the taproom. K followed the hint, for he was shivering and wanted to see human faces." Here he is in the process of learning, of confirming what Gerstaecker already knew: that the meaning is so bound up with process as to be not yet: he is learning how foolish was his discourse seven chapters earlier:

> "I'm surprised that you have the nerve to drive me round on your own responsibility. Are you allowed to do that?" Gerstaecker paid no attention but went on walking quietly beside the little horse. "Hi!" cried K, scraping some snow from the sledge and flinging a snowball, which hit Gerstaecker full in the ear. That made him stop and turn round; but when K saw him at such close quarters—the sledge had slid forward a little—this stooping and somehow ill-used figure with the thin, red, tired face and cheeks that were different—one being flat and the other fallen in—standing listening with his mouth open, displaying only a few isolated teeth, he found that what he had just said out of malice had to be repeated out of pity, that is whether Gerstaecker was likely to be penalized for driving him. "What do you mean?" asked Gerstaecker uncomprehendingly; but without waiting for an answer he spoke to the horse and they moved on again.

And K moves on to the point where he will become what all along he should be, a mainstay to Gerstaecker. His role is to seek his role; in this sense he is, the more gloriously though only metaphorically, a land-surveyor (the less perceptive villagers have never heard of this job title). This role's pain is a spiritual training course, and its absurdity, its radical incompletion, is only the stigma of human limitation. K's hope knows its full freedom in the consequence of despair. The allegory refuses to mediate between its detail and the significance of detail, because that would limit this vision of K's freedom by giving him a certitude, even a certitude of pain. This certitude critics who cannot face his heroism invent for him. But as Kierkegaard says of Abraham's problem, "We are confronted by a paradox which is higher than all mediation."

"The story of Abraham," he continues, "contains therefore a teleological suspension of the ethical. As the individual he became higher than the universal. This is the paradox which does not permit of mediation. It is just as inexplicable how he got into it as it is inexplicable how he remained in it. If such is not the position of Abraham, then he is not even a tragic hero but a murderer." The ethical and its universal are also transcended by Kafka's fictive Abraham in *The Castle*. Kafka refrains from giving the allegory a schematic key, from providing the limiting mediation. Thus can K be, in the phrase of Kierkegaard which Goodman stresses, a "knight of infinity." In the terms of the novel this must be so, for otherwise *The Castle* would be the diabolical hallucination of gloom some critics take it to be, a kind of super-Calvinistic supplement to *In the Penal Colony*. As Kierkegaard again puts it, "So either there is a paradox, that the individual stands in an absolute relation to the absolute, or Abraham is lost."

But Kafka's novels are more than an illustration of Kierkegaard, though *The Trial*, the least profound of the three, is barely more; though *Amerika*'s superabundance of free incident almost floats it away from theological romance into the picaresque. In *The Castle*, Kierkegaard's system becomes a vision of appearance and reality through the dreaminess of the plot's causality, through the marvelously rendered village and its inhabitants, through the poetic detail at moments of intensity, through the controlled pace, at once inexorable and dilatory, itself an insight into the way lived time can seem.

As Blanchot puts it, "Self-knowledge (in the religious sense) is one of the modes of our condemnation: we only raise ourselves by it, but it alone prevents us from raising ourselves; before we attain it, it is the necessary way; afterward, it is the insurmountable obstacle. This venerable idea, which comes from the Cabbala, by which our loss is seen as our salvation and vice versa, may perhaps help us understand why art can succeed where intellect fails: it is that which is not true enough to become the way, too unreal to change itself into an obstacle. Art is an 'as if.' "

A mythical plot evokes theology almost automatically, as in a romance like *Wuthering Heights*, where characters are half-schematized into the Satanic. The meaning of fuller theological romance, Kafka and Melville, is achieved through the reference of the symbols and the symbolic action to the moral categories envisioned thereby.

Without more or less explicit moral theology, romance must provide its own significance, and to that end it multiplies detail. The beginnings of fictional romance provide us with the alternatives: either the structure of *Don Quixote* or the extensive documentation of Rabelais. An untheological romance finds its insight in a vast documentation which the plot coordinates. One type of union between documentation and myth is provided by Balzac's use of history as rhetoric. Peacock surrounds his comedy of humors, a satire so close to drama that it continually breaks into dramatic form, with a learned documentation which both characterizes his quirky people and provides a shimmering appearance in which they may play out their reality. His romance is to Jane Austen as Kafka's is to Dostoevsky.

In the romance of *Finnegans Wake* the reference of
the allegory is back to itself, back at the same time to a vast
range of historical incident which the documentation has
included in the novel. The portmanteau words are the
mechanism of this analogy. Their distortion becomes a
convex mirror which makes every incident in this novel infinitely analogical to every other. "Sir Tristram, violer
d'amores," in its sequence, identifies HCE with the lover
of Isolde, with Sterne's protagonist, and so on (and any
with any other, or any pair, or any triad, and so on).
"Violer d'amores" makes rape (violate) the same as seduction (playing the viola); thus an ancient musical instrument,
and by analogy its whole historical period, enters the comparison. This process is literally infinite. But vast documentation and infinitely self-schematizing romance are only one
pair of partners, one comic alternative. *Finnegans Wake*
is a limit for romance, though it has not thereby exhausted
the possibilities of the genre.

XIII

PLATITUDE, SENTIMENT, AND VISION

The observational character of fictional language makes novels less composed than poems. It is quality of language more than length or scope that makes even the *Odyssey* more composed than even a story by Chekov. Thus in fiction the observations, coming through less entirely than in the tense conjunctions of poetic statement, are not so dependent on unifying emotional context. Novels may employ sentimentality as a way of observation, while poems may not. It is very hard for a successful poem, through its necessarily formal (and rhythmic) literary surface, to contain a tone of direct sentiment without abstracting it: Dostoevsky and Dickens use sentiment to heighten the intensity of their jeremiads against injustice, whereas in the equally sad, equally scarifying poetic prophecies of Jeremiah, the poetry controls the sentiment into a kind of objectivity. We are as sad in Jeremiah as in Dostoevsky (who often quotes him); but the poetry puts our sadness at one remove.

"Un immense bonhomme, mais de second ordre," Flaubert said of Balzac, led perhaps to this conclusion by Balzac's platitude and sentimentality. One can search Balzac's work in vain for the perceptions about spiritual differences we find in Henry James or Chekov or Dostoevsky or Turgenev, for profound social subtleties (not mere gradations)

like those exhibited by Jane Austen or Trollope, for motives explored as in Stendhal's novels or *Adolphe,* even for
the depths of Hardy's or Gide's unifying concepts; for
that sensitivity to human situations which is given us consistently by a score of living novelists. One could, in fact,
define where the themes of all these novelists begin as
where Balzac leaves off. "La transformation des choses et
des hommes en bigoterie est un mystère inexplicable"—a
"mystère" another novelist might have tackled.

The platitude of Balzac's single plots is served by an
equal platitude of style. His novels are as full of aphorisms
as Tacitus, but they reflect a wisdom akin to that of a village gossip, as many of his plots are stories a gossip might
include in her repertory.

This platitude is not simply a limitation in Balzac
(though we must admit it to be that); it is a consequence of
the historical style. Direct statement, through Balzac's unity
of theme and fidelity to the historical *parti pris,* becomes
itself a rhetorical device, a giant trope, unnoticed because
universal in *La Comédie Humaine.*

Balzac, as Flaubert's predecessor, is like Homer naive
only in retrospect. His tropes and images are merely illustrative as in the style of a historian. I should like to examine
his platitude and his sentiment in this passage from *Modeste
Mignon:*

> Jean Butscha, pauvre enfant naturel abandonné, de qui
> le greffier Labrosse et sa fille avaient pris soin, devenu pre-
> mier clerc à force de travail, logé, nourri chez son patron
> qui lui donne neuf cents francs d'appointements, sans aucun
> semblant de jeunesse, presque nain, faisait de Modeste une
> idole, il eût donné sa vie pour elle. Ce pauvre être, dont les
> yeux semblables à deux lumières de canon sont pressés entre
> des paupières épaisses, marqué de la petite-vérole, écrasé par
> une chevelure crépue, embarrassé de ses mains énormes, vivait
> sous les regards de la pitié depuis l'âge de sept ans: ceci ne
> peut-il pas vous l'expliquer tout entier? Silencieux, recueilli,
> d'une conduite exemplaire, religieux, il voyageait dans l'im-

mense étendue du pays appelé, sur la carte de Tendre,
Amour-sans-espoir, les steppes arides et sublimes du Désir.

(Jean Butscha, poor illegitimate foundling, whom the
clerk Labrosse and his daughter had taken care of, became
first clerk through hard work, boarding with his employer
who paid him nine hundred francs a year, with no trace of
youth, nearly a dwarf; idolised Modeste; he would have
given his life for her. This poor creature, whose eyes like
two cannon flashes were crammed between thick eyelids,
marked by smallpox, crushed by thick hair, embarrassed
by his enormous hands, had lived under pitying eyes since
the age of seven: does not this fact wholly explain him to
you? Silent, composed, of exemplary conduct, religious, he
travelled the immense extent of the country called, on the
map of Tenderness, Love-without-hope, the arid and sublime
steppes of Desire.)

Balzac does not render Butscha as Flaubert rendered the
clubfoot in Madame Bovary. He is created by a series of
evocations.

Platitude spills over into sentiment. Our sympathy is
aroused as gratuitously as in a charity folder, right at the
start with "pauvre enfant naturel abandonné." The rhythm
of the expressed emotion almost sinks under "il eût donné
sa vie pour elle," catching its breath after the pause with
a repetition of the first phrase's evocation in "ce pauvre
être." Balzac, with his virtues, is not the kind of novelist
who makes analysis and scene effective enough to do his
work; for them he substitutes a mere rhetorical question
(does not Butscha's history explain him?), and mytholo-
gizes Butscha by locating him on the *carte de Tendre*.

But Balzac's plot, like his style, takes on an exaggera-
tion from the wrenching of particular person or house to
the general. The obviousness of the references to the over-
all scheme gives plot and style the air of platitude.

Fiction tends to use idea. For Balzac, as for Dostoevsky
and Dickens, sentimentality is the direct emotion accom-

panying a social platitude. His narrating sentiment is the solvent of the more intense, splendidly fictive emotions of Pons or Vautrin or Rosalie de Wattville or de Rubempré. Pons's acid, Max de Gilence's alkali, become diffused through the whole *Comédie* by the narrator's stream of sentiment. No doubt Balzac would have been a better novelist than he (or anyone else) is, if he had only purged his style of heavy-handed obviousness. As it is, his clumsiness is so fused with his theme as to be a partial success.

Dickens' sentimentality allows him to get an easy—at times too easy—emotional dimension into his characters. Santayana seconds Gissing in warning us against reading them as caricatures, though they are so hallucinatory that they would seem to be either caricatures or of such insubstantial stuff that they scarcely have more roundness than what E. M. Forster (*Aspects of the Novel*) allows Mr. Pickwick. ("It is a conjuring trick; at any moment we may look at Mr. Pickwick edgeways and find him no thicker than a gramophone record.") The eye that could so recreate the world as to give the London fog almost palpable presence in the lives of *Bleak House*, that could bake Miss Havisham's fantastic wedding cake, was procreative of people who seek dimly and fantastically, through the faery labyrinth of the modern city, the substance of their lives. Often in *Great Expectations, Bleak House, Martin Chuzzlewit, The Old Curiosity Shop*, the substance is a hidden parentage, an obscured connection, involving perhaps some miraculous treasure like a pot of gold at the end of the book which has been rainbowing around it. What distorts the people is their secret lives, their pregnant gestures, the fantastic reality of their illusion. And this world, through the illusions of the people who move in it, is pervaded by gigantic fantasy. Sally Brass removes from the safe "a dreary waste of cold potatoes, looking as eatable as Stonehenge." It seems almost more than a metaphor when Mr. Merdle's physician says of that suicide-to-be financier, "He has the constitution of a rhinoceros, the digestion of an ostrich, and the concentration of an oyster." Dickens' sentimentality puffs the illusion; it creates the fog, the shades of the prison house in *Little Dorrit*, the hallucinatory rationalism of Gradgrind and Bounderby. For Dickens even hard cash has something supernatural about it, something other than even the philosophical integers of money in Balzac: money in Dickens is either paradisal in its power or crusted and begrimed with an evil as dank as that of the embankment where Bill Sikes meets his filthy death.

The sentimentality gives Dickens' style an almost poetic refinement, as Robert Liddell strikingly shows by printing a passage as if it were Jacobean verse:

> Which, Mr. Chuzzlewit, is well beknown to Mrs. Harris
> As has one sweet infant (though she *do* not wish it known)
> In her own family by the mother's side,
> Kep' in spirits in a bottle;
> And that sweet babe she sees at Greenwich Fair,
> A travelling in company with the pink-eyed lady, Prooshan
>   dwarf, and living skelinton,
> Which judge her feelin's when the barrel-organ played,
> And she was showed her own dear sister's child,
> The same not bein' expected from the outside picter,
> Where it was painted quite contrairy in a livin' state,
> A many sizes larger,
> And performing beautiful upon the Arp,
> Which never did that dear child know or do;
> Since breathe it never did, to speak on, in this wale
> And Mrs. Harris, Mr. Chuzzlewit,
> Has knowed me many a year, and can give you information
> That the lady which is widdered can't do better
> And may do worse than let me wait upon her,
> Which I hope to do.
> Permittin' the sweet faces as I see afore me.

Here sentiment is the instrument of insight, beautifully clean in its designations; in its rhetoric and associations it is far from the drugged bathos of blind sentimentality.

Sentimentality serves the plot of a Dickens novel, as well as the style. His plots manipulate the emotions of the audience in such a way as to reveal the underlying disposition, and therefore connection, of the involved characters. In *The Old Curiosity Shop*, for example, Dick Swiveller responds to the pressure of a feeling about the good which he scarcely understands in any analytic sense, as Sally Brass holds up like a pillar of salt and Sampson Brass gives way like a block of poisoned mush in the heat of feeling. The cause of Little Nell's death seems, quite simply— more than that her grail wandering on the countryside presages death—that the feelings released, and therefore played out, at the exculpation of Kit and death of Quilp, have left her remote. The obscure causal world of Dickens' perception is governed by sentiment, and for Little Nell, as for us, death is the only meaningful end, even though the poetic justice of allowing her to live would be more in accord with traditional sentimentality. Dickens' own sentimentality acts as a mode of perception. It would capitulate to readers' demands in everything but its own felt rightness.[1] Thus, too, David Copperfield leaves the Murdstones, and is left by them, because they are, in feeling, intolerable. Likewise the pressure brought to bear by Uriah Heep on Mr. Wickfield is intolerable, and (therefore) the result of fraudulent *feeling* on Uriah's part; embezzlement is the consequence, not the cause, of this feeling. And the mass exodus to Australia of Peggoty, Little Emily, Martha, and the Micawbers, takes place because England is intolerable, not because all of them could not somehow make out there. Dickens' sentiment creates the feeling, which is the felt

---

[1] Except in the case of *Great Expectations*, whose altered ending I find, with other critics, inferior to the original one.

motive for the happenings in his novels (as in no others).

The sentimental unreality of the plot is a means of showing the illusory quality of a world very real. Dickens, read without a view to his intuitive delicacy, is heavy-handed; read for his true meaning (often, it would seem obscured to himself) he is incomparably deft and light. This meaning relates with sufficient observed insight to the real world to have served to reform education and poor laws and the courts of chancery. But Dickens' social concern is only the context of a fantasy that shows the nightmare of evil and the dream of good, rather than their Dostoevskian psychological action in waking life.

His fund of characterization, then, is not the great gift in a void which it is often assumed to be. The characters are profound and sharply visioned not because Dickens has mysteriously caricatured them by some hobbyish gift but because they belong to a world of hallucination equally profound and vivid. This world is a fictive world, one that in its unique way envisions the illusion in reality through the melting and distorting lens of sentimentalism.

Dreiser's platitude in its idea of life chemistry recalls Balzac's "chemistry of the will"; Dreiser's sentimentality has the same ring, perhaps partly derives from Dickens'. The reality of Dreiser's world, however, plots itself on a straight, rather conventional, line and not analogically as in Balzac. Sentimentality is not put to Dickens' fantasizing, but to the work of transmogrifying reality into a more petrified version of itself. Dreiser's sentiment is not air-launching but earth-binding. Exaggerating a character's attitudes and actions makes the character massive:

> In a tremulous state of dissatisfaction with himself—
> that any such grisly thought should have dared to obtrude
> itself upon him in this way—he got up and lit the lamp—
> re-read this disconcerting item in as cold and reprobative

way as he could achieve, feeling that in so doing he was putting anything at which it hinted far from him once and for all. Then, having done so, he dressed and went out of the house for a walk—up Wykeagy Avenue, along Central Avenue, out Oak, and then back on Spruce and to Central again —feeling that he was walking away from the insinuating thought or suggestion that had so troubled him up to now. And after a time, feeling better, freer, more natural, more human, as he so much wished to feel—he returned to his room, once more to sleep, with the feeling that he had actually succeeded in eliminating completely a most insidious and horrible visitation. He must never think of it again! He must never think of it again. He must never, never, never think of it—never.

"Poets, like lovers, must be bold and dare." Dreiser lumbers through these platitudes of analysis, amassing clichés into over-all insight. In a sense, he suffers, like Hawthorne, from a provincial style. But take away that style, and what happens to the fictive grandeur of Clyde Griffiths and Sister Carrie, Frank Cowperwood and Eugene Witlaw? In this passage, as in Balzac, the gross obviousness of Clyde's reaction to the first thought of murder takes Antaean strength from his specific situation, from Lycurgus (as earlier from Chicago, and, at the very end, San Francisco). The documentative list of streets serves to link his feelings to this scene: it is "an *American* tragedy." America makes Clyde Griffiths, or any of Dreiser's protagonists, a Paul Bunyan of the moral life. The crude massiveness of Dreiser's style apes the crude massiveness of the America in which he was himself successful as a journalist. America is made present in his novels through the platitudinous style, through the realism of his documentation, as France is made present in the novels of Balzac, though without Balzac's depth or extent. His plots are so usual, indeed, that without his deplored style Dreiser, for all his knowledge of character, would be far less striking as a novelist. Like other novelists, he cannot only succeed against his own platitude and sentiment, but harness them to substantiate his meaning.

XIV

THE LIFE OF FICTION

In order to envision a process in fiction, the novelist must have lived far enough, or intensely enough, into process in reality to see a real moral life taking shape behind social appearances. Defoe and Cervantes began writing fiction even later in life than Proust. Hemingway began writing young, but not before having lived through the First World War. The sea for Melville, journalism and disease for Stephen Crane, were an unusually early ordeal. Fitzgerald could succeed young by virtue of the precious and extravagantly sacrificial paradigm he made of the life that furnished his material. The young Radiguet and Alain-Fournier confine themselves to adolescence or fantasy. After the minor achievement of *A Portrait of the Artist as a Young Man*, whose composition Joyce was forced to spread out over ten years, he developed not only technique but the concrete experience which would enable him to write *Ulysses*; confronting Stephen with Bloom took as long as building style and inventing the *Odyssey* analogy.

It must be his own secret life that the novelist observes; its process of social manifestation then becomes the pattern of his books, which he must build observation by observation. He translates his other, pre-novelistic, life into the life of his books more directly than do the poet and the dramatist. It is as much a rule for them to professionalize from the time they come of age as it is a rule for the novelist to bide his time.

The actor Shakespeare of the *Sonnets* feels an anguish of distance between himself and the noblemen who more closely resemble Lear, Othello, Prospero, even Hamlet. The out-at-elbows sharper Malory lives in a different world from Launcelot. Cervantes, though, projects in Don Quixote the idealism of his own aging self. Literature and life become the dimension of appearance and reality for Don Quixote because they have been so for his creator.

The private implications of social life occupy the novelist: it is his own secret life that he writes about, and this secrecy is at once something private and something necessarily social. The poet, by contrast, publicizes his ideas—if, like the Romantics, he publicizes his life at all. Aristotle speaks not at all of the poet's life, and Plato's *Ion* so generalizes it that it bears less direct resemblance to the process of social existence. Cowper and Crabbe, in the low pitch of their verse as in their private subject matter, seem close to fiction. Wordsworth in *The Prelude* is silent about Annette Vallon; Keats translates Fanny Brawne into an idealized silence. Maud Gonne appears in the poems of Yeats, but as a moral lesson and a type. Hoelderlin in his own existence lives out the plot of *La Nouvelle Héloïse*, but in the poetry his love becomes a Diotima idealized as elusively as Dante's Beatrice; Stendhal, whose secret life was perhaps to have missed this plot, turns a more concrete version of it into the fiction of *Le Rouge et le Noir*.

In the privacy of his writing condition, the novelist tends to attain a public self unlike that of dramatist or poet. The silently expanding circle of readers, holding the novel in a thousand solitary armchairs, conjures up an image of the novelist who likewise sits in his solitary room heaping up the pages of his vision of experience—and writing against a deadline, or even for a serial, occasionally knowing at the point of publication little more about the sequel than the public itself does. This experience is unknown to the dramatist, who must collaborate with actors and a present

audience, to the poet who has impersonality. The real
Byron is at once less known for himself and less concealed
in his work than the real Dickens. Normally the vast audience which is available to the novelist either ignores the
poet or adores his idealized person.

The industrial revolution, which isolated the individual
and complicated society, raised the novel's conditions a
pitch higher: observation became more ramified, privacy
and subjectivity more total.

The city, in a word, haunted fiction, and became the
supreme subject of fiction. Flaubert and Proust are un-
thinkable without Paris, Stendhal without Milan and Rome,
Kafka without Prague, Tolstoi and Dostoevsky without
Petersburg and Moscow, Joyce without Dublin, James
without international life, Chekov and Turgenev without
cosmopolis. Spengler is not the first to notice that the novel
is a characteristically megalopolitan form—the communion
of swarming privacies, the surface play of idea over that
constellation of objectified motives we call a metropolis.
Even George Eliot's provincial life is really the province
invaded by what amounts to London sophistication. And
the national life of Faulkner's county seat is the key dimension of its local life. Even when Harvard or Chicago or
Heidelberg are referred to, what Faulkner's characters
confront is the post-Civil War urbanization of national life.
Melville's whalers are setting up an ideal, against an urban
industrial development, as Charles Olson (*Call Me Ishmael*)
points out; whaling as big business. And Ishmael sets out
from the Manhattan where first Pierre and then Melville
himself end up. The Mississippi of *The Confidence Man*
is invaded by the metropolitan types, which Huck and Jim
are as yet the one too young and the other too lowly to encounter—till much of the way down the river.

The cosmopolite has lost at once a sense of community and a fixed moral ethos. So anguishing can be the novelist's observation of the protean forms of city life, so bewildering the lack of moral categories, that the city novelist like Dickens or Dostoevsky may be ridden all his life by excruciating if heuristic psychological handicap. Petersburg drives Gogol mad, into the arms of religious fanaticism. Who knows but that the Gogol-like Kafka was moving in his last Berlin isolation toward a banal Zionism which would have clinched his wish to destroy his novels? Dostoevsky, more harrowed denizen of Gogol's metropolis of white nights, is strong enough to include the truth of religion in his fictive vision, and actually so is Kafka. But Tolstoi, bolstered though he was by the aristocrat's sense of community in Moscow and Petersburg, allowed his vision of appearance and reality to transmogrify into a fanatic castigation of appearance. Even this supreme moralist among novelists succumbed to the flux he had once controlled: the partially reasonable claims of his social religion cannot obscure the perversity of their maker.

The dramatist Racine's conversion first from great secular plays and then from the stage in general; the poet La Fontaine's penitential assumption of a hair shirt during the last year of his life—these react not to the instability of their art form, as Gogol and Tolstoi seem to be reacting to the evanescence and urban solitude of fiction. Racine felt the social role of the theatre to be pernicious; La Fontaine, his subject matter to be frivolous. Racine and La Fontaine are penitential as men; Gogol and Tolstoi go insane perhaps partly because of the instability of appearance and reality in the root condition of their art.

Writing more or less explicitly about his own life, the novelist tends to autobiography. Henry Miller and Céline simply transcribe artistically their observed experience. In writers like Proust autobiography can itself become a formal part of the novel's structure.

In the tension between life and work we do not always find the formal finish of the very greatest novels. "The cult of experience" in a romantic novelist like Thomas Wolfe has intoxication with actuality substitute for vision. The writer who is impassioned over the inductive implications of his fictional observations, or over the paradigmatic character of his own life, pushes the formal art of fiction into extreme, if legitimate, shapes. D. H. Lawrence lives his books and lives beyond his books. Henry Miller, not accidentally one of Lawrence's most sympathetic critics, degenerates from autobiographical novelist to chronicler and pamphleteer.

Gide's hesitations, and his partial failures—especially the characteristic failure of reflexivity in *Les Faux Monnayeurs*—spring from too direct an identification of fiction with its necessary preliminary experience. As Blanchot says (*La Part du Feu*) Gide's novels are a "littérature d'expérience," stages of his moral life: "Artist or creator of his own life . . . he is entirely at the disposition of the *experience* to which he surrenders himself, and yet he does not push it far enough to make anything else impossible; in the end he always meets, in the moment of forgetting himself, the moment that recalls him to himself, and at the extreme point of innovation the sanction of a traditional rule; in the strangest boldness of spirit, he meets a regret and a taste for measure and equilibrium." *Expérience* in French means both experience and experiment; but the novel must model its experience beyond experiment. Thus, "Gide is the meeting place for two conceptions of literature: that of traditional art which values most highly a delight in producing masterworks; and that of literature as experiment which throws 'works' to the wind and is prepared to ruin itself to attain the unattainable."

D. H. Lawrence campaigns for a resacramentalization of the process of personal relations, distorting the form of his novels. Malraux makes of the novel's observed events a mirror of, and a program for, political reality. As again Blanchot succinctly puts it, in words which apply most aptly to *L'Espoir* (which is his immediate subject), "Malraux's novels are not novels: they are at once too close to their author and too close to events, too closed on a single being and too dissipated through the actuality of the world." Still, we recognize this excessive privacy, and excessive publicity, not for something unfictional, as Blanchot would have it, but for a limit to fiction itself, necessary to novels which are to "see and describe," as Blanchot continues, "the most important events, those which reveal his epoch and decide the future . . . but the movement of this interior universe coincides with that of history; in its own way it also creates history, that is the direction of history." Malraux in his novels turns history's process of metamorphosis into a kind of fictive art, and he has gone on to interpret visual art in the light of historical metamorphosis. His life, too, is more than his novels, and that excess determines the conditions of his writing, bringing them so close to the limits of the genre that Blanchot can call them not novels at all.

On the very limit itself of the novel's generic disposition to let its creator live an excessive parable are the writings of that *aventurier* whose life Malraux finds so archetypical, T. E. Lawrence. The ambiguity of his life (did he act to write or write to record action?) reflects exactly that of his work. Is *The Mint* a novel? And what is the nature of the relation between historiography and personal experience in *The Seven Pillars of Wisdom*? Is it a historical novel à la Henry Miller and Malraux, or a piece of history? This question is radically ambiguous, because in Lawrence we find the point at which history and fiction meet.

That they do so in his writing is significant, because

Lawrence's life is an anguished parable of ideological conditions archetypical of the fictive mind and of what writes fiction, the modern temper.

T. E. Lawrence, more sophisticated than Henry Miller and Thomas Wolfe, realizes, like Goethe in *Dichtung und Wahrheit,* the necessarily artificial, because selective, character of autobiography. Yet Valéry's malaise attacks him: ("If I say Duchess F went up the stairs in a fiction, and I mean Duchess G, I am already lying.") He is comfortable only in the narration of fact, feeling at the same time, like all the romantic autobiographers from Rousseau on, that the sequence of his life has extraordinary meaning.

While Rimbaud left splendid artifices realized as unmagical behind him in his past and probably thought of his rejection as a talisman of superiority both to the writers left in Paris and to the blacks with whom he traded, Lawrence thought of his inability to produce splendid artifices as a humbling limitation on all his action.

In the unity of his acts and his writings, for all his lack of the wilder romantic errors (literature as magic-artifice or gospel-reality), he exhibits in a pure, almost desperate, form, the sundering tensions of fictive ideas. This is the irony of the triumph of *The Seven Pillars,* the agony of his minting.

As an autobiographer Lawrence agonizes between "I can't write it, because in literature such things haven't ever been, and can't be. To record the acts of Hut 12 would produce . . . not a work of art but a document," and "The irony was in my loving objects before life or ideas. . . . It was a hard task for me to straddle feeling and action; I had one craving all my life—for the power of self-expression in some imaginative form—but had been too diffuse ever to acquire a technique. At last accident, with perverted humour, in casting me as a man of action, had given me a place in the Arab Revolt, a theme ready and epic to a direct eye and hand, thus offering me an outlet in literature, the techniqueless art. Whereupon I became excited only over mechanism. Memory gave me no clue to the heroic." The modesty of the second statement is curious if compared with his painstaking composition of *The Seven Pillars*, and if he believes the first statement, written from the Air Force, why did he write *The Mint*? Lawrence tries to assert and deny at the same time the genius order and his membership in it. Which did he believe? Both ambivalently and neither. In his imagination he held partial belief, just as in his action he held partial involvement.

The state of partial belief in idea, or partial involvement in action, vacillates between the reality of our common humanity and the illusion of the difference of the genius order. Among alien people partial involvement comes easy, if only because total involvement is impossible; a craving for such superiority, perhaps, helped to draw young Lawrence first to the ideal past of Crusader castles, then as a traveler to the Near East, then into direct contact with the alien Arab Revolt (which he was able to join, he says, by deliberately antagonizing his colleagues in Egypt so that they would be anxious for him to leave), then as an emissary to Versailles who gave up all action as humanly relative when he found that his pure purposes were compromised by the wills of others, then briefly as a projected publisher of fine editions, then as an author who refused the human limitations of fame and the necessity of money, then as a private in the Air Force, committing "mind-suicide," holding himself there "till the burnt child no longer feels the fire," seeking, like a god, freedom from the past which one might imagine could have furnished his novelistic material. Finally there was scrupulous anonymity, peace in what he called a secular equivalent to monasticism, in the society of the disillusioned and the precision of working with photographs, machine tools, speedboats.

"I did not believe finally in the Arab Movement," he says, and the reason is repeatedly given. He feels, and is, superior to the Arabs, even in his primitive admiration of their "intuition which left our centrifugal minds gasping." "They knew only truth and untruth, belief and unbelief, without our hesitating retinue of finer shades." Is this praise or blame? Both at once, in the ambiguity of a partial belief which made him feel always like an actor among the Arabs, "my sham leadership a crime," "the godless fraud inspiring an alien nationality," "the event for me sorrowful and the phrase meaningless."

So he felt about the Air Force. "Do you ever feel like a unicorn strayed among sheep?" he said after examining his motives in a letter. "Angels, I think, we imagine. Beasts, I think, we are. And I like the beasts for their kindliness and honesty, without really managing to make myself quite like them." In the famous Chapter C of *The Seven Pillars* he probes his own motives through the comparison of himself with the sacrificed Savior. Lawrence was both immolating his active and intellectual powers to his pride, and, unlike most romantics, scrutinizing his own fallacies. In the power of that scrutiny, beyond even Rimbaud's (though Lawrence is the lesser writer), his excellence lies. He has the honesty of a saint in admitting his diabolical fallacies, and in this virtual confession we have what verges on autobiographical fiction.

The metaphorical correlatives of his illusion—the evanescent appearances of reality—we find in the frequent mirage or mirage-like images of *The Seven Pillars:* "The irrational tenth was like the kingfisher flashing across the pool, and in it lay the test of generals," "The road was bestial with locusts, though from a distance they looked beautiful, silvering the air with the shimmer of their wings," and "But when at last we anchored in the outer harbour, off the white town hung between the blazing sky and its reflection in the mirage which swept and rolled over the wide lagoon, then the heat of Arabia came out like a drawn sword and struck us speechless."

He interprets the sword for us in a letter, "The sword was odd. The Arab Movement was one: Feisal another (his name means a flashing sword); then there is the excluded notion, Garden of Eden touch; and the division meaning, like the sword in the bed of mixed sleeping, from the Morte d'Arthur . . . and the sword also means clean-ness [hyphen Lawrence's] and death."

The sword was odd indeed that could identify cleanness and death. This identity is realized also in those Blackmur (*The Expense of Greatness*) shows us in his writing, as between subsistence and the stuff of life, leisure and death, etc. Blackmur has well qualified Lawrence's literary achievement: ". . . the weakness is basic only; and in the worlds of the mind what is basic is not necessarily conclusive, what totters at the bottom does not always fall; the towers of imagination fling up, like Lawrence's active pains and joys, out of quicksand and stand firm in light and air. It may be there is a type of imagination, of which Lawrence would be an exemplar, incapable equally of the bottom reality and the top ideal, yet tortured by both, which exhibits its strength solely in the actual confronting world —the flux—and is confounded only in those terminals which, so to speak, it could never reach." "In Lawrence the intention everywhere counts, which is to say is questionable, uncomposed." That is, in my terms, his being at once a novelist and not a novelist is both his weakness and his strength.

Lawrence's failure of action is the breach between his purpose and his act due to the shifting of the purpose itself: reality's process was so evasive that one could not recognize its appearances. The corresponding breach in his writings is the failure to integrate, to "compose" as Blackmur says, which causes him to verge on the enumerative and the anecdotal. Blackmur notes that he did not quite ever create a character, "not even his own." And he envied David Garnett most for his ability to write novels.

Why else than because he himself felt this breach did he hyphenate the word "clean-ness"?

A breach exists between two sides. These two sides in *The Seven Pillars* and *The Mint* are the closely observed natural detail and the moral generalization, both almost obsessively characteristic of Lawrence's writing, as of fictional statement. They always combine or become interchangeable in achieved fiction. Lawrence keeps them separate, preserving the unfiction of his fictional material. Detail never becomes analogy, moralization never points toward plot.

Observed natural detail and moral generalization almost pull asunder, too, in the novels of Hemingway and Céline. The succession of nearly repetitive events in *The Seven Pillars* has no parallel more close than the structure of Hemingway's early novels. Yet Hemingway's observed natural detail integrates better than Lawrence's; and his moral perspective always enters his work as a structural element, whereas it confuses Lawrence's artistic attitude. Hemingway's certitude is aesthetically superior, if morally inferior, to Lawrence's vacilliation.

The minting never takes place in *The Mint;* it never rises to fiction; though Lawrence's style has improved since *The Seven Pillars,* the degeneration of his choice implicit in the self-generating progress of his confusion was mirrored in his autobiographical writing as a solipsistic concern with anecdotes and individual landscapes. The moral observation operates as powerfully as ever, but in a vacuum; he ironically notes that corporateness is the only spiritual quality of a military unit, and yet he fails to express the growth of that corporateness which was his book's stated purpose, as the title announces it. The duality between body (observed natural detail) and spirit (moral generalization) was felt as an obsession rather than unified in writing.

We do have a marginal unity in *The Mint,* between moral passion and detailed observation, but surely Lawrence was capable of a greater unity even than the one Céline

realizes in the similar *Mort à Crédit*. If Lawrence had succeeded, he would surely have left a literary monument
whose peculiar fictive unions would be worthy of comparison with the strange, powerful junction of lushness with
martyrdom that Fromentin notes in certain paintings of Ru-
bens; with the poetic union of calm and violent images
in *Pericles* and *Cymbeline*. And the literary achievement,
the recorded action, we actually possess of Lawrence is so
painfully heroic that we are perhaps unable to say with
any finality that the element of failure is the man's fault and
not the time's.

D. H. Lawrence, T. E. Lawrence, Malraux, live beyond
their fiction, making it something other than tightly constructed artifice. The way of excessive observation of the
private life is countered by the way of deprivation, that of
the novelists who in one way or another missed some of the
reality of their own life in order to give a generalized
vision of the private life's process. Perhaps because in the
Renaissance, and still more after the industrial revolution,
religion had become partly displaced into secular forms—
even into art—the novelist and his modern fellow the romantic poet must often immolate themselves almost religiously to deprivation: of rooted place (D. H. Lawrence,
Shelley, Byron), of a satisfying career (Stendhal, Samuel
Butler, Melville), of will and status (Proust, Coleridge),
of youthful development (Defoe, Fielding, Stendhal, Trollope), of stable childhood and mature confidence (Dostoevsky, Dickens), of respectability (Joyce, *les poètes maudits*),
of a public (Stendhal, Joyce, Kafka, Blake, Emily Dickinson) even of virtue (Proust, Baudelaire) and of sanity
(Tolstoi, Gogol, Hoelderlin). And there are many combinations of these deprivations which paradoxically enable
the novelist to envision the life he has missed experiencing.
    With a sure psychological sense for his needs, Balzac

engaged himself to a woman completely removed from the stream of the society he wrote about, a woman who wrote him from the private circle of his readers, beginning her correspondence through the public newspaper. Did Balzac sense in her someone whose peculiar personality would delay marriage by various subterfuges for years after the long awaited death of her husband? Balzac also saddled himself with debts through commercial speculation, unconsciously to gain material, and probably also out of the deeper necessity for a spur to writing, just as Dostoevsky gambled away his last resources and contracted himself involvedly against successive manuscript deadlines in order, perhaps, to create a condition for writing like the climate of his fiction. It is as if Balzac got himself into debt like that lesser historical novelist he admired, Walter Scott, because to write about the past imaginatively one must be mortgaged to one's own past.

His devotion to reconstructing the past involved Balzac in an extreme version of the paradox of observation by deprivation. Perched on his *butte*, saddled sixteen hours a day to his desk, he built up out of his seclusion from society an image of society's private interconnections. This is his most inexplicable condition, perhaps the secret of his life he said no one could probe, remarked first by Théophile Gautier and made so much of by James. "He did *not* live, save in his imagination, or by other aid than he could find there." [Italics James's.] Writing for practically all his waking hours over nearly all his maturity, he had "visibly no time for the real thing."

James, too, observed pastness from the depth of a missed life. "There is one thing," he said to an aspiring writer of fiction who later became a critic, "that, if you really intend to follow the course you indicate, I cannot too emphatically insist on. There is one word—let me impress upon you—which you must inscribe upon your banner, and that," he added after an impressive pause, "that word is

Loneliness." The vision of the "portentous intelligent stillness" exacted from its creator a silence in all but his literary
works; those literary works whose final condition of composition was to be uttered verbally to a secretary, the public
and the private joined in the single act. James sealed himself
off from the place of his birth and the significant congress
of his compeers into a fructifying deprivation similar to
that of his master.

In excess or deprivation, the novelist is thrown upon
his own life in a way no more demanding for him than for
other artists, but in a way whose peculiarity is influenced
by—and itself shapes—the art form he has chosen.

⚔ XV ⚔

THE INVISIBLE STILTS OF TIME

PROUST

Proust puts his own life, reflexively, at the center of his novel, *A la Recherche du Temps Perdu*. The work was so grafted onto the life that even after he had begun it, he altered its whole center of gravity, so far as can be judged, to include a new love affair. And he set a final section in a war that was still several years in the future when he had published his first section. The book grew as he did, and concerned itself with its own growth.

The Marcel of imagination converges with the Proust of real life in the double-I perspective of the novel. This reflexivity can only be ended or broken down if you say that Marcel decides in the novel to begin writing after the First World War, whereas Proust had begun beforehand. But this is to judge the imagined by reference to a literal event, which by definition it is not bound by.

What separates, and unites, imagination and reality is time; the aging Proust will be separated from the young Marcel until through the passage of time one joins and becomes the other. Thus time can be a real window on eternity, and at the same time a transitory appearance. The process of a secret life makes the appearance reality. Marcel is at once more deeply subjective—more of a reflector— than any character in fiction, including Strether, and more

282

objective—more objectified—than even the Flaubertian narrator which one side of Proust's technique makes him. "A la fois Joseph et Pharaon," Proust says, "je me mis à interpréter mon rêve."

The unity of the double perspective corresponds to time's victory over itself, that *le temps* is *retrouvé* in spite of all paradises being lost. In the single light of their seemingly uneventful temporality the characters can undergo sea change and assume gigantic stature; time serves, Proust says at the end, to "les faire ressembler à des êtres monstrueux."

The purpose of the recapitulating vision gives every sentence the generality and resonance of philosophical discourse, which it imitates, without losing the concreteness of fictive representation. The dialectic between subjective perception of the present and objective involuntary memory of the past inflates and deepens, abstracts and orchestrates, the novel's style; this surpasses the already Proustified passage imagined as being from the journal of the Brothers Goncourt, that passage which seemed so shallow as to make Marcel despair at once of the meaningfulness of literature and existence of his gift.

Here is the "journal cité," the pretended Goncourt description of *foie gras* and potato salad:

> Même le foie gras n'a aucun rapport avec la fade mousse qu'on sert habituellement sous ce nom, et je ne sais pas beaucoup d'endroits où la simple salade de pommes de terre est faite ainsi de pommes de terre ayant la fermeté de boutons d'ivoire japonais, le patiné de ces petites cuillers d'ivoire avec lesquelles les Chinoises versent l'eau sur le poisson qu'elles viennent de pêcher.

> (Even the *foie gras* had no relation to the pale paste usually served under that name, and I do not know many places where ordinary potato salad is made with potatoes as firm as Japanese ivory buttons and possessing a patina like that of those little ivory spoons the Chinese use to pour water on fish that has just been caught.)

This observer's eye, though clear and precise, lacks *pro-fondeur;* it substitutes for the aura of qualities in a Proustian description mere analogies with art objects; the Orientalism here serves as a kind of gratuitous rarefaction of the trivially poeticized food. Here, by contrast, is Proust's description of asparagus:

> . . . mais mon ravissement était devant les asperges, trempés d'outre-mer et de rose et dont l'épi, finement pignoché de mauve et d'azur, se dégrade insensiblement jusqu'au pied— encore souillé pourtant du sol de leur plant—par des irisa-tions qui ne sont pas de la terre. Il me semblait que ces nuan-ces célestes trahissaient les délicieuses créatures qui s'étaient amusées à se métamorphoser en légumes et qui, à travers le déguisement de leur chair comestible et ferme, laissaient aper-cevoir en ces couleurs naissantes d'aurore, en ces ébauches d'arc-en-ciel, en cette extinction de soirs bleus, cette essence précieuse que je reconnaissais encore quand, toute la nuit qui suivait un dîner où j'en avais mangé, elles jouaient, dans leurs farces poétiques et grossières comme une féerie de Shakespeare, à changer mon pot de chambre en un vase de parfum.

> (. . . but what fascinated me would be the asparagus, tinged with ultramarine and rosy pink which ran from their heads, finely stippled in mauve and azure, through a series of im-perceptible changes of their white feet, still stained a little by the soil of their garden-bed: a rainbow-loveliness that was not of this world. I felt that these celestial hues indicated the presence of exquisite creatures who had been pleased to as-sume vegetable form, who, through the disguise which cov-ered their firm and edible flesh, allowed me to discern in this radiance of earliest dawn, these rough sketches of rainbows, this extinction of blue evenings, that precious essence which I should recognize again when, all night long after a dinner at which I had partaken of them, they played, lyrical and coarse in their jesting as the fairies in Shakespeare's *Dream*, at transforming my chamber pot into a vessel of perfume.)

Marcel sees the asparagus first of all through his "ravisse-ment," itself an emotion reflecting through the lost paradise of time; and the rhythm of his description is impregnated with the novel's high nostalgia. Allusion to eternity is explicit in "irisations qui ne sont pas de la terre," in "nuances célestes"; it is hinted also in "azur," "essence précieuse," "farces poétiques et grossières comme une féerie de Shakespeare," "ébauches d'arc-en-ciel," and perhaps also in the association of religious asperging, which the French "asperges" would suggest. The eye of the impressionist painter, a like exalter of process, informs this description. Time vivifies these vegetables beyond those denoted with such lifeless precision in the journal of the Goncourts, just as the "réalistes" of such journals—and novels—are, Proust asserts, the least realistic of all, reality being shrivelled to mockery without the necessary dimension of time; the merely denoted is "comme tout ce qui est réalisé, stérilisant."

Not with the superficial "mémoire volontaire" and "intélligence" of a "géomètre" does Proust have powers of observation, but as the "personnage intermittent" who uses his *mémoire involontaire* to make the past present, and thus to have both past and present transcended in a kind of putative eternity, a "synthetic absolute," in Thomas McFarland's fine phrase.[1] The abstraction of what McFarland goes on to call Proust's "impure apriori knowledge" in the Kantian sense—the immediacy of memory—invests the thousands of poetic details in the world of this novel with an eternal fourth dimension of time; so art enhances even a scullery maid into the Charity of Giotto, and the demimondaine Odette de Crécy becomes the Jethro's daughter of Botticelli's Sistine Chapel mural.

These poetic substances in Proust are Flaubertian metaphors, with the crucial difference that the protagonist comes to realize their figurative signification, as Flaubert's protagonist in his very conception cannot. The novel dramatizes Marcel's realization. The pitch of the narrative weaves a

---

[1] "Proust: the Philosophic Implications of Classicism," *Halcyon*, II, Winter, 1948.

marvelous intellection about their metaphorical properties. The effect is to make Marcel articulate of what he would else be mute, the aesthetic significance of his experiences; he is, then, himself the novelist, and, for poetic detail as for character, the schema of subject being object is an angle of vision which extends his perception into infinity. Thus every object is impregnated with every other through time; time is the impregnation. "Tout Combray et ses environs, tout cela qui prend forme et solidité, est sorti, ville et jardins, de ma tasse de thé." The cup of tea in which he dips his madeleine awakens and interprets his childhood past: the significance of the madeleine is in him, and he sees his eternity by the reflection of that significance.[2] "Un plaisir délicieux m'avait envahi, isolé, sans la notion de sa cause. Il m'avait aussitôt rendu les vicissitudes de la vie indifférentes, ses désastres inoffensifs, sa brièveté illusoire, de la même façon qu'opère l'amour, en me remplissant d'une essence précieuse: ou plutôt cette essence n'était pas en moi, elle était moi. J'avais cessé de me sentir médiocre, contingent, mortel." (A delicious pleasure invaded me, isolated, with no hint of its cause. It had immediately rendered the vicissitudes of life indifferent, its disasters inoffensive, its shortness illusory, in the same way that love works, filling me with its precious essence: or rather, that essence was not in me: it was me. I had ceased to feel myself mediocre, contingent, mortal.)

His modality was no longer that of a Kantian contingency, then, but of the eternity his heart intermittently perceives through the transitoriness of time and all its lovely mirrors—foods and landscapes and paintings and music and the associations of people, "la richesse du monde des possi-

[2] The madeleine is associated with eternity by the derivation of its name and the capitalization Proust gives its first appearance; so too it was first taken communion Sunday morning; similarly, hawthorn is associated with the month of May, the spires of Martinville are those of a church, the revelatory "dalles inégales" those of the baptistery of St. Mark.

bles par rapport au monde réel." He apprehends what surrounds him as Platonic metaphor, with the difference that its significance in heaven he refers not to heaven but reflexively back to earth. The recapitulation of time is the proof of eternity, and not the death which we can only surmise—as Proust repeatedly surmises—will itself make us see face to face what we see in his novel as through a many-colored glass darkly.

The development of the abstractions which dominate the style is the one experience undescribed by Marcel, as his growth to old age is tacitly represented through the expanding series of self-analyses which constitutes the novel's narrative progress. "On a dit que le silence était une force." It is as if the concretization of Flaubert were wedded to the past-reflexivity of James to produce a hybrid poetic analysis of life, except that Proust seems somehow less stylized than either writer, as Cervantes than Rabelais, through the initial simplicity of his conception.

As Pierre-Quine says of his style, he is "like certain philosophers who work in the abstract and feel the need to return to the concrete world." The verbal side of the fourth dimensional qualification of present by past is the airy superstructure of "peut-être que," "soit que," "tandis que," of "comme," "tel que," "de même"; of the reciprocal angles of references in alternating between the *passé défini* and the *passé indéfini*, which, Proust says, gives Flaubert a Kantian modality. "Dans tout amour," he says in another connection, "l'oeuvre . . . nous apprend que le général gît à côté du particulier, et à passer du second au premier par une gymnastique qui fortifie contre le chagrin en faisant négliger sa cause pour approfondir son essence."

Proust deepens the essence by the "gymnastique" of constant ratiocination, of generalizing over the particular event; the concrete and particular are present, the abstract and general measure the distance between it and the past, the relation between concrete and abstract, apparent present and real past, grows into an identity of self-transcendence. The disquisitions and interpretations of Proust's moralizing style keep the sequentiality of time acutely present, as their infinite divisions are all the time being subsumed in the eternal unity of the novel's theme. Otherwise, as he says of time's most excruciating emotion, love, "le tourment qui l'avait forcé de sortir de chez lui avait perdu de son acuité en perdant de son vague." Having learned from Baudelaire that vagueness and intensity can go together, his vocation brings it upon him through his life's fullest experience that they must go together. The intensity is in the divisions of sequentiality that get meaning exactly from the vagueness of union when *le temps perdu* becomes *le temps retrouvé*. Of course all along it is becoming *le temps retrouvé* in that end which is a beginning, that beginning which is an end; the old Marcel is recalling *Du Côté de chez Swann*, and the end of *Le Temps Retrouvé* is the point at which the first of the series begins.

Thus the ideas, the vast compendium of moral maxims in Proust, which make the whole tradition from La Rochefoucauld to Chamfort look like fragments, never lose their moorings to the concrete situation they are abstracting from; nor does the concrete situation ever emerge without its tissue of ideas: the situation is the tissue, as time recapitulates into eternity. The never mentioned undertone that validates these ideas is the eternity that transcends them, just as it is eternity that endows with all its urgency the transitoriness of love. Bergotte's yellow wall is in time, but it is an earnest of a better world.

The plot, which the ideas discuss, is plotless. It is a parable without being schematized into parable. It merely exists as a pure process of life in time, eventless except in those larger cosmic events which are the very substance of life as this novel conceives it.

There is no causal pattern in the plot, not even the mysterious nexus of a Dostoevsky. Its double perspective allows it to make any event at once purely fortuitous and deeply congruous in relation to any other. Just as in the most purely temporal art, music, one note follows another and makes of the two not merely an addition but something new, something that like the Vinteuil phrase strikes a chord in the spirit; so *A l'Ombre des Jeunes Filles* combines with *Du Côté de Chez Swann* not causally but in pure temporal process. The meaning of childhood's yearning begins to be given as the child emerges into the world of puberty, into "the shadow of flowering young girls." That second novel in itself is an image, a large pluri-significant metaphor, of Marcel's adolescence; and in context it modulates in the maturity of *Le Côté de Guermantes*—where, and when, Marcel has arrived at a point of time which allows him to enter the complete, rather abstract, fullness of worldly concerns and relations. Two previous novels have struck chords which qualify this arrival. But after a person has become mature, there is a kind of sickening of the spirit; the darkness of this world, the sadness of time, the ineradicable inherence of evil age-old and age-thick, darken the ennui one already feels as one realizes, as a kind of foretaste of death, that the relations of one's maturity are the relations one will take to the grave. People have hidden depths, flayed by the bituminous temporal rain, the sad sulphur, of their iniquities. *Le Côté de Guermantes* gives way to—and is qualified by—the seemingly interminable stretches of the longest section, *Sodome et Gomorrhe*. Inversion, loving an image of oneself, becomes the actualized symbol of social disease, the sickness unto death of social process.

The possibility of a dedicated love gains further urgency against this time weariness. And Albertine—prepared for as far back as Marcel's childhood devotion to Gilberte (which really gained its strength as a presage of the other, mature love); kissed in *A l'Ombre des Jeunes Filles en Fleur;* a fleeting consolation through the thousand pages of social maturity—has finally moved in with Marcel to dominate the Indian summer of his existence, in *La Prisonnière.* The very title, though, suggests that this period is a mere cell in time whose artificiality is implicit in the vast web of intellection Marcel spins to explain his love and the jealousy which is at once its renewing force and its seed of destruction. The next note of the chord becomes *Albertine Disparue,* the mistress fled because time is fleeting—and because, as the jealousy foreknew in spite of itself, she is herself involved in the mendacity and selfishness and unattainability of social disease, of homosexual connection. Sudden death takes her before reconciliation. Time the wounder is time the healer, and the end of this section spells his gradual solace, bringing him face to face with the next to last "intermittence du coeur," the sense of lack of vocation, which is really a foretaste of the vocation this whole series expresses. His approaching death, the *intermittence* foretasted in the final social gathering, is not a rebirth but the conquest of death in the understanding of the meaning of time. Life becomes cognizant of itself at the same time, and because, it is drawing to a close. It is *Le Temps Retrouvé,* the resolving note of the chord of seven, of the septet which like the *septuor* of Vinteuil crystallizes in a temporal sequence the meaning of time as a window on eternity.

The conventional image of Proust's composition is not a temporal art, music, but a spatial, that of a stained-glass window in a church, a *rosace.* This spatial metaphor is a useful one so long as one remembers that it is a metaphor, that Proust's juxtapositions, *pace* Joseph Frank,[3] are the

---

[3] "Spatial Form in Modern Literature," in *Criticism: the Foundations of Modern Literary Judgment,* ed. Mark Schorer, Josephine Miles, and Gordon McKenzie (New York, 1947).

very opposite of spatial. For the window is growing through its juxtapositions. And, to continue the image, not only does Marcel set one incident beside another, and then a third. Not only does he combine them. All themes, all pieces of glass, are set in the Combray section of *Du Côté de chez Swann*, even in the "Overture," as Scott-Moncrieff calls it, of the very beginning. And all colors reflect each other till they blend at the end. Bergotte enchants Marcel because he renders the evanescence of his experiences with the hawthorn. And Gilberte, whose house has hawthorns growing outside, infatuates him because she knows Bergotte. Swann, his parents' old friend, is valued first as the father of Gilberte, next because of his acquaintance with Bergotte; so M. de Norpois is valued because he will take Marcel to see Berma, whom Bergotte admires. Marcel does not know that Swann's love is deeply analogous to his own, nor does he know till later that M. de Norpois is the lifelong lover of Mme. de Villeparisis, whose friendship becames the bridge to Saint-Loup. Nor can he know before the fulness of time that Saint-Loup, Marcel's entrée into the circle of the Guermantes, will become the real husband of Gilberte, remaining at the same time the lifelong lover of the prostitute Rachel Quand du Seigneur in the house Bloch has first led Marcel to on a despairing rebound from Gilberte; that this very Rachel will draw, at the final party, her children away from the dying Berma. He cannot know that Odette de Crécy, painted by the Elstir he meets because of Albertine, the fashionable woman who has enhanced the Champs Elysées as Madame Swann the mother of Gilberte, will in her last evolution become the final mistress of the aging Basin de Guermantes. Nor that the last Princesse de Guermantes will be none other than the *arriviste* Madame Verdurin whose banal salon provided a meeting ground first for Swann and Odette, then for the violinist Morel and the Baron de Charlus.

One can go on and on and on. Every relation leads to

every other. "Le visage humain est vraiment comme celui
du Dieu d'une théogonie orientale, toute une grappe de vi-
sages juxtaposés dans des plans différents et qu'on ne voit
pas à la fois." Every section of glass refracts the colors of
all the others, with which it blends without losing its specificity, into a dazzling mortal vision of eternity. "Ainsi, à
chacun des moments de sa durée, le nom de Guermantes,
considéré comme un ensemble de tous les noms qu'il admet-
tait en lui, autour de lui, subissait des déperditions, récrutait
des éléments nouveaux, comme ces jardins où à tout moment des fleurs à peine en bouton et se préparant à rempla-
cer celles qui se flétrissent déjà se confondent dans une
masse qui semble pareille, sauf à ceux qui n'ont pas toujours
vu les nouvelles venues et gardent dans leur souvenir l'image
précise de celles qui ne sont plus." (Thus, at each of the
moments of its duration, the name Guermantes, considered
as an ensemble of all the names it admitted into it, all about
it, underwent losses, recruited new elements, like those gar-
dens in which at every moment flowers scarcely budded,
preparing to replace the wilting ones, are already confused
in an indistinguishable mass, except to those who have not
always had the new arrivals before their eyes and who cherish in memory the exact image of the ones which are no
more.)

Time's transcendence crystallizes in the works of art perceived by Marcel, in the process of aesthetically envisioning
life, places and people. This novel makes of aesthetic perception a theological "way of affirmation," to adapt Charles
Williams' phrase (*The Figure of Beatrice*) for the process
by which man asserts not his "terrible difference" from
God but his "terrible likeness." One perceives the eternal
in people if one is sensitive to art, preeminently to the
process which the novel reflexively presents. *À la Re-*

cherche du Temps Perdu is itself the chief art object, though the novels of Bergotte are deeply analogous, just as the death of Bergotte is analogous to Marcel's, as Swann is analogous to Marcel in his love for Odette and in his profession as art critic. The painting of Vermeer is for Swann what Elstir's paintings later become for Marcel, a window on the meaning of time. People inform the paintings, the paintings inform the people who so resemble paintings by Rembrandt or Vermeer or Botticelli or Giotto or Benozzo Gozzoli or Ghirlandaijo. And Charlus becomes like a literary figure, the white-haired King Lear. There is music, too, that pure art; the music of Vinteuil charges the life of Swann and later Marcel, impregnates the life it expresses as it expressed the life, that of Vinteuil, which it impregnated. For life learns to imitate art, Proust says; its process tends toward what it holds all the time, the crystallization which art may present.

Behind the configurations of art lies the evolution of love, that otherness—that incarnation of transience—which dominates life. "Tout regard habituel est une nécromancie et chaque visage qu'on aime le miroir du passé. . . . Notre oeil, chargé de pensée, néglige, comme ferait une tragédie classique, toutes les images qui ne concourent pas à l'action et ne retient que celles qui peuvent en rendre intelligible le but." (Every habitual look is a necromancy and every beloved face a mirror of the past. . . . Our eye, laden with thought, neglects, as a classic tragedy would, all images not concurrent with the action, retaining only those which can make the end intelligible.) Marcel must know life before he can fully love; but he must love before he can write the novel which will consummately express his life. Love, which might conquer time, is itself subject to time—not only to the finality of death, but to the fact that, as Proust reiterates, one creates, in a sense, the love object anew with every morning; what one has is not a single love but an invisibly divided series of new, resembling loves for the same person. Time undermines time because *l'habitude*, the drug of love, which obscures this process of recreation, grows from love, just as it grows from the intellect it drugs.

Love lies behind the society whose splendid surface cannot take cognizance of it: in this the Duc de Guermantes' unconcern over Swann's approaching death is as crass as the Verdurins' spite at Swann's preoccupation with Odette. Society is a school of elegance, but elegance precludes the love which enhances most deeply the private life, and Marcel leaves the Guermantes' party at midnight for the arms of Albertine. High society itself appears, at the last, a meaningless shell, the elegance of aristocracy all too separable from the actual aristocrats who supposedly embody it; the social appearance has vanished, having been lived through in process. The long final *soirée* shows the only reality left, that of the amorous relationships which have caused the aristocracy so to permute.

All those whom one loves, including the tutelary past in the form of one's parents or grandmother, are subject to sickness and death. Illness is the cross of this novel, the counterpoise to its affirmation of aesthetic epicureanism. The body knows time through involuntary memory but is subject to time through disease. Marcel is always sick and must undergo two years in a sanatorium before being released to begin his immortal novel. Even the rather imperceptive Tante Léonie suffers religiously; her sufferings are surrounded in the presentation by the churchgoing of those about her; her medicine stands on the same shelf with a statue of the Virgin, and the veins in her forehead are compared by the narrator to a crown of thorns.

This is the sickness of eternity, the bodily pangs which almost always accompany death, Swann's or Bergotte's or the grandmother's, even the rapid accident of Albertine. The sickness of time is a moral sickness, sexual inversion, seen not predominantly as a moral evil but as a moral disease, in terms of sickness and health rather than in terms of good and evil. The society is sick unto death with its own lack of otherness.

The most sensitive to love, to eternity, to art, eschew homosexuality. Charlus is the very parody of the sensitive man, as he is crassly egoistic and sadistic in his personal relations. Marcel, Swann, Saint-Loup, Elstir, the grandmother, the all or all but untainted, are the most wide awake to the meaning of time. The others are not time's masters but its slaves. They are the ones who murder time's crystallization in art by the parody of temporary fashion, who crucify illness by selfishness, who ignore in love its eternal dedication. They have, though, an eternal dimension unperceived by themselves, as, like Marcel perhaps, they enter the Mantegna-sky scaffolding of the Gare St. Lazare, "sans lequel ne pouvait s'accomplir que quelque acte terrible et solennel comme un départ en chemin de fer ou l'érection de la Croix"; as they breathe an Elysian elixir in the Bois de Boulogne or the opera or the church at Combray or the salon of the Duchesse de Guermantes; as they, like Charlus, wander about the Wagnerian hell of Paris during an air-raid; as they sit like medieval constellations in the Rivebelle restaurant when at rose twilight the tree against the sky has seemed like the pink veins of an onyx's arborescence; as they move like marvelous fish inside the glassed-in "tank" of the hotel at Balbec. Marcel's novel sees for everyone, from Albertine and Saint-Loup and Charlus as vast as Milton's Satan; through Berma, Rachel, Gilberte, Odette, Morel, Cottard, Brichot, the Verdurins, the Guermantes, Bloch; down to Françoise and Aimé, a past that like his own is rediscovered as extending monstrously back in time. At last they gather all into the coinherence of a love where they belong, though they rigidly disown it to their deathbed; or till, in Proust's superb Giacometti-like final metaphor, they fall from the invisible stilts of time:

> Je venais de comprendre pourquoi le duc de Guermantes, dont j'avais admiré, en le regardant assis sur une chaise,

combien il avait peu vieilli bien qu'il eût tellement plus d'années que moi au-dessous de lui, dès qu'il s'était levé et avait
voulu se tenir debout, avait vacillé sur des jambes flageolantes
comme celles de ces vieux archevêques sur lesquels il n'y a
de solide que leur croix métallique et vers lesquels s'empres-
sent des jeunes séminaristes gaillards, et ne s'était avancé
qu'en tremblant comme une feuille, sur le sommet peu pra-
ticable de quatre-vingt-trois années, *comme si les hommes
étaient juchés sur de vivantes échasses, grandissant sans cesse,
parfois plus hautes que des clochers,* finissant par leur rendre
la marche difficile et périlleuse, et d'où tout d'un coup ils
tombaient. Je m'effrayais que les miennes fussent déjà si
hautes sous mes pas, il ne me semblait pas que j'aurais encore
la force de maintenir longtemps attaché à moi ce passé qui
descendait déjà si loin. Du moins, si elle m'était laissée assez
longtemps pour accomplir mon oeuvre, ne manquerais-je pas
d'abord d'y décrire les hommes (cela dût-il les faire ressembler à des êtres monstrueux) comme occupant une place si
considérable, à côté de celle si restreinte qui leur est réser-
vée dans l'espace, une place au contraire prolongée sans me-
sure—puisqu'ils touchent simultanément, comme des géants
plongés dans les années, à des époques si distantes, entre les-
quelles tant de jours sont venus se placer—dans le Temps.

(I now understood why it was that the Duc de Guermantes, whom, as I looked at him sitting in a chair, I mar-
velled to find showing his age so little, although he had so
many more years than I beneath him, as soon as he rose and
tried to stand erect, had tottered on trembling limbs, like
those of aged archbishops who have nothing solid on them
except their metallic cross, with the hearty young divinity
students flocking assiduously about them, and had wavered
as he made his way along the difficult summit of his eighty-
three years, *as if men were perched on giant stilts, sometimes
taller than church spires,* constantly growing and finally
rendering their progress so difficult and perilous that they
suddenly would fall. I was alarmed that mine were already
so tall beneath my feet; it did not seem as if I should have
the strength to carry much longer attached to me that past
which already extended so far down. If, at least, there were
granted me time enough to complete my work, I would not
in the first place fail therein to describe men, even should
that give them the semblance of monstrous creatures, as oc-

cupying in Time a place far more considerable than the so restricted one allotted them in space, a place, on the contrary, extending boundlessly—since, giant-like, plunged in the years, they touch, simultaneously, epochs of the lives, with countless intervening days between so widely separated from one another,—in Time.)

The time which is the very essence of the novel, manipulated by Sterne and others, is rendered by Proust in the very actuality of its process; it is rendered as intimating, in all aesthetic surface and spiritual depth, the conquest of natural time by the represented quality of time. We would not have seen ourselves tottering on stilts as high as bell towers, stilts that grow and grow, had not Proust made himself at once the botanist, the moralist, and the metaphysician of that growth. He is our stilts of time.

☙ XVI ☙

THE MEANING OF FICTION

The people who emerge from Proust's simple but infinite doubling of an apparent present with a real past, of the actual with the remembered, of art with life—these people sense time and are sensed in time. Their lives seem particularly long not because they really are so more than any other lives, or even because the book is long. In his deliberate and processive attention to his view of their long lives, Proust permits them a variety of postures, a multiplicity of roles and relations, a gamut of stages in development.

It is people like these that the particular means of the novel can afford us. The inward evasion, and gradual growth of a Don Quixote, the spiritual abysses and exaltations of a Dmitri Karamazov, rise from the free form of a genre which allows unparalleled latitude, minuteness, and slowness of presentation. The view of man that results may do one kind of justice to human variety and depth. A whole moral intuition may be brought to bear on a small series of gestures by the novelist, a whole subtlety of personal reaction may be portrayed as coloring a dish or a landscape or a gift or a kiss.

Fiction affords an image of character that catches at once the single evanescent factor, the cut of dress, the heaviness of a tread; and also the total moral bearing of a life seen over the long haul of decades, or over the short haul of *Ulysses'* single day.

A novel, its finger on the very pulse of change in people, can even be consistently inconsistent. So *Sons and Lovers* can show Morel as mean at one moment, generous at another; subtle at one moment, surlily stupid at another. Lawrence's characters, in their desire for Laurentian freedom, exemplify just one sort of fictive openness. Miriam can both inspire Paul and hold him back, Paul himself can both totter under his dead mother and urge himself on, at the end, to a new life which the book has been consistently, if not with strict coherence, preparing. The novel as a form permits not only vacillation but sudden lifting from an appearance to a reality.

The protean character of the interior life, the complexity of detail in social commitments, become bodied forth for us as we read an authentic novel. The purpose of fiction is to elucidate by slowly following the thread of an imagined life's myriad turns the "vastness" of man, in Dostoevsky's phrase, to portray what James called "the Medusa-face of life." The greater leeway, the sometimes humdrum deliberateness, of the genre, is justified in the extent and variety of an individual life that it can handle. No deeper than poetry, of course, and no more compelling than drama, the novel still may deal more inclusively with existence and yet not be obliged to provide the sort of structure to its material which the rhythm and the poetic diction of an epic must give.

The process of such interior lives must involve interconnections from perception to perception. Otherwise how would the process be perceived as a process? To represent process a novel, however loose it may get, needs a structure of interconnections, needs, in short, a plot. Novels like *Finnegans Wake* border on poetry not only because of their verbal technique but because of the way their near plotlessness verges on a lyric structure. *Finnegans Wake* is a romance whose myriad plots are one, of a simplicity so archetypical that the causal pattern is all but absent. Rather, the absence of cause is the hidden side, the secret life, of its omnipresence. *A la Recherche du Temps Perdu* contains less of romance than any fiction; its pattern is so nearly plotless, so processive, that it needs a transcendental reflexivity to keep itself fiction at all, instead of a mere treatise about time on the one hand or a dry series of scenes like *Jean Santeuil* on the other.

Process is by its very nature fine-meshed, and its causal sequences are minutiae which only the slow accretion of observations could render. Joyce's archetypes, Proust's time dialectic, Fielding's gestures of enlightened or unenlightened self-interest, Tolstoi's sense of over-all personal destiny, the protean reflexes of the specializing sensibility—all give process minute by minute, sentence by sentence, its very water shapes.

A process built of insights, the meaning of time seen through its pace of transient manifestations, becomes, in fiction, a means of representing those intangible states between appearance and reality, what Lukàcs (*Die Theorie des Romans*) calls an "equilibrium of becoming and being." Poetry, contrastingly, through the dominance of its rhythm, through the inevitable heightened selectiveness of its diction, through the coherence of its metaphorical or argumentative structure, turns what Lukàcs calls the novel's "self-knowledge and hence self-exaltation of subjectivity" into something external and formal.

Spleen de Paris, for example, is a series of prose poems in narrative, a procession of little cosmoses, from which the process of time is absent either in sequence or (as the parables of Kafka) by the implication of dialectic. In any poetry, as in this series of small stories by a poet, subjectivity is public, a persona; it is public even in a poem which would borrow the autobiographical device, the anecdotal leisureliness, the concern with process, of the novel. Even in *The Cantos*, which fuses the medium of poetry with some of the means of fiction, we have an ordering of process into the abstracted and public. "Rain also is of the process," Pound has himself say at Pisa. Process is named, typified, structurally and rhythmically imitated, but not represented as in fiction. *The Cantos* publicize the private archetype into personæ; in even so poetic, even so socially comic, a novel as *Finnegans Wake*, the public and national archetype is a secret life. Is not all a runic letter on the dung heap which the chicken has scratched into illusory insignificance? The weight of the past on HCE is what the letter concerns and will define. The letter, in fact, is understood to be none other than the whole elusive and cryptic *Finnegans Wake*. *The Cantos* are difficult and allusory, but not cryptic in this sense: " 'Tis endless now senne eye or erewone last saw Waterhouse's clogh. They took it asunder. I heard thum sigh. When will they reassemble it? . . . My sights are swimming thicker on me by the shadows to this place. I sow home slowly now by own way, moyvalley way." This refers its abstractions and analogies to process; *The Cantos* structures process into abstractions and analogies.

In fiction reality is made to coalesce with appearance. In history, even so fictive a plot as the relation between Tiberius and Sejanus in *The Annals* bodies forth its reality simply, coloring the public manifestations of the actors with so little reference to the private life that it remains a perpetual puzzle; we must take the evidence of Tacitus and ourselves build for Tiberius a private life; and Jonson makes of Sejanus something quite other, a dramatic figure with the tragic flaw of overweening pride.

Process in fiction must perpetually fuse appearance and reality. "The process," Lukàcs says, "which we must conceive as the inner form of the novel, is the journey of problematic individuality to itself, the way from troubled perplexity to a reality of clear self-knowledge which is simple in its existence though actually heterogeneous and, for the individual, unconscious." And, in slightly different terms,

"The largest discrepancy between idea and reality is time, the issue of time as duration." Not a "discrepancy," though but a shuttle of mediation. Time does not widen, it adapts, the distance between appearance and reality. The novel's temporal process lies between appearance and reality, rendering them both as a structure of resembling life observations. What had been an idle adjunct to poetry or philosophy or history, a mere entertainment, became thereby a great art form with a universe of meaning peculiar to itself. Simply because it was born so recently, we tend to think the novel might die, though it holds possibilities as endless as those of poetry and drama. There is no more reason for fiction to die than for these other genres; and, in the unlikely eventuality of its temporary disappearance as a mode of expression, it might very well be revived, like the drama, in different forms; once a Cervantes has been its Aeschylus, some other could be its Marlowe, still another its Hebbel or its Ibsen.

How are we to judge among novels? If we assume that a work of art has a meaning, then we may judge it finally by what it means. When we say that one novel is better than another we must be signifying that what it means is more extensive, or deeper, or both. The decision may be unconscious; at its best it may wholly or partially evade formulation. None of us can be any more discriminating as critics than Homer, who was acting, however unconsciously, as a literary critic, when he selected from his rhapsodic tradition the lines and the halves of lines which he would use to compose *The Iliad* and *The Odyssey*. The most sensitive reading may simply and properly identify the meaning with the work. But criticism must imply or explain the question of meaning.

Our first criterion in judging a novel should be that of

unity. This is not the coherence of skillful motivation and economy of presentation, the novel's stock-in-trade equivalent for the Ibsenesque tightness of modern drama. Nor is unity some particular plot structure felt to be economically managed. It is simply the singleness of vision in every intuitive statement, and in the whole, which is given a novel by the "esemplastic power of the imagination."

Even stylistic unity can be lacking in a work which we may still consider a genuine novel. The particular character of fictional language leaves room for a stylistic imprecision which would destroy a poem by the very fact. Fiction may present its observations through an unconscious common speech—even, as in the case of Dreiser or James Jones a bad literary dialect—as well as through the sublime stylistic modulations of Flaubert, Proust, Joyce. Still, so special and intermittently successful a writer as (to take a contemporary example) Jerome Weidman, so general a one as Balzac, may well obscure the unity they do possess by failing to shake off a kind of overriding stylistic clumsiness.

Another criterion is that of range. Not "how much ground is covered," or Mann, always intuitive in a limited compass, would be credited with a spurious extra cubit of stature for his excellent novella expanded into a philosophistic pseudoepic, *Der Zauberberg*; for the fake world wisdom of his Joseph series; for the fine minor novel *Doktor Faustus*, which masks as an apocalyptic fictive panorama. It is hard to describe what an authentic range is without begging the question. This criterion might best be formulated as "whose world will include whose?" We may see, I believe, that Balzac, who could incorporate Trollope's or George Eliot's worlds, is a greater novelist than either, but that he could not incorporate Dostoevsky's or Tolstoi's. Tolstoi, too, could incorporate Conrad's world, but not Proust's.

Another criterion, difficult to define since we are dealing with qualities best apprehended directly, is what I would call intensity or sharpness of focus, what Edmund Wilson means (*The Wound and the Bow*) when he speaks of the "burning glass" of Hemingway's intuiting style. Stendhal is far sharper in focus than Gide and Constant. Jane Austen is more intense—and thus, I feel, superior—to Trollope, whose range is greater; she is superior because this intensity of emotional effect derives, if authentic, from a concentration of fictional meaning. Such intensities as are gained in the fine minor novels of Graham Greene come not from insight but from melodrama; they are evocative, but, in their intensity, unmeaningful. Related to intensity is sensibility; one may call sensibility the fineness, intensity the penetration, of fictive meaning. And often the heightened sensibility, of Stendhal or Proust or Jane Austen, makes for heightened intensity; fineness allows for penetration.

In modern times the novelist's approach and vision have come to deal so effectively with social reality that the sociologist may sometimes make by conceptual analysis of data a kind of observation like the novelist's. It may be said with equal justice that Zola used a sociologist's approach to substantiate the social groups of his novels, that David Riesman informs *The Lonely Crowd* with a vision of society which is essentially novelistic. The fictional achievement of *La Nausée* reproduces more faithfully the kind of mental process discussed in *L'Être et le Néant* than do Sartre's plays (or the thesis novels of *Les Chemins de la Liberté*). Proust, it is said, and many another novelist, anticipated Freud; that great unveiler of a reality behind the appearances of the dreaming and the waking life was able to delineate, in the spare style of such clinical histories as "The Case of Dora," an almost Kafkan, and convincingly fictive, world. Of course in being directed towards a different sort of meaning,

Freud's writing comes to a different meaning from that of fiction: appearance and reality he keeps firmly apart.

Into the Bible's absoluteness of meanings, with the help of our own fictive art's natural vision, we are able to read back what amounts to the meaning of fiction. Here is the sacrifice of Abraham (Gen. 22: 1-13):

And it came to pass after these things, that God did tempt Abraham, and said unto him, "Abraham": and he said, "Behold, here I am." And he said, "Take now thy son, thine only son Isaac, whom thou lovest, and get thee into the land of Moriah; and offer him there for a burnt offering upon one of the mountains which I will tell thee of." And Abraham rose up early in the morning, and saddled his ass, and took two of his young men with him, and Isaac his son, and clave the wood for the burnt offering, and rose up, and went unto the place of which God had told him. Then on the third day Abraham lifted up his eyes, and saw the place afar off. And Abraham said unto his young men, "Abide ye here with the ass; and I and the lad will go yonder and worship, and come again to you." And Abraham took the wood of the burnt offering, and laid it upon Isaac his son; and he took the fire in his hand, and a knife; and they went both of them together. And Isaac spake unto Abraham his father, and said, "My father": and he said, "Here am I, my son." And he said, "Behold the fire and the wood: but where is the lamb for a burnt offering?" And Abraham said, "My son, God will provide himself a lamb for a burnt offering"; so they went both of them together. And they came to the place which God had told him of; and Abraham built an altar there, and laid the wood in order, and bound Isaac his son, and laid him on the altar, upon the wood. And Abraham stretched forth his hand, and took the knife to slay his son. And the angel of the Lord called unto him out of heaven, and said, "Abraham, Abraham": and he said, "Here am I." And he said, "Lay not thine hand upon the lad, neither do thou any thing unto him: for now I know that thou fearest God, seeing thou hast not withheld thy son, thine only son, from me." And Abraham lifted up his eyes, and looked, and behold behind him a ram caught in a thicket by his horns; and Abraham went and took the ram, and offered him up for a burnt offering in the stead of his son.

Here, as nowhere in the mere art of fiction, are perfectly fused the romance of legend—all the symbolic meanings which Auerbach touches on in analyzing this passage —and the most delicate fictional perceptions. There is, for example, Abraham's finely realized set of relations with his servants and his son, existing mutely under the designations of the style—the polite dismissal of the servants before the sacrifice, the exaction of filial obedience in making Isaac carry the wood, the restrained answer to the breathless matter-of-factness of Isaac's questions, held back silently till the very ascent itself. And all the relations, heavenly and earthly, take on irony, pathos, and spiritual depth from the echoing progression of the three *Hinneni*'s (Here am I) spoken by Abraham, first to God, then to Isaac, then to his guardian angel. Fiction as well as symbolism, and much else, lies in the tacit distinction of lambs: the white young animal in Isaac's mind; the human lamb in Abraham's; and what actually appears, the old curly-horned beast (ram, Hebrew *ayil*, curled horned). This animal, like the ass here, or anywhere in the Bible, is endowed with allegorical attributes (lamb = sacrifice; ass = unquestioning duty), but it also lives and breathes beyond the animals of pastoral or romance; it has all the mute presence of the animals in Cervantes and Kafka.

This is history in which God's purpose is presented as so manifest that every act is symbolic. And one dimension to that symbolism, I would urge, is the fictive, the process of a secret real life underlying the appearances of the narrative. The text leaves to our perceptions what it mutely presents—"in the background," as Auerbach says—the terrible intensity of this experience for Isaac. Doubtless his terror here helps to charge the yearning timidity with which he approaches the veiled Rebecca at twilight somewhat later. Doubtless it renders more pathetic and profound his later domination by Rebecca, in which an almost fictive situation combines to make Isaac, too, sacrifice his first-born, in his death-bed blessing, to allow the ascendency of Jacob. And Jacob will show in his crafty side the third-generation version of Abraham's wisdom; he will go through, too, what, in fictional terms, is the metamorphosis of Abraham's encounter with God, wrestling with the angel, his head pillowed on stone, envisioning the ladder in heaven with "the angels of God ascending and descending on it."

Not at first heavenward but earthward is directed the gaze of Cervantes, that Jacob who has left an Israel of progeny. Their continuing achievement allows us to read further meanings out into the world, back into other books, including the Book itself.

☙ INDEX ❧

Edited by Alexander Brede
Designed by S. R. Tenenbaum
Set in Linotype Janson and Garamond display
Printed on Warren's Olde Style Antique Wove
Bound in Holliston's Zeppelin cloth
Printed and bound in the United States of America